Basic MathsBytes

Basic MathsBytes®

© Sue Chandler and Ewart Smith 2001

The right of Sue Chandler and Ewart Smith to be identified as joint authors of this work has been asserted by them in accordance with sections 77 and 78 of the Copyright, Designs and Patents Act 1988

All rights reserved. No part of this book, including interior design, cover design and icons, may be reproduced or transmitted in any form, by any means (electronic, photocopying, recording or otherwise) without the prior written permission of the publisher or under licence from the Copyright Licensing Agency Limited. Further details of such licences (for reprographic reproduction) may be obtained from the copyright Licensing Agency Limited, of 90 Tottenham Court Road, London W1P 0LP.

First published in 2001 by:
Summerfield Publishing Ltd
P O Box 16
Evesham
Worcestershire
WR11 6WN
Great Britain

01 02 03 04 05 / 5 4 3 2 1

A catalogue record of this book is available from the British Library.

1-901-995-37-2

Basic MathsBytes is a registered trademark under exclusive licence to Summerfield Publishing Ltd from Summerfield Business Services Ltd.

Limit of liability/Disclaimer of Warranty: The authors and publishers have used their best efforts to ensure the accuracy in this book suitable to the usage expected. However Summerfield Publishing and the authors make no representation or warranties with respect to the accuracy or completeness of the contents of this book and specifically disclaim any implied warranties of merchantability or fitness for any particular purpose and shall in no event be liable for any loss of profit or any other commercial damage, including but not limited to special, incidental, consequential, or other damages.

This publication includes images from WordPerfect® Office 2000 which are protected by the copyright laws of the US, Canada and elsewhere. Used under licence.

Every effort has been made to acknowledge copyright holders. The publishers apologise to anyone whose rights may have been overlooked and will endeavour to rectify any errors or omissions at the earliest opportunity.

Diagrams and illustrations
by Hardlines, Charlbury, Oxford

Typeset by Tech Set Ltd, Gateshead, Tyne & Wear
Printed in Italy by G. Canale & C.S.p.A.

GCSE – Foundation Tier

Basic MathsBytes

Sue Chandler and Ewart Smith

Advisory Team:
Alisdair Nicholas *Hendon School*
Lee Turner *Pershore High School*
Terry James *Ebbw Vale Comprehensive School*

SUMMERFIELD PUBLISHING LIMITED

CONTENTS

A Whole Numbers — 1
Place value   Addition and subtraction   Multiplication and division
Brackets and order of operations   Names for numbers   Indices
Investigation — 7

B Symmetry and Coordinates — 8
Line symmetry   Rotational symmetry   Coordinates   Conversion graphs

C Angles and Parallel Lines — 12
Angles   Angle facts   Parallel lines   Compass directions and bearings

D Collecting and Illustrating Data — 17
Pictograms   Making frequency tables   Bar charts   Scatter graphs
Time series and stem-and-leaf diagrams
Investigation — 22

E Transformations — 23
Reflection   Rotation and translation   Enlargement

F Sequences — 26
Continuing a sequence   Finding the pattern   Describing the pattern
Investigation — 29

G Fractions — 30
Meaning of fractions   Equivalent fractions   Adding and subtracting fractions

H Decimals — 33
Meaning of decimals   Adding and subtracting decimals   Multiplying and dividing by whole numbers
Changing fractions to decimals   Multiplying and dividing by decimals   Using a calculator

I Using Numbers — 39
Units of length, mass, capacity   Time and speed   Travel graphs   Money
Negative numbers

J Using Fractions — 44
Finding a fraction of a quantity   Fractional change   One quantity as a fraction of another
Ratio   Ratio and proportion   Scale drawing   Pie charts

K Percentages — 52
Meaning of percentage   Percentages as fractions
Percentages, fractions and decimals

L Probability 55
Probability scale   Finding and using probability   Sums of probabilities   Two events
Investigation 59

M Triangles, Quadrilaterals and Polygons 60
Angles of a triangle   Quadrilaterals   Special quadrilaterals   Polygons
Congruence and tessellation

N Perimeter and Area 66
Perimeter   Area by counting squares   Areas of squares and rectangles
Areas involving mixed units   Areas of compound shapes
Investigation 71

O Using Percentages 72
Percentage of a quantity   Percentage increase   Percentage decrease
One quantity as a percentage of another   Mixed percentage questions

P Algebra 77
Function machines and formulas in words   Adding and subtracting letter terms
Multiplying letter terms   Using negative numbers   Making and using a formula
Substituting positive and negative numbers   Solving equations   Graphs of straight lines

Q Areas of Triangles and Parallelograms 85
Area of a triangle   Areas of compound shapes involving triangles   Area of a parallelogram

R Summarising Data 88
Mode and median   Mean and range   Comparing distributions
Investigation 91

S Solids 92
Faces, edges and vertices   Nets   Surface area   Plans and elevations

T Circles 96
Circumference of a circle   Area of a circle

U Volumes 98
Counting cubes   Volume of a cuboid   Using volumes

V More Algebra 101
Making equations   More equations   Curved graphs   Using brackets

A WHOLE NUMBERS
PLACE VALUE

1. Use all these three number cards.

   5 7 3

   a Write the largest number you can make.
   b Write the smallest number you can make.
   c Write all the numbers that you can make.
   d Write the answers for **c** in order, from smallest to largest.

2. Write these numbers in figures.
   a Two hundred and fifty
   b Two hundred and five
   c Five hundred and twenty five
   d Three hundred
   e One thousand and six
   f One thousand and sixty

3. What does the digit 5 stand for in 3650?

4. What does the digit 7 stand for in 87 400?

5. Arrange the digits 2, 0, 3, 2 to make the largest possible number.

6. Arrange the digits 1, 9, 7, 9 to make the smallest possible number.

7. Write these numbers in words.
   a 65   b 406   c 290

8. Write these numbers in words.
   a 1500   b 2020   c 12 056

9. Which digit gives the number of tens in 2437? How many tens are there altogether?

10. Which digit gives the number of units in 150?

11. Which digit gives the number of hundreds in 2786? How many hundreds are there altogether?

12. Write these numbers in order of size with the smallest first.

    2508, 905, 70, 509, 1919

13. Look at the number 65 298.
    Which digit gives the number of
    a hundreds   b thousands?

14. Look at the number 40 409.
    a How many units are there?
    b How many tens are there?
    c How many hundreds are there?
    d How many thousands are there?

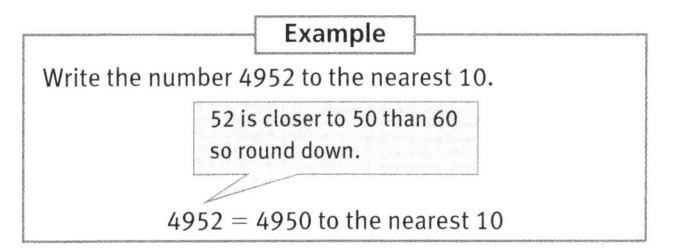

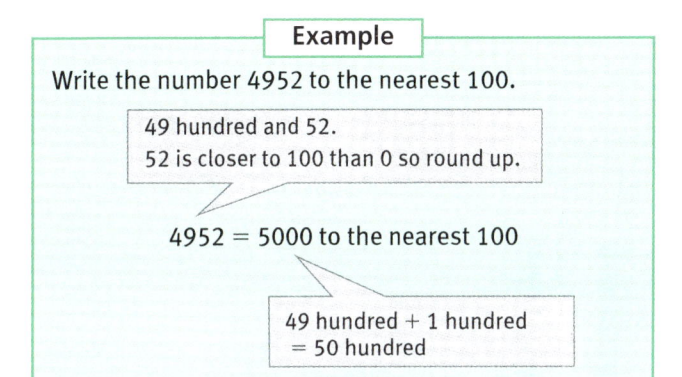

> **Example**
>
> Write the number 4952 to the nearest 10.
>
> 52 is closer to 50 than 60 so round down.
>
> 4952 = 4950 to the nearest 10

15. Write these numbers to the nearest ten.
    a 168   b 72   c 593   d 487

16. Write these numbers to the nearest hundred.
    a 180   b 527   c 1560   d 205

17. Write these numbers to the nearest thousand.
    a 2311   b 2031   c 4955   d 5199

> **Example**
>
> Write the number 4952 to the nearest 100.
>
> 49 hundred and 52.
> 52 is closer to 100 than 0 so round up.
>
> 4952 = 5000 to the nearest 100
>
> 49 hundred + 1 hundred = 50 hundred

18. Write these numbers to the nearest 10.
    a 398   b 96   c 1950   d 998

19. Write these numbers to the nearest 100.
    a 1599   b 3970   c 99   d 9999

20. 47 980 people went to a match at Wembley.
    a How many is this to the nearest 100?
    b This headline was in the newspaper.
        50 000 CHEER ENGLAND!
    What did the paper do to the number?
    c The headline in another paper was
        48 000 SEE ENGLAND WIN
    What did this paper do to the number?

21. Use **three** of these cards for each number.

    5 0 3 6

    a Write the largest number you can.
    b Write the largest number that is to the nearest 10.
    c Write the smallest number that is to the nearest 10.

A WHOLE NUMBERS
ADDITION AND SUBTRACTION

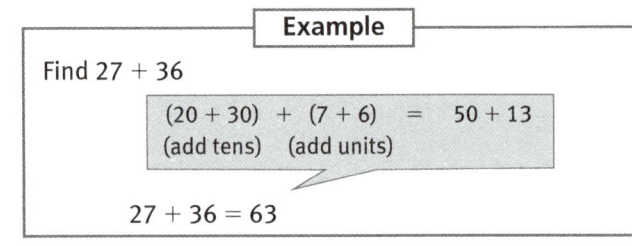

Example

Find 27 + 36

(20 + 30) + (7 + 6) = 50 + 13
(add tens) (add units)

27 + 36 = 63

Write down the answer.
1. a 40 + 18   b 25 + 75
2. a 30 + 27   b 36 + 64
3. a 84 + 10   b 59 + 41
4. a 47 + 30   b 19 + 81
5. a 47 + 53   b 147 + 53
6. a 76 + 24   b 276 + 24

Example

Estimate 79 + 52 by writing each number to the nearest 10.

79 + 52 ≈ 80 + 50 = 130

Estimate by writing each number to the nearest 10.
7. a 38 + 29   b 68 + 47
8. a 59 + 25   b 23 + 41
9. a 47 + 92   b 87 + 98
10. a 88 + 59   b 43 + 57

Example

Find 57 + 64

Estimate: 60 + 60 = 120

(50 + 60) + (7 + 4) = 110 + 11

Exact: 57 + 64 = 121

First estimate then find exactly
11. a 48 + 26   b 26 + 57
12. a 172 + 19   b 58 + 44
13. a 63 + 77   b 84 + 119

Write down the number that fits the box.
14. a 7 + ☐ = 10   b 10 − 7 = ☐
15. a 4 + ☐ = 10   b 10 − 4 = ☐
16. a 6 + ☐ = 12   b 12 − 6 = ☐
17. a 3 + ☐ = 11   b 11 − 3 = ☐
18. a ☐ + 8 = 15   b 15 − 8 = ☐
19. a ☐ + 9 = 16   b 16 − 9 = ☐

First estimate then find exactly
20. a 54 − 32   b 36 − 14
21. a 65 − 18   b 28 − 19
22. a 132 − 71   b 257 − 84

Example

Find 25 + 79 + 56

Estimate: 30 + 80 + 60 = 170   Exact: 25
                                        79
                                        56

                                       160

First estimate then find exactly
23. 12 + 27 + 44
24. 32 + 15 + 85
25. 73 + 49 + 9
26. 67 + 18 + 31
27. 73 + 105 + 5
28. 83 + 17 + 120

First estimate then find exactly
29. 237 + 155
30. 1552 + 319
31. 571 − 29
32. 835 − 552
33. 2110 − 1506
34. 1992 − 850
35. 25 + 47 − 19
36. 12 + 18 + 6 + 55
37. 123 + 188 − 20
38. 4114 + 3878
39. 8 + 16 + 112 − 51
40. 1120 + 1667 − 2005

41. Use each of the digits 1, 3, 4, 5, 6, 7, one in each box to make this sum correct. ☐☐ + ☐☐ = ☐☐

42. Mrs Smith bought new computer equipment.

    This is her bill.
    a. Round each sum to the nearest £100.
    b. Use your rounded sums to estimate the total.
    c. Find the exact total.
    d. Mrs Smith paid £900 in cash. Find the change.
    e. The printer is 420 mm wide.
       The scanner is 340 mm wide.
       The computer (with speakers) is 740 mm wide.
       They are placed side by side on a table.
       What length of table do they occupy?
    f. The hard disk has 5000 Mb of space.
       The software takes up 286 Mb of space.
       What space is left when the software is loaded?

```
18  3  00         1645
Computer         £489
Scanner          £138
Printer          £ 89
Software         £127
Total
```

A WHOLE NUMBERS
MULTIPLICATION AND DIVISION

Find
1. 31×10
2. 87×100
3. 7×1000
4. 561×100
5. 2070×100

Find
6. $200 \div 10$
7. $800 \div 100$
8. $120 \div 10$
9. $3800 \div 100$
10. $12\,000\,000 \div 1000$

Example
Find 23×200
Multiply by 2:
$23 \times 2 = 46$
Then multiply by 100:
$46 \times 100 = 4600$
$23 \times 200 = 4600$

Find
11. 7×200
12. 4×300
13. 6×400
14. 7×600
15. 4×60
16. 3×4000

Write down the number that fits the box.
17. a $4 \times \square = 8$ b $8 \div 4 = \square$
18. a $6 \times \square = 42$ b $42 \div 6 = \square$
19. a $\square \times 8 = 56$ b $56 \div 8 = \square$
20. a $\square \times 9 = 63$ b $63 \div 9 = \square$
21. a $5 \times \square = 35$ b $35 \div 5 = \square$

Example
Find $6000 \div 300$
Divide by 100:
$6000 \div 100 = 60$
Then divide by 3:
$60 \div 3 = 20$
$6000 \div 300 = 20$

Find
22. $400 \div 20$
23. $800 \div 400$
24. $1600 \div 80$
25. $240 \div 60$
26. $80\,000 \div 200$

Example
Find 42×60
$42 \times 6 = 252$
$252 \times 10 = 2520$
$42 \times 60 = 2520$

Find
27. 23×20
28. 41×300
29. 26×30
30. 750×60
31. 400×56

Example
Estimate 362×42
Round each number to the nearest 10.
$362 \times 42 \approx 360 \times 40 = 14\,400$

Estimate
32. 305×18
33. 156×33
34. 59×129
35. 88×370
36. 277×76

Estimate then find exactly
37. 28×42
38. 56×42
39. 166×23
40. 57×221
41. 577×83

Find
42. $63 \div 3$
43. $156 \div 4$
44. $215 \div 5$

Find, giving the remainder
45. $97 \div 7$
46. $311 \div 9$

Example
Find $460 \div 30$
Divide by 10: $460 \div 10 = 46$
$460 \div 30 = 46 \div 3$
$= 15 \text{ r } 1$

Find
47. $540 \div 20$
48. $600 \div 400$
49. $670 \div 50$
50. $5900 \div 200$
51. $4780 \div 30$

Example
Estimate $534 \div 82$
Divide by 10, then divide by 8 (leave out the remainder).
$534 \div 82 \approx 500 \div 80$
≈ 6

Estimate
52. $257 \div 26$
53. $493 \div 32$
54. $502 \div 29$
55. $447 \div 81$
56. $899 \div 38$

Find, giving the remainder
57. $521 \div 36$
58. $803 \div 21$
59. $441 \div 27$
60. $9115 \div 48$
61. $5001 \div 52$

62. Find the cost of 53 pens.   47p
63. Estimate the price of one pin.   36 pins £2.88
64. Find the cost of 20 000 pads of paper.   57p

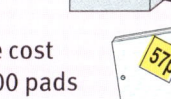

A WHOLE NUMBERS
BRACKETS AND ORDER OF OPERATIONS

Brackets first then **O**rder is do **D**ivision and **M**ultiplication before **A**ddition and **S**ubtraction.
BODMAS

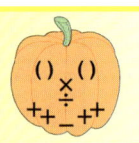

Example
Find $(25 + 13) \times 20$

Do the sum in the bracket first.

$38 \times 20 = 760$

Work out
1. $(6 + 12) \times 4$
2. $(20 - 8) \div 6$
3. $2 \times (4 - 1)$
4. $25 \times (18 + 22)$
5. $14 \div (12 - 5)$
6. $(6 + 5) \times (4 - 2)$
7. $7 \times (15 \div 3)$
8. $50 \div (17 + 33)$
9. $(25 + 15) \div (12 - 7)$
10. $(8 + 62) \times (126 + 74)$

Example
Find $2 + 4 \times 2$

Do the multiplication first.

$2 + 4 \times 2 = 2 + 8$
$\qquad\qquad = 10$

Work out
11. $5 + 4 \times 4$
12. $15 - 3 \times 2$
13. $4 \times 6 - 15$
14. $17 \times 2 - 12$
15. $24 + 5 \times 12$

Example
Find $7 - 48 \div 8$

Do the division first.

$7 - 48 \div 8 = 7 - 6$
$\qquad\qquad = 1$

Work out
16. $25 + 36 \div 6$
17. $17 - 27 \div 9$
18. $45 - 25 \div 5$
19. $8 + 81 \div 9$
20. $64 - 64 \div 4$

Work out
21. $2 \times (17 - 6)$
22. $2 \times 17 - 6$
23. $30 - 12 \times 2$
24. $(30 - 12) \times 2$
25. $15 - 12 \div 3$
26. $(15 - 12) \div 3$

27. Jon worked out $4 + 2 \times 6$ as 36.
    He checked using his calculator.
    He keyed in [4][+][2][×][6][=]
    The display showed 16.
    Which is the right answer and why?

Example
First estimate, then use a calculator to find
$$367 + 24 \times 16$$

Estimate: $367 + 24 \times 16 \approx 400 + 20 \times 20$
$\qquad\qquad\qquad\qquad\quad = 400 + 400 = 800$

Calculator: 751

First find an estimate, then use your calculator to find exactly
28. $251 + 16 \times 42$
29. $76 \times 31 - 121$
30. $156 \div (103 - 91)$
31. $945 \div 21 + 277$
32. $165 - 60 \div 12$
33. $(75 + 127) \times 34$

34. Lynne estimated $43 \times (185 - 159)$ as about 1200.
    When she keyed in
    [4][3][×][1][8][5][-][1][5][9][=]
    the display showed 7796.
    What mistake has she made?

35. Saeed had to work out $741 - 164 \div 4$
    His estimate was 150.
    His calculator result was 700.
    Which is wrong and why?

4

A WHOLE NUMBERS
NAMES FOR NUMBERS

> An even number ends in 0, 2, 4, 6 or 8.
> An odd number ends in 1, 3, 5, 7 or 9.

1 Look at these numbers.

200, 214, 227, 288, 121, 112

  a Write down those that are even numbers.
  b Write down those that are odd numbers.

2 Does 2 divide exactly into any even number?

3 Write down all the even numbers between 9 and 19.

4 Write down all the odd numbers between 50 and 60.

5 How many odd numbers are there between 6 and 16?

> A factor divides a number exactly.

6 Write down all the factors of 6. (Have you remembered 1 and 6?)

7 Find all the factors of 12.

8 a Is 6 a factor of 72?
  b Is 9 a factor of 95?

9 a Why is 5 not a factor of 5016?
  b Why is 5 a factor of 5010?

10 How can you tell if 3 is a factor of 5016?

11 a Find all the factors of 171.
   b Find all the factors of 30.

> You can find a multiple of a number by multiplying it by any other whole number.

12 Which of these numbers are multiples of 3?

1, 6, 8, 12, 14, 21

13 Write down all the multiples of 7 between 10 and 30.

14 How do you know that 1770 is a multiple of 5?

15 Is 60 a multiple of 5?

16 Write down all the multiples of 8 between 1 and 50. (Did you remember 8?)

> A prime number can only be divided exactly by itself and 1.

17 Write down all the prime numbers between 1 and 10.

18 Write down all the prime numbers between 10 and 20.

19 Which of these numbers are prime?

1, 2, 4, 6, 9, 11, 13, 15, 21.

20 2 is a prime number. Are there any other even prime numbers? Give a reason.

21 Write down the factors of 12. Which of these are prime?

22 Find the factors of 30 that are prime numbers.

23 Look at these numbers.

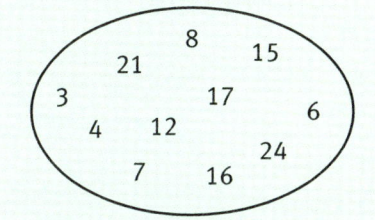

(8, 15, 21, 17, 3, 6, 4, 12, 24, 7, 16)

  a Write down those that are prime numbers.
  b Write down those that are even numbers.
  c Write down those that are multiples of 4.
  d Write down those that are factors of 24.

24 Find the largest number that is a factor of both 8 and 12.

25 Find the highest common factor of 6 and 9.

26 Find the lowest number that is a multiple of both 3 and 5.

27 Find the lowest number that is a multiple of both 8 and 12.

28 Find the largest prime number that is a factor of 18.

29 Find the largest prime factor of 45.

30 There is only one prime number that is a multiple of 7. Which is it?

31 There is only one prime number that has a factor of 13. Which is it?

32 Find two prime numbers between 1 and 20 such that one of them is 10 more than the other. (There are two answers, can you find them both?)

5

A WHOLE NUMBERS

INDICES

Example

Find 3^2.

$3^2 = 3 \times 3$
$= 9$

3^2 is called '3 squared'.

1. Find 4^2.
2. Find 2^2.
3. Find 5 squared.
4. Find the square of 10.

9 is a square number because $9 = 3 \times 3$.

5. Write down the square numbers between 1 and 50.
6. Which of these numbers are square numbers?
    18, 81, 144, 46, 36, 27
7. Write down the square number that is nearest in size to 20.

Example

Find 4^3.

$4^3 = 4 \times 4 \times 4$
$= 16 \times 4$
$= 64$

4^3 is called '4 cubed'.

8. Find 2 cubed.
9. Find 3^3.
10. Find 10^3.
11. Find the cube of 5.

Example

Find 3^4.

$3^4 = 3 \times 3 \times 3 \times 3$
$= 9 \times 3 \times 3$
$= 27 \times 3$
$= 81$

12. Find 2^4.
13. Find 10^4.
14. Find 3^5.
15. Find 2^5.
16. Find 10^2.
17. Find 10^5.
18. Find 10^6.
19. Find 2^6.

*$\sqrt{9} = 3$ because $9 = 3 \times 3$
$\sqrt{9}$ is called the square root of 9.*

20. Find $\sqrt{4}$.
21. Find $\sqrt{36}$.
22. Write down the square root of 25.
23. What is the square root of 100?
24. Find $\sqrt{64}$.

Example

Find 4×10^3.

$4 \times 10^3 = 4 \times 1000$
$= 4000$

Find

25. 2×10^2
26. 5×10^4
27. 26×10^3
28. 53×10^2
29. 671×10^5
30. 2×3^3
31. 4×5^2
32. 5×7^2

33. From the numbers in the box,

    | 4 16 25 27 36 75 100 |

    write down those that are
    a. cubed numbers
    b. square numbers larger than 50
    c. square roots of numbers less than 100
    d. multiples of 25
    e. factors of 100.

34. Find 5×3^3
35. Find $6^2 - 3^2$
36. Find $\sqrt{36} - \sqrt{16}$
37. Find $4^2 \times 5^2$
38. Find 54×10^5
39. Find 20^2
40. Find $10^4 \div 10^2$
41. Find $6^2 \div 3^2$
42. Find $\sqrt{100} \times \sqrt{25}$
43. Find $\sqrt{100} \div \sqrt{25}$
44. Find $8^2 - \sqrt{49}$

MIXED QUESTIONS ON WHOLE NUMBERS

45. Write down a number smaller than 50 that is
    a. a multiple of 5 and also a multiple of 6
    b. a factor of 26 and also a factor of 39.

46. The number 29 400 is divided by 300. What is the value of the digit 9 in the answer?

47. Find 26×200 and write the answer using
    a. figures   b. words.

48. A piece of tape is 176 cm long. It is cut into pieces each 24 cm long.
    a. How many pieces can be cut from the tape?
    b. What is the length of the piece of tape left over?

A WHOLE NUMBERS
INVESTIGATION

This is a number square.
Look at the shaded numbers. They make a cross.

1	2	3	4	5	6	7	8	9	10
11	12	13	14	15	16	17	18	19	20
21	22	23	24	25	26	27	28	29	30
31	32	33	34	35	36	37	38	39	40
41	42	43	44	45	46	47	48	49	50
51	52	53	54	55	56	57	58	59	60
61	62	63	64	65	66	67	68	69	70
71	72	73	74	75	76	77	78	79	80
81	82	83	84	85	86	87	88	89	90
91	92	93	94	95	96	97	98	99	100

1. Copy the shaded cross.
   a. Add the three numbers in the vertical strip of the cross.
   b. Add the three numbers in the horizontal strip of the cross.
   c. Find the difference between these sums.

2. Now try question **1** on three other crosses with different numbers in the middle.
   Do you still get the same answer?

3. Copy and complete this sentence.
   'Some numbers on the grid cannot be middle numbers because ....'

4. Look at the numbers in the vertical strip of any cross.
   a. How do you get from the middle number to the number above it?
      Answer this by copying and completing this sentence:
      In any cross, the number above the middle number = middle number ....
   b. How do you get from the middle number to the number below it?
      Answer this with a sentence like the one you used for part **a**.
   c. Now explain the relationship between the sum of the three numbers in the vertical strip of any cross and the middle number.

5. Now look at the numbers in the horizontal strip of any cross.
   Use reasons like those given in question **4** to explain what happens when you add the three numbers in the horizontal strip of any cross.

6. Now explain why you got the answers that you did for question **2**.

7. Can you make your explanations for questions **4** to **6** shorter?
   Try copying and filling in these crosses:

	37					
47	48			n	$n+1$	

8. Now try answering questions **1** to **7** with crosses that have five numbers in each strip.

9. Can you make a cross with any number of squares in each strip? Give a reason for your answer.

10. What happens if you take a cross of any size then add the numbers in the vertical strip, add the numbers in the horizontal strip and find the difference between the two sums? Explain your answer.

B SYMMETRY AND COORDINATES

LINE SYMMETRY

1 How many lines of symmetry does each shape have?

a   b 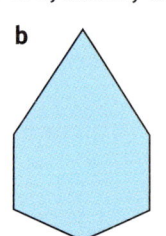   c

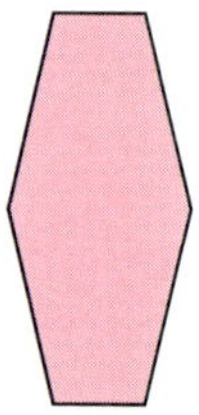

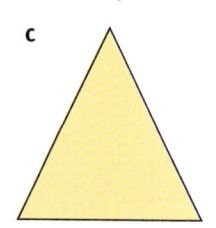

d 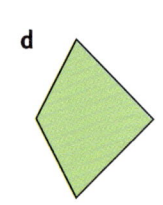   e

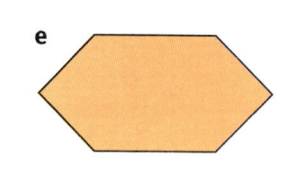

2 Copy each diagram.
  Complete the diagram so that the shape has symmetry about the broken line.

a   b

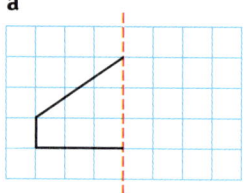

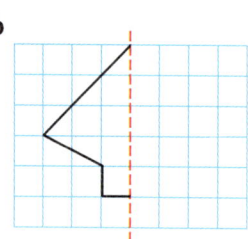

c 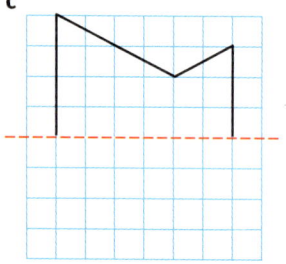   d

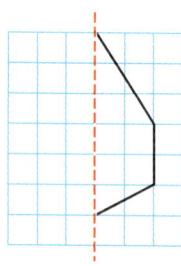

e 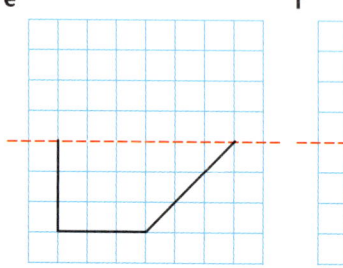   f

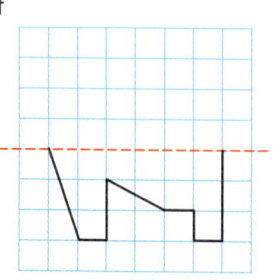

3 Copy each diagram.
  Draw all the lines of symmetry on your diagram.

a   b

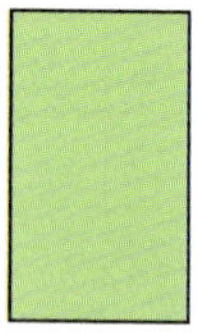

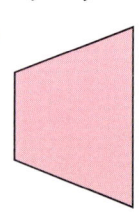

c 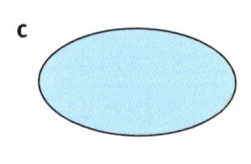   d

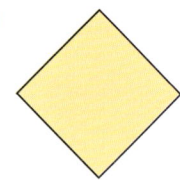

4 Copy and complete each letter so that each dashed line is a line of symmetry.

5 Copy this drawing on to squared paper.
  Complete it so that the two broken lines are lines of symmetry.

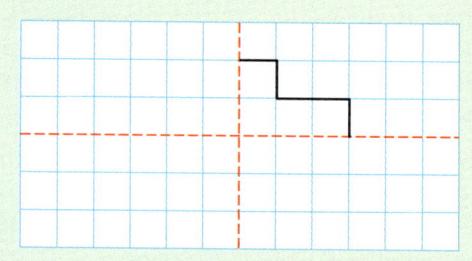

6 Copy this drawing on to squared paper.
  Complete it so that the two broken lines are lines of symmetry.

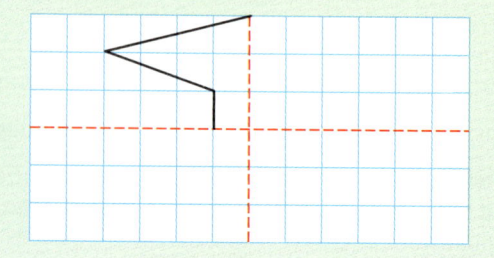

B SYMMETRY AND COORDINATES
ROTATIONAL SYMMETRY

1 What is the order of rotational symmetry of each of these diagrams?

a b 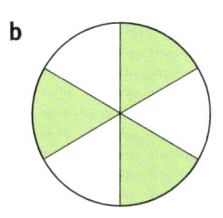 c 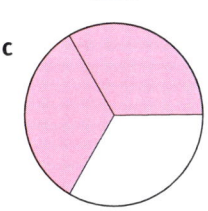 d 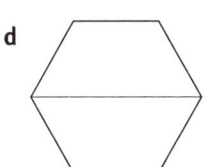 e 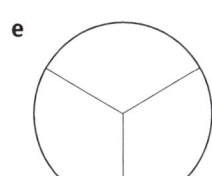 f 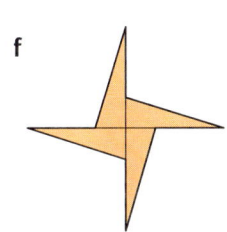 g 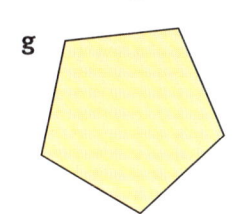 h

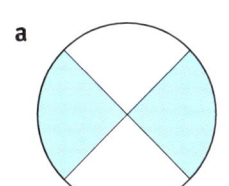

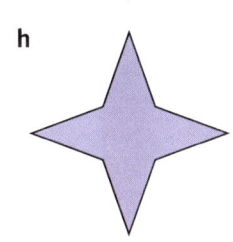

2 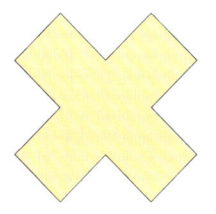 For this shape state
  a the order of rotational symmetry
  b the number of lines of symmetry.

3 Copy this shape.
Complete the shape so that it has rotational symmetry of order 2 about A.

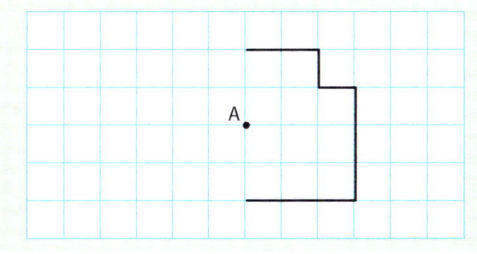

4 Copy this shape.
Complete the shape so that it has rotational symmetry of order 4 about the cross.

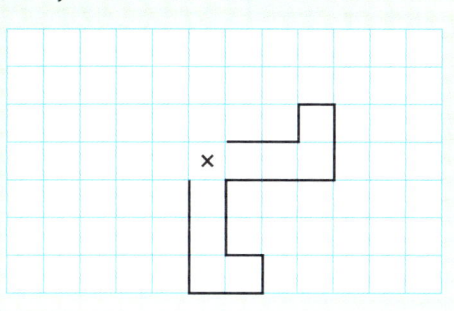

5 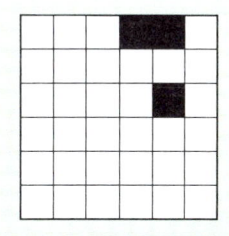 This is a blank for a crossword.
  a How many black squares are there in the quarter of the blank that is filled in?
  b The crossword is to be completed so that it has rotational symmetry of order 4 about its centre. How many black squares will there be in each of the other three quarters?
  c Copy and complete the crossword blank by shading the correct squares.

6 This is a blank for a crossword.
  a How many black squares are there in the quarter of the blank that is filled in?
  b The crossword is to have rotational symmetry of order 4 about its centre.
  How many black squares will there be in each of the remaining quarters?
  c Copy and complete the crossword blank by shading the correct squares.

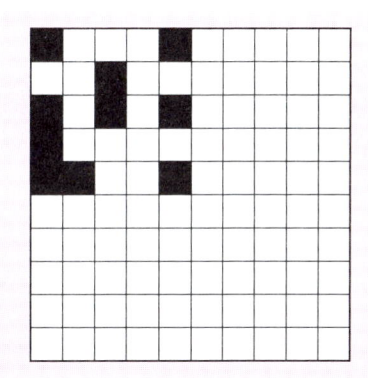

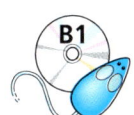

B SYMMETRY AND COORDINATES

COORDINATES

1

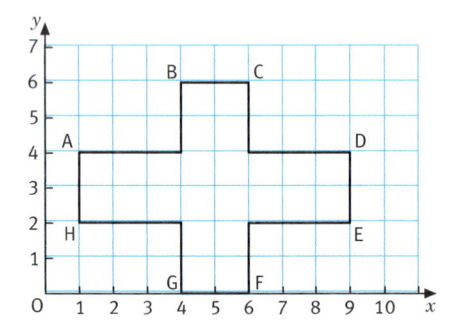

a The coordinates of A are (1, 4) and the coordinates of B are (4, 6).
Write down the coordinates of the other points marked by letters.

b What is the order of rotational symmetry of this shape?

2

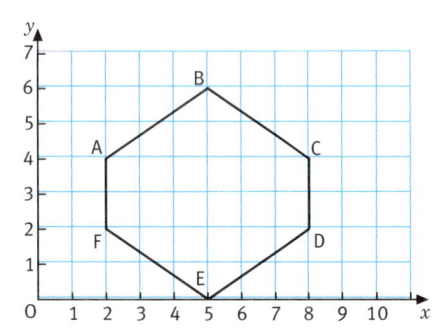

a Write down the coordinates of A.
b Write down, in alphabetical order, the coordinates of all the other points marked with capital letters.
c How many lines of symmetry does this shape have?

> The midpoint of the line joining two points is the point half way between the ends.

3

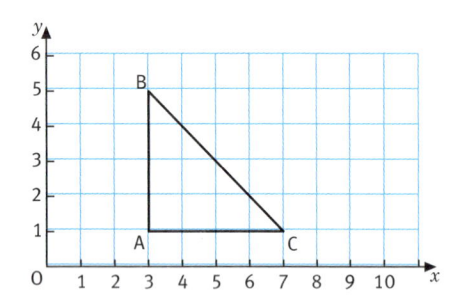

a Write down the coordinates of A, B and C.
b How many lines of symmetry does this shape have?
c Write down the coordinates of the midpoint of the line joining A and B.
d Write down the coordinates of the midpoint of the line joining A and C.
e Write down the coordinates of the midpoint of the line joining B and C.

4

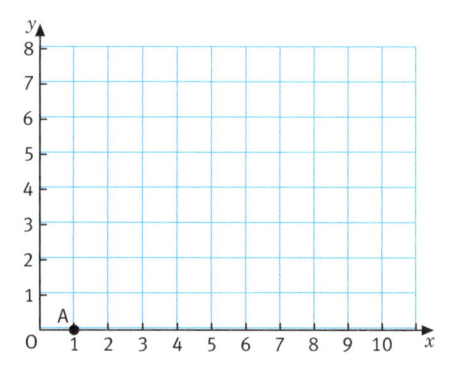

a Copy this diagram.
b Write down the coordinates of A.
c Mark the point B with coordinates (5, 8). Join AB.
d Write down the coordinates of the midpoint of AB.
e Does the point (4, 6) lie on this line?

5

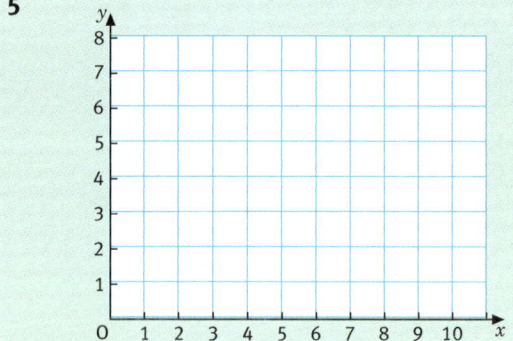

a Copy this diagram.
b Plot the points A(3, 4), B(6, 7), C(9, 4) and D(6, 1).
c Join these points in alphabetical order.
d What name do we give to this shape?
e How many lines of symmetry does the shape have?
f What is the order of rotational symmetry?

6 Use your diagram from question **4** for this question.
The points D and E lie on the line AB.

a The x-coordinate of D is 2.
What is the y-coordinate?
b The y-coordinate of E is 6.
What is the x-coordinate?
c For every point on the line there is a simple connection between the y-coordinate and the x-coordinate.
What is this connection?
d If the straight line is extended what is the value of y when x is 10?

B SYMMETRY AND COORDINATES
CONVERSION GRAPHS

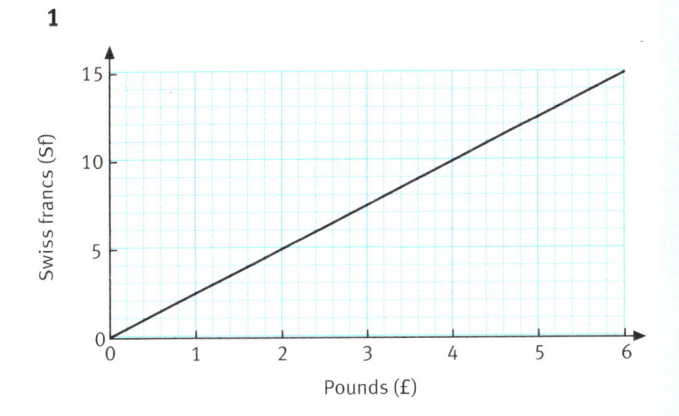

1

This graph converts between pounds Sterling and Swiss francs.

a Use the graph to find how many Swiss francs Kim would get for
  i £4
  ii £5.20
  iii £3.40.

b How many pounds would Mike get for
  i 5 francs
  ii 9 francs
  iii 14 francs?

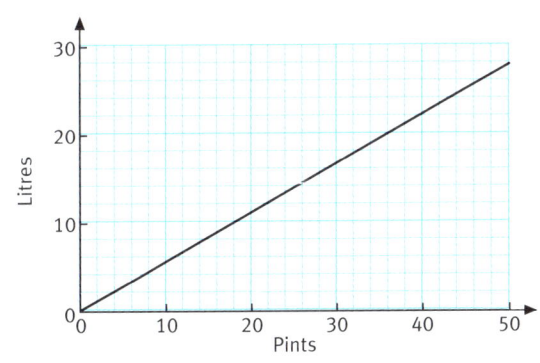

2

This graph converts between pints and litres.

a About how much is 40 pints in litres?

b Ed buys 10 litres of petrol. About how many pints is this?

c Sabina has 18 litres of water in her bucket. She needs 24 pints to mix with some fertiliser for the garden.
Does she have enough?
Give a reason for your answer.

3 The table shows the distances between some towns in miles and in kilometres.

Towns	Distance in miles	Distance in kilometres
Bickly and Ackford	5	8
Stanton and Eveley	15	24
Laxton and Southleigh	25	40

a Plot these values on a copy of the grid. Draw a straight line through your points.

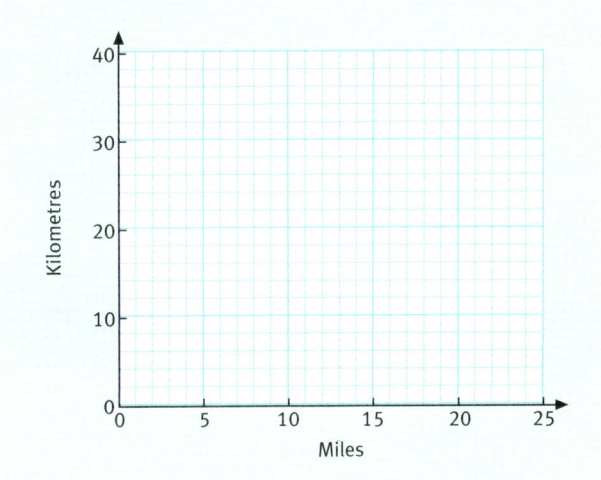

b Use your graph to find
  i 34 km in miles
  ii 12 miles in kilometres.

4 a Copy the table.

Pounds Sterling (£)	0	50	100
Euros (€)			150

b £100 is equivalent to 150 Euros. Complete the table.

c Draw a conversion graph to convert between pounds sterling (£) and Euros (€).
Use 1 cm to represent 10 units on both axes.
Plot pounds sterling across the page.
Plot Euros up the page.

d Use your graph to convert
  i 120 Euros into pounds
  ii £50 into Euros.

C ANGLES AND PARALLEL LINES
ANGLES

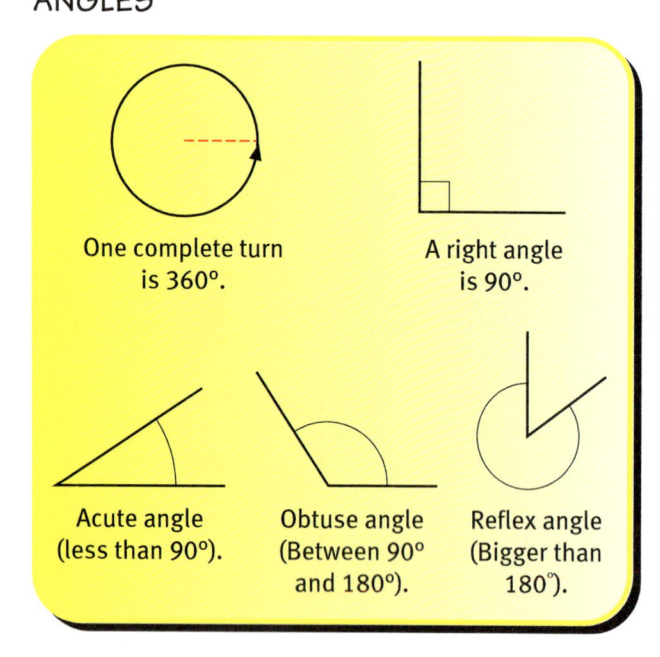

One complete turn is 360°.

A right angle is 90°.

Acute angle (less than 90°).

Obtuse angle (Between 90° and 180°).

Reflex angle (Bigger than 180°).

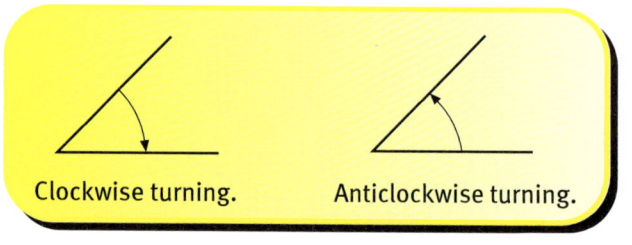

Clockwise turning.

Anticlockwise turning.

11 Which arrows in questions **1** to **10** show anticlockwise turning?

Use a protractor to measure the size of each angle.

What type is each angle: acute, right angle, obtuse or reflex?

1

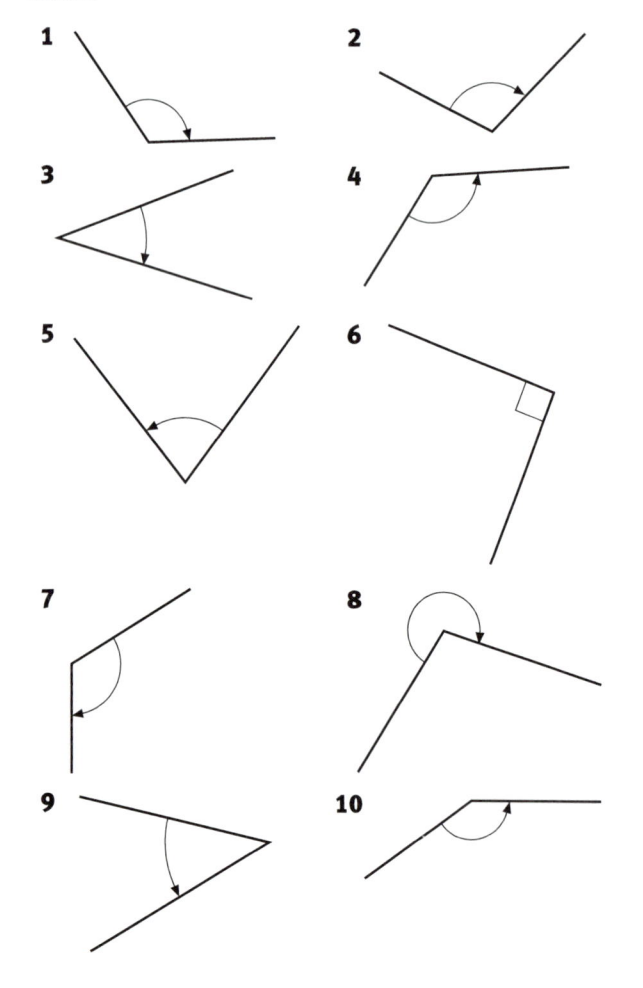

2

3

4

5

6

7

8

9

10

12

13

14

15

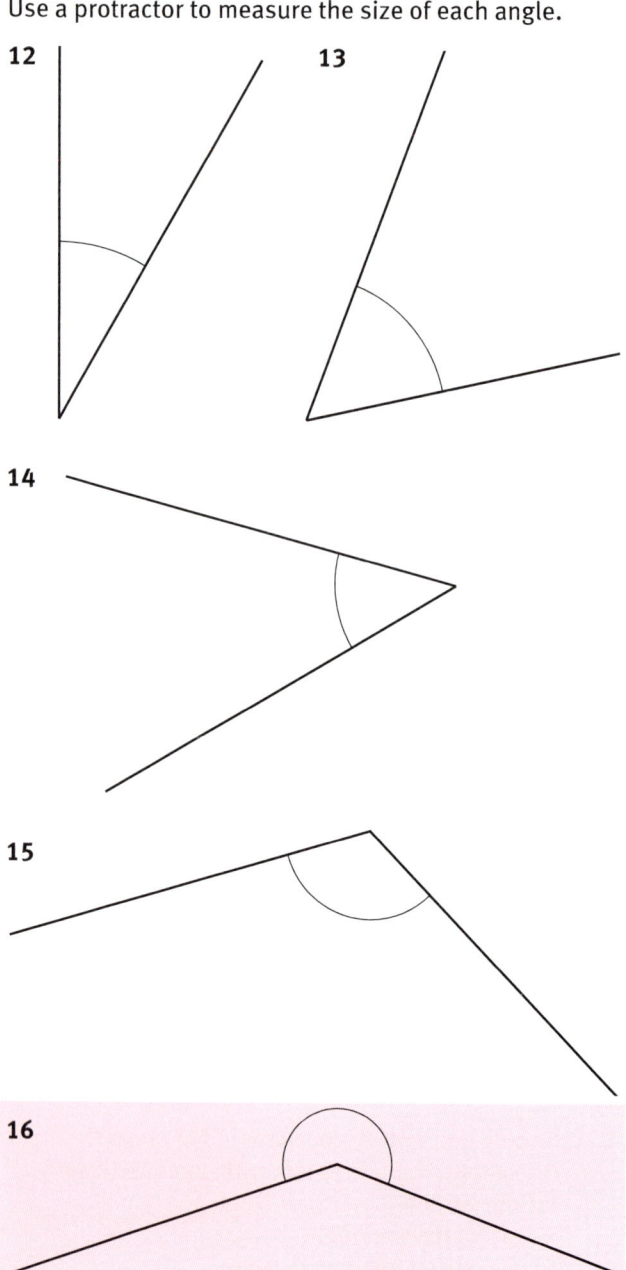

16

Use a protractor to measure the size of each angle.

17

18

19

20

Draw the following angles as well as you can by estimating.
Measure each angle using a protractor after you have estimated it.

21 90°   **22** 30°
23 120° **24** 60°
25 45°   **26** 70°
27 75°   **28** 150°
29 260° **30** 130°

Estimate the size of each angle.

31   **32**

33   **34**

35   **36**

37   **38**

Use a protractor to draw the following angles accurately.

39 25°   **40** 83°
41 125°   **42** 74°
43 37°   **44** 160°
45 136°   **46** 15°

47 274°   **48** 210°

13

C ANGLES AND PARALLEL LINES
ANGLE FACTS

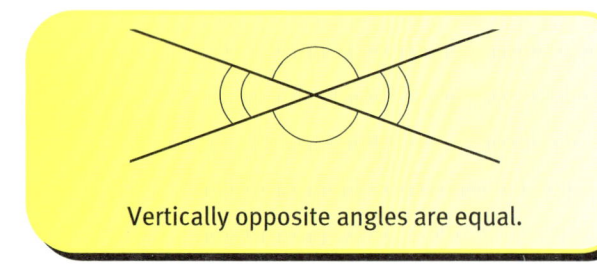

Vertically opposite angles are equal.

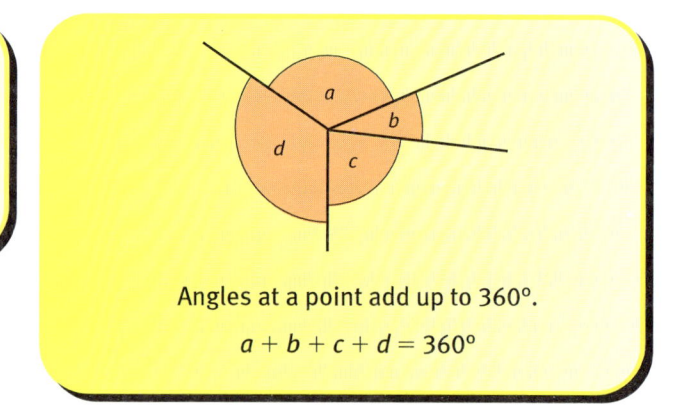

Angles at a point add up to 360°.

$a + b + c + d = 360°$

Find the size of each angle marked with a letter.

1. 120°, d
2. 50°, e
3. f, 45°
4. g, 138°

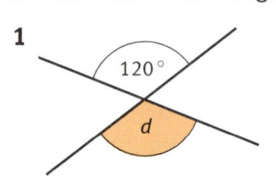

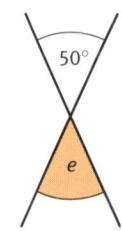

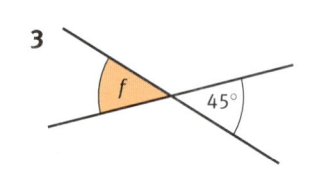

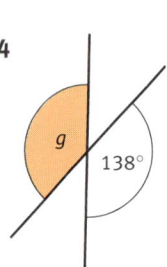

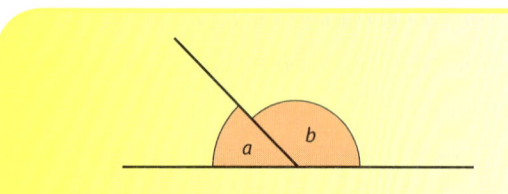

Angles on a straight line add up to 180°.

$a + b = 180°$

Find the size of each angle marked with a letter.

5. h (right angle)
6. i, 130°
7. 80°, j
8. 110°, k

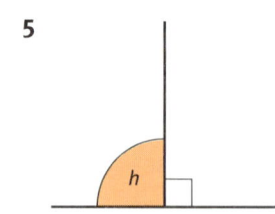

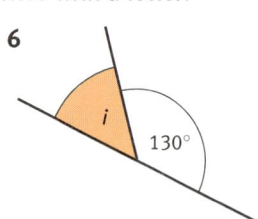

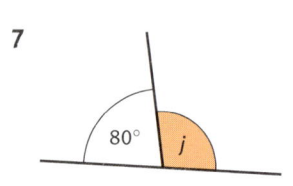

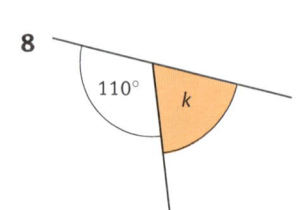

Find the size of each angle marked with a letter.

9. m, 40°
10. 240°, n
11. p, 120°
12. q, 150°
13. r, s, 130°
14. t, u, 65°
15. v, 95°, 150°
16. 75°, 45°, w, 100°
17. y, 70°, x, z
18. a, 200° (right angle)

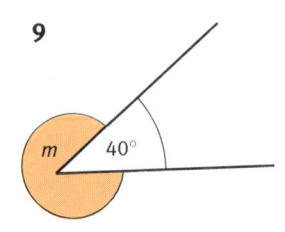

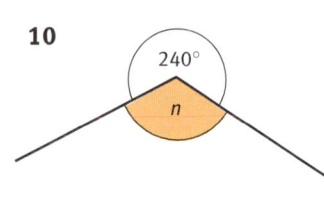

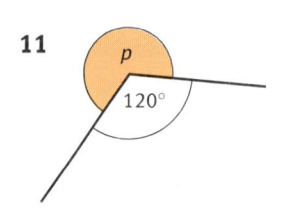

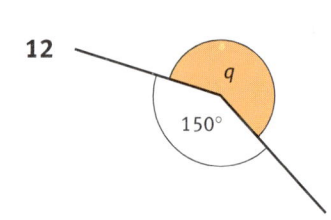

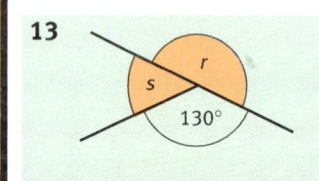

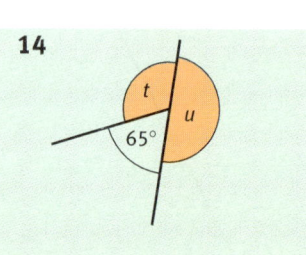

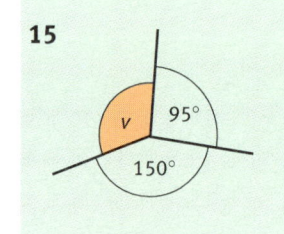

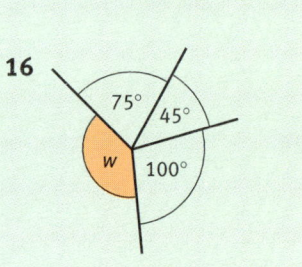

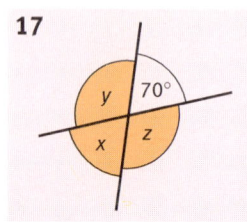

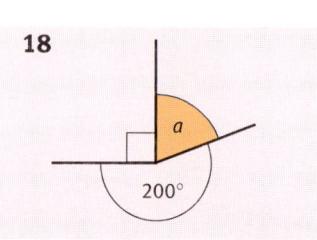

C ANGLES AND PARALLEL LINES
PARALLEL LINES

1

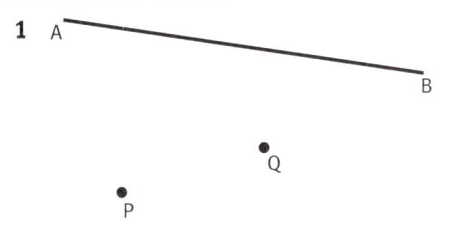

A •———————————• B

• Q

• P

a Copy the diagram.
b Draw a line through P that is parallel to AB.
c Draw a line through Q perpendicular to AB.

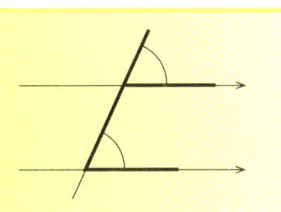

> The marked angles are **corresponding angles**.
> Corresponding angles are equal.
> Look for the letter F, which may be upside down or on its side or backwards.

Find the size of the angle marked with a letter.

2 74°, d

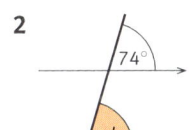

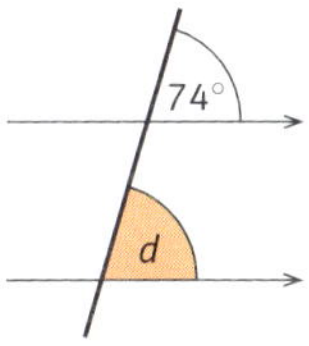

3 110°, e

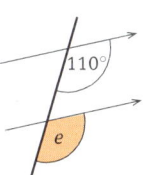

4 65°, f

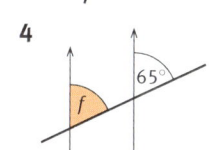

5 105°, g

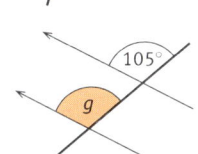

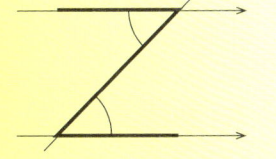

> The marked angles are **alternate angles**.
> Alternate angle are equal.
> Look for the letter Z, which may be on its side or backwards.

Find the size of the angle marked with a letter.

6 65°, h

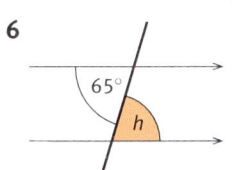

7 i, 120°

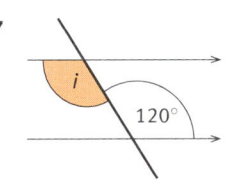

8 70°, j

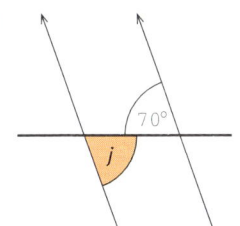

9 95°, k

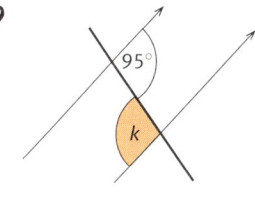

10
a Which angle corresponds to p?
b Which angle corresponds to r?
c Which angle is alternate to v?
d Which angle is alternate to q?

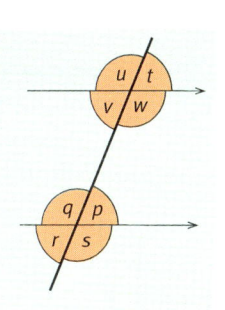

e $p = 65°$. Find q.
f $u = 120°$. Find w.
g $t = 75°$. Find p.
h $v = 80°$. Find t.
i $q = 110°$ Find w.
j $p = 75°$ Find v.

In questions **11** to **18** find the size of each marked angle.

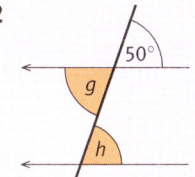

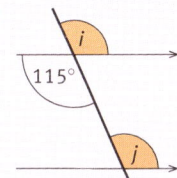

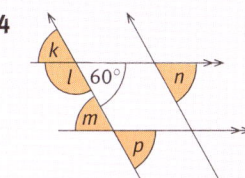

11 130°, d, e, f

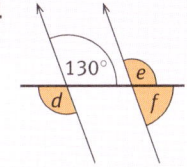

12 50°, g, h

13 115°, i, j

14 k, l, 60°, m, n, p

15 q, 65°, r

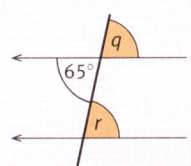

16 t, u, s, 110°

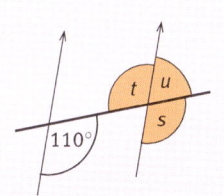

17 75°, v

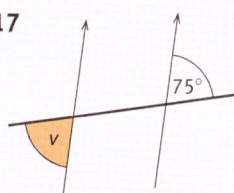

18 x, w, 70°

15

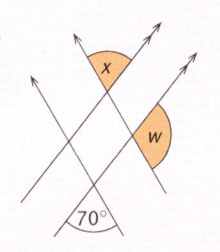

C ANGLES AND PARALLEL LINES
COMPASS DIRECTIONS AND BEARINGS

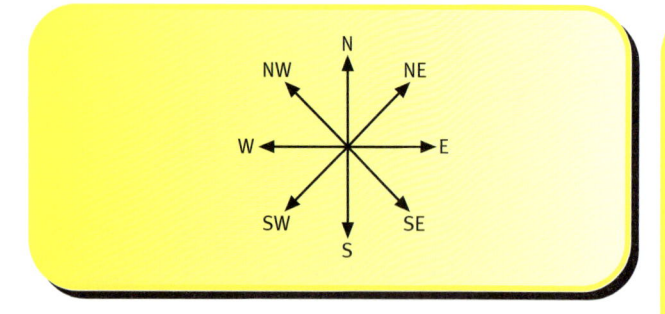

A three-figure bearing is the angle turned through clockwise from north.

From A the bearing of B is 210°.

From C the bearing of D is 055°.

1 Peter, Sara and Harry are standing in the positions shown below.

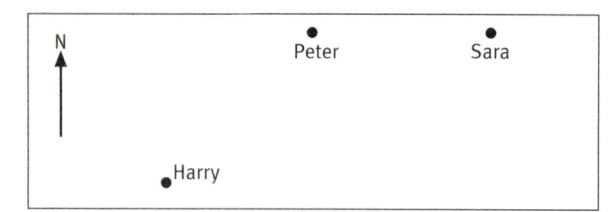

a In what direction is Sara from Peter?
b In what direction is Peter from Sara?
c In what direction is Harry from Peter?
d In what direction is Peter from Harry?
e Sara stands facing north. She turns clockwise through 90°. In what direction is she now facing?
f Harry stands facing south. He turns anticlockwise through 90°. In what direction is he now facing?
g Peter stands facing east. He turns clockwise through 45°. In what direction is he now facing?
h Sara stands facing west. She turns anticlockwise through 180°. In what direction is she now facing?

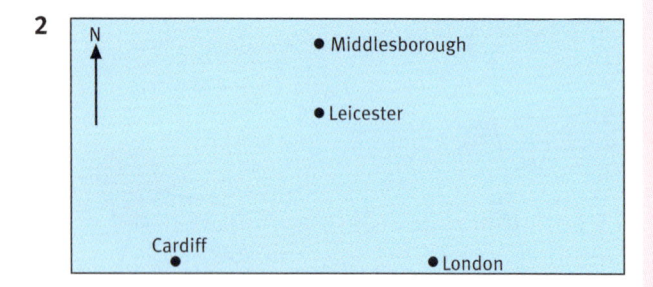

2

a Write down the name of the place that is west of London.
b Write down the name of the place that is due north of Leicester.
c Write down the compass direction of London from Cardiff.
d Write down the compass direction of Cardiff from Leicester.

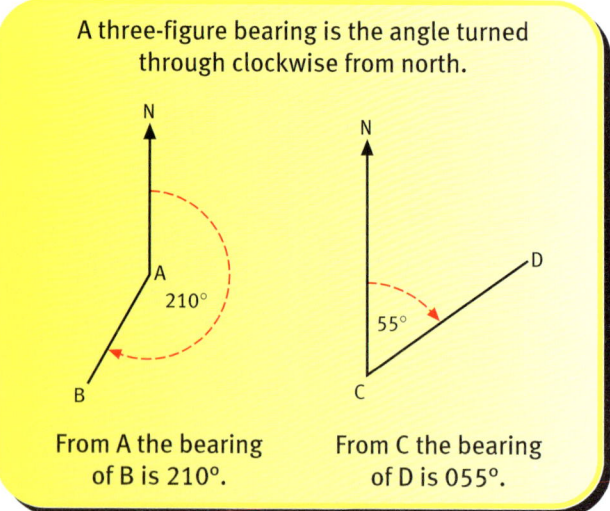

In questions **3** to **8** draw a freehand sketch to show each bearing.
Start by drawing a line to show due north.
Mark the given angle in your sketch.

3 From a ship S the bearing of a yacht Y is 045°.
4 From a point P the bearing of a radio mast M is 120°.
5 From a point H the bearing of a church C is 225°.
6 The bearing of a town A from a town B is 075°.
7 From a boat B the bearing of a port P is 300°.
8 The bearing of a tree T from a hilltop H is 180°.

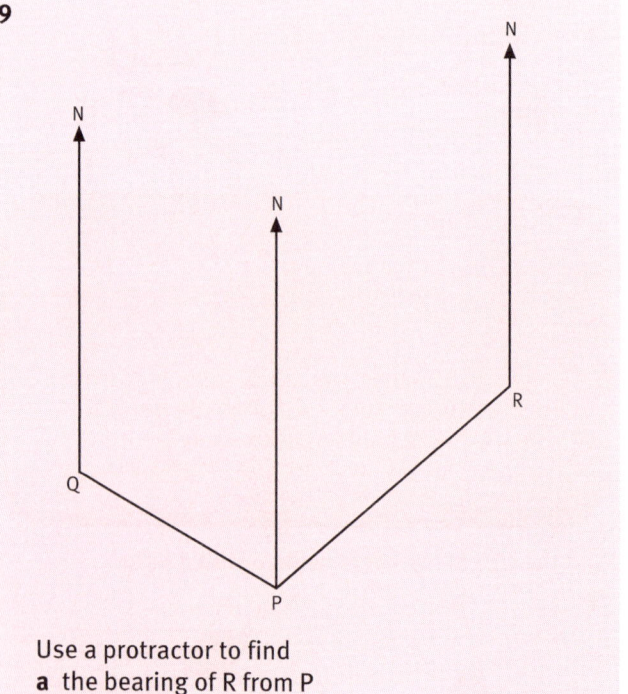

9

Use a protractor to find
a the bearing of R from P
b the bearing of Q from P
c the bearing of R from Q.

16

D COLLECTING AND ILLUSTRATING DATA

PICTOGRAMS

1   **Year 10 pupils taking lunch in the school canteen**

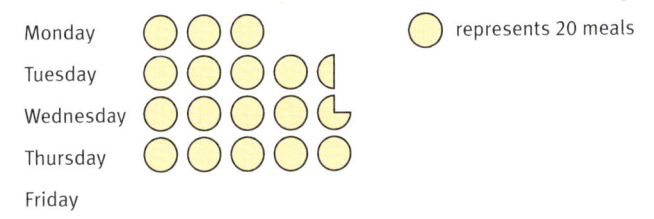

Monday: ○ ○ ○
Tuesday: ○ ○ ○ ○ ◐
Wednesday: ○ ○ ○ ○ ◔
Thursday: ○ ○ ○ ○ ○
Friday:

○ represents 20 meals

a How many meals were served on Monday?
b How many meals were served on Tuesday?
c How many more meals were served on Thursday than on Wednesday?
d 65 meals were served on Friday.
   Show this on a copy of the pictogram.

2   **The most popular subject among Year 10 pupils**

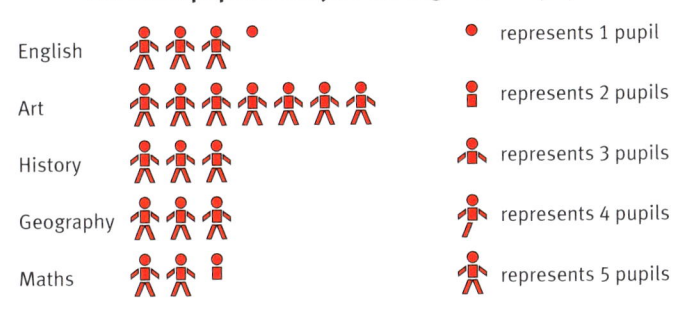

English: 👤 👤 👤 •
Art: 👤 👤 👤 👤 👤 👤
History: 👤 👤 👤
Geography: 👤 👤 👤
Maths: 👤 👤 👤

• represents 1 pupil
▮ represents 2 pupils
👤 represents 3 pupils
👤 represents 4 pupils
👤 represents 5 pupils

a Which is the most popular subject?
b How many pupils are shown in total in the diagram?
c Twenty-three pupils did not have a favourite subject.
   Draw a line of 'stick people', to show how you would represent these.

3   **Number of letters delivered in Coronation Street**

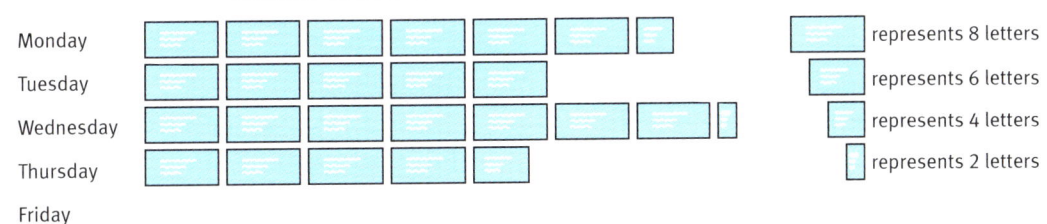

Monday: ▭ ▭ ▭ ▭ ▭ ▭ ▭
Tuesday: ▭ ▭ ▭ ▭
Wednesday: ▭ ▭ ▭ ▭ ▭ ▭ ▯
Thursday: ▭ ▭ ▭ ▭ ▭
Friday:

▭ represents 8 letters
▭ represents 6 letters
▭ represents 4 letters
▯ represents 2 letters

a How many letters were delivered on Tuesday?
b How many letters were delivered on Monday?
c How many letters were delivered, in total, on Monday, Tuesday, Wednesday and Thursday?
d How many more letters were delivered on Wednesday than on Thursday?
e Thirty-six letters were delivered on Friday.
   Show, in your workbook, how you would represent this number on the pictogram.

4 James carried out a survey to find out where the cars in the school car park had been made.
The results of the survey were:
     United Kingdom 17, Europe 32, Japan 24, Rest of the world 7
Draw a pictogram to represent this information.
Use 🚗 to represent 4 cars, 🚗 to represent 3 cars, 🚗 to represent 2 cars and 🚗 to represent 1 car.

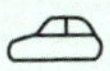

D COLLECTING AND ILLUSTRATING DATA

MAKING FREQUENCY TABLES

1 The list shows the number of pens owned by each pupil in Class 10K.

    1 0 3 4 2 1 1 2 1
    2 1 0 3 1 1 0 1 1
    1 4 0 1 2 1 0 3 1

   a How many pupils gave information to make this list?
   b Copy and complete the following table.

Number of pens	Tally	Frequency
0		
1		
2		
3		
4		

2 This is a list of the favourite colours of forty-eight members of a Youth Club.
   They could choose from the colours red (R), yellow (Y), blue (B), green (G) and pink (P).

    G B Y G R P Y B B Y P B
    B R B R G B P R Y R R Y
    R B R B R G G B G B R G
    R Y B R R R B B Y Y G R

   Make a frequency table for this list.

3 These are the scores (out of 30) achieved by twenty-seven pupils in a test.

    20 5 11 19 15 26 18 17 9
    17 27 23 17 23 25 18 13 12
    24 2 7 6 22 12 19 29 30

   Copy and complete this frequency table.

Score	Tally	Frequency
0–6		
7–12		
13–18		
19–24		
25–30		

4 The size of the workforce at twenty-five factories is

    12 34 23 36 38
    43 19 26 43 21
    19 45 32 41 29
    30 18   9 24 44
    22 46 37 48 16

Make a frequency table for this data.
Use the groups 0–10, 11–20, 21–30, 31–40 and 41–50.

5 These are the scores in sixteen different football matches.
The score of the home side is given first.

   3–2, 0–1, 2–0, 1–1, 2–0, 0–1, 3–1, 1–1,
   2–1, 1–0, 5–0, 2–0, 1–0, 2–3, 2–0, 1–0

   a Copy and complete this frequency table which shows the number of goals scored by each of the thirty-two teams.

Number of goals scored	Tally	Frequency
0		
1		
2		
3		
4		
5		

   b How many teams scored goals?
   c How many teams scored more than 1 goal?

D COLLECTING AND ILLUSTRATING DATA
BAR CHARTS

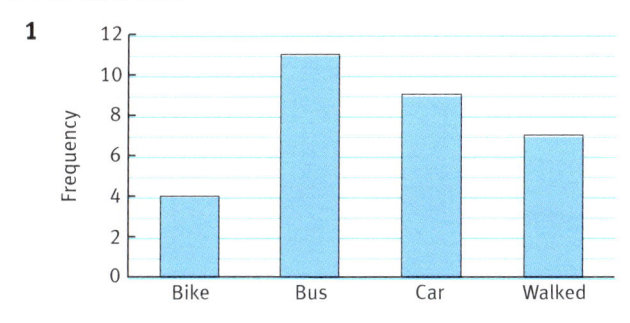

1 This bar chart shows how the pupils in Class 10K came to school this morning.
  a How many pupils came by bus?
  b How many pupils walked?
  c How many pupils are there in Class 10K?

2 The bar chart shows the shoe sizes of a class of 16-year-old girls.
  a How many girls are there in the class?
  b Which size is the least common size of shoe?

3

Number of kittens	0	1	2	3	4	5	6
Frequency	2	6	0	11	4	3	1

The table shows the number of kittens born to each cat in a cattery during the last six months.
  a Draw a bar chart to show this information.
  b Work out the number of cats that had 3 or more kittens.
  c Copy and complete this frequency polygon for the data.

4 300 office staff spent their last holiday leave as follows:

Stayed at home 80, In the UK 100, In Europe 50, In the USA 30, Elsewhere 40.

Show this information on a bar chart.
Use 1 centimetre to represent 20 people.

5 The marks of thirty pupils in a test are listed below.

45 24 32 21 32 52 26 44 32 35
35 23 54 39 19 35 22 56 45 38
28 34 28 43 38 49 29 15 30 31

  a Copy and complete this frequency table.

Mark	Tally	Frequency
11–20		
21–30		
31–40		
41–50		
51–60		

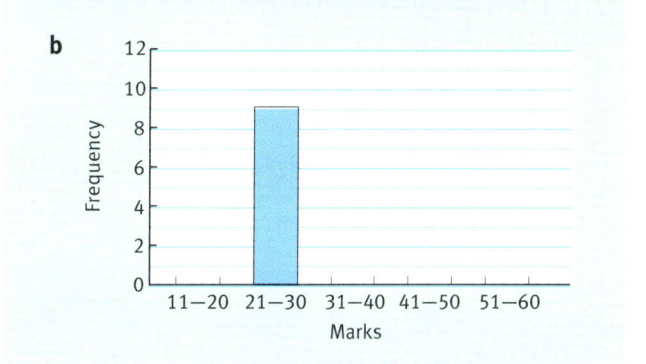

  b Copy and complete the bar chart to illustrate the distribution of the marks.

6 This list shows the number of people attending a weekly dancing class during the first half of the year.

32 14 36 35 31 27 25 19 17
26 35 37 31 39 16 27 32 33
31 38 29 19 34 37 31 27

  a Make a frequency table for this data.
     Use the groups 9–16, 17–24, 25–32 and 33–40.
  b Draw a bar chart to illustrate this information.
  c Draw a frequency polygon for this data.

D COLLECTING AND ILLUSTRATING DATA
SCATTER GRAPHS

1

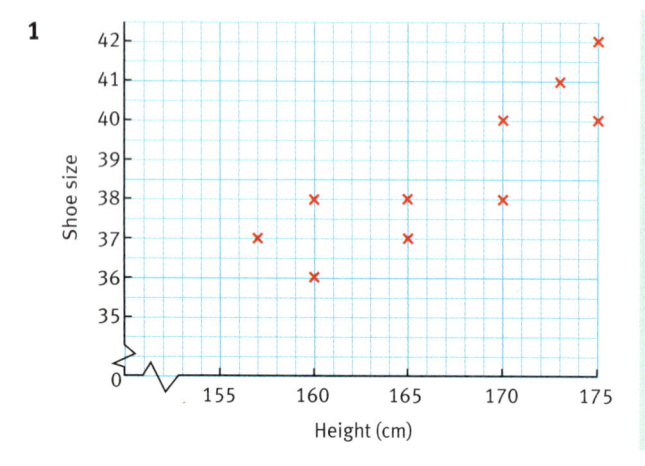

This graph shows the relationship between the heights and shoe sizes of a group of students.

a How many students gave details of their height and shoe size?

b Which of the following statements best fits this data?
   A There is no relationship between height and shoe size.
   B Tall people tend to take a large size of shoe.
   C People with large feet tend to be short.

c Draw a line of best fit.

d Sam's height is 170 cm.
   What shoe size is he likely to take?

e Peter takes a size 40 shoe.
   About how tall is he likely to be?

2 This table shows the heights and weights of 8 people.

Height (cm)	150	152	158	160	163	165	170	175
Weight (kg)	58	62	64	62	65	66	65	70

a Plot this data on a graph.
   Use 1 cm to represent 5 cm on the horizontal axis and 1 cm to represent 2 kg on the vertical axis.
   Start the horizontal axis at 150 cm and the vertical axis at 56 kg.

b Describe the correlation between the heights and weights of this group of people.

c Draw a line of best fit.

d John is 165 cm tall. About how heavy is he likely to be?

3 This table shows the number of rooms and the number of people living in each of eight houses.

Number of rooms	3	4	4	5	5	6	6	7
Number of people	2	3	4	1	5	3	4	5

a Draw a scatter graph for this data.
   Use 1 centimetre for 1 unit on each axis.

b Helen lives in a house with 4 other people.
   Is the house likely to have more than 4 rooms?

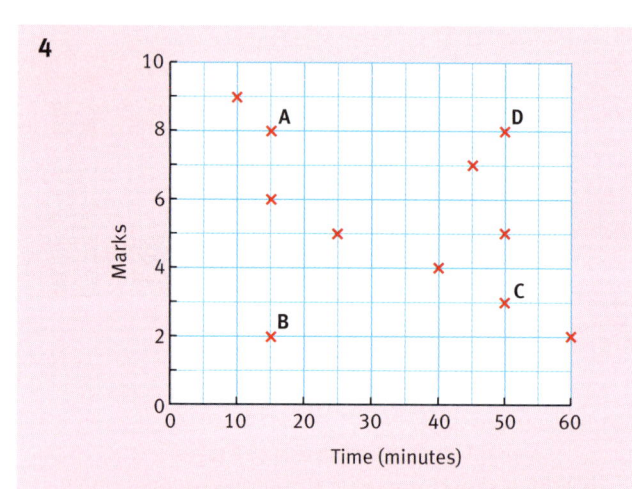

4

The scatter graph shows the relationship between the number of minutes a group of pupils spent on their science homework and the number of marks they were given for this homework.
Write down the letter of the point that best fits each sentence.

a Kerry spent a lot of time doing her homework but didn't score many marks.

b Sue did her homework quickly and scored high marks.

c Doug did well by spending a lot of time at his homework.

Bryn's performance is marked with the letter B.

d Write a sentence to describe this.

e How would you describe the relationship between marks and time?

D COLLECTING AND ILLUSTRATING DATA
TIME SERIES AND STEM-AND-LEAF DIAGRAMS

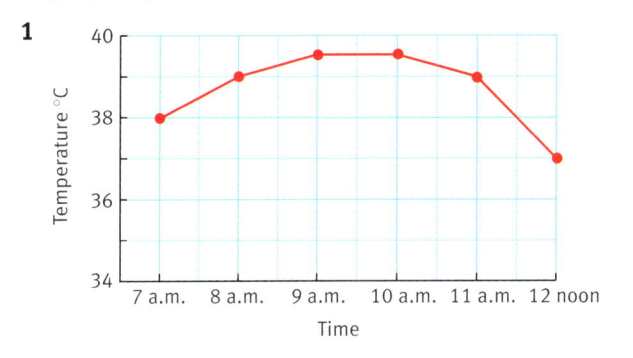

1 The graph shows Carol's temperature one morning. Her temperature was taken every hour.
  a What was Carol's temperature
    i at 7 a.m.   ii at 11 a.m.?
  b What was the highest temperature taken?
  c During which hour did her temperature rise most?

By 12 noon Carol's temperature had returned to normal.
  d What is Carol's normal temperature?
  e How long did it take for her temperature to fall from its highest level to normal?

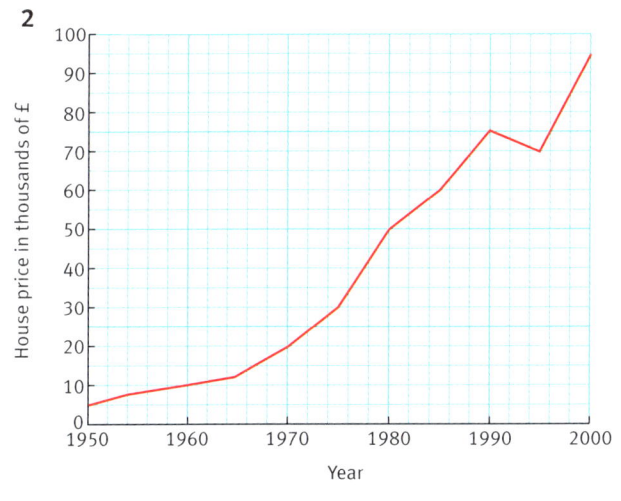

2 The graph shows the price of a standard house in Walter Street at 5-year intervals from 1950 to 2000.
  a What was the price of a house in
    i 1970   ii 2000?
  b In which 10-year period did the price increase most?
  c By how much did the value change
    i between 1970 and 1990
    ii between 1965 and 1995?
  d Was there any 5-year period when the price fell? Explain how you decided on your answer.
  e How would you describe the trend in house prices?

3 Twenty boys were asked what they spent on lunch yesterday.
This stem-and-leaf diagram shows the distribution of these amounts.

Amount spent on lunch   1|26 means £1.26

0	00 90
1	26 35 50
2	00 10 50 85 85
3	50 65 77 80 80 90
4	10 15 25 60
5	05 10

  a How many boys spent more than £3?
  b How many boys spent less than £2?
  c How many boys spent nothing?
  d How many boys spent £2.85?
  e How many boys spent between £3 and £4?

4 Jenny counted the number of words in each sentence in an article in the *Daily Record*.
These are the results in order of size.

5 5 6 6 6 7 8 8 8 8 8 9
9 10 10 11 12 13 17 17 20 21 21 25

  a Jenny made this stem-and-leaf diagram but left out the last four numbers.

Number of words   1|2 means 12

0	5 5 6 6 6 7 8 8 8 8 8 9 9
1	0 0 1 2 3 7 7
2	

Copy this stem-and-leaf diagram and add in the last four numbers.
  b How many sentences were in the article?
  c How many sentences had more than 10 words?
  d Which of these groups contains most sentences: 0–9 words, 10–19 words, 20 or more words?

5 Jack measured 25 leaves from a holly bush. These are his measurements in order of length.

25 mm   29 mm   30 mm   31 mm   37 mm
38 mm   38 mm   39 mm   40 mm   41 mm
42 mm   42 mm   43 mm   43 mm   43 mm
44 mm   44 mm   45 mm   46 mm   46 mm
47 mm   48 mm   51 mm   51 mm   52 mm

Draw a stem-and-leaf diagram to show these measurements. Use the digit giving the number of tens for the stem and the digit giving the number of units for the leaves.

D COLLECTING AND ILLUSTRATING DATA
INVESTIGATION

'Petrol consumption of a car is linked to engine size.' Investigate.

1. Start by writing your own hypothesis, that is write down in your own words, what your investigation is going to test.
   For example: 'My hypothesis is that cars with large engines do fewer miles per gallon than cars ....'

2. Now decide what questions you need to answer. Write these down in your own words.
   For example: 'For each car I look at, I need to find out
   - a the size of its engine
   - b its petrol consumption.'

   To answer **a** you need to know what figures to use for the engine size.
   To answer **b** you need to know how petrol consumption is measured.

3. You need to decide which cars to consider. For example, do you look at cars that are the same make and body shape but come with several different engine sizes, like the Vauxhall Vectra; do you look at cars from one manufacturer only or from several different manufacturers? How many cars do you need altogether? When you have discussed these points, write down a sentence giving your decision. For example, 'I have decided to investigate cars that ....'

   Next you have to find the information about the engine size and the petrol consumption of different cars. You can look in car magazines such as *What Car* or you could use information on an internet site such as www.autotrader.co.uk.

4. Write the information in a table like this one.

Name of car	Ford Ka (Hatchback 3D)				
Engine size (litres)	1.3				
Petrol consumption (combined m.p.g.)	48				

5. Next represent your information on a scatter graph.

6. Your scatter graph will show what the relationship is between the engine sizes and petrol consumptions of the cars you looked at so you can now give an opinion on your hypothesis and you must write this down. Whatever conclusion you come to it must be based on **your** investigation **and** it must be supported by reasons. Write a sentence such as: 'The evidence shows that there is no connection between engine size and the amount of petrol used by Ford cars because the points on the scatter graph ....' or 'My investigation shows that, for the cars I looked at, the larger the engine the higher the petrol consumption because ....'

E TRANSFORMATIONS

REFLECTION

1

a Write down the coordinates of
  i X ii Y iii Z.

b Copy the diagram.
  On your copy draw the reflection of triangle XYZ in the line AB.

c What are the coordinates of the reflection of Z?

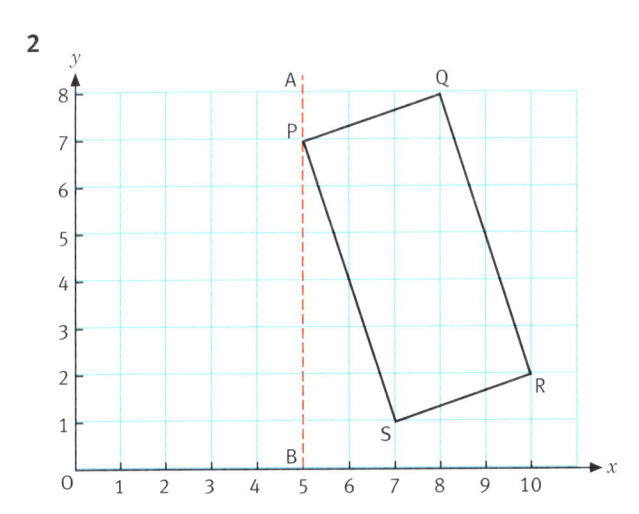

2

a Write down the coordinates of
  i P ii Q iii R iv S.

b Copy the diagram. On your copy draw the reflection of rectangle PQRS in the line AB.

c What are the coordinates of the reflection of
  i Q ii S?

d What are the coordinates of the **midpoint** of the reflection of the line PS?

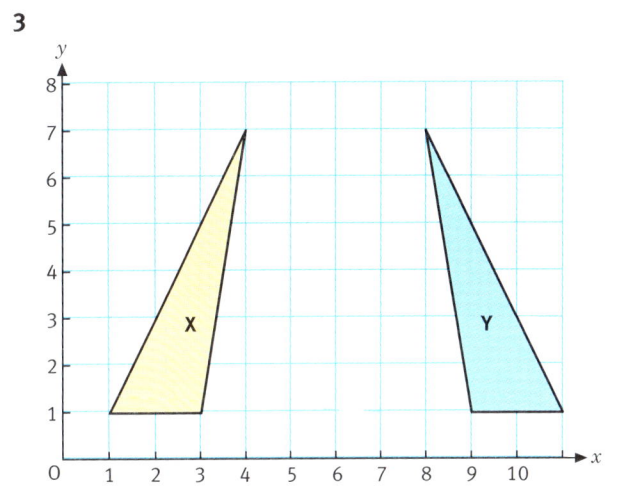

3

The triangle marked **X** is a reflection in a mirror line of the triangle marked **Y**.

a Copy the diagram and draw the mirror line on your copy.

b Write down the coordinates of the vertex at the obtuse angle in triangle **Y**.

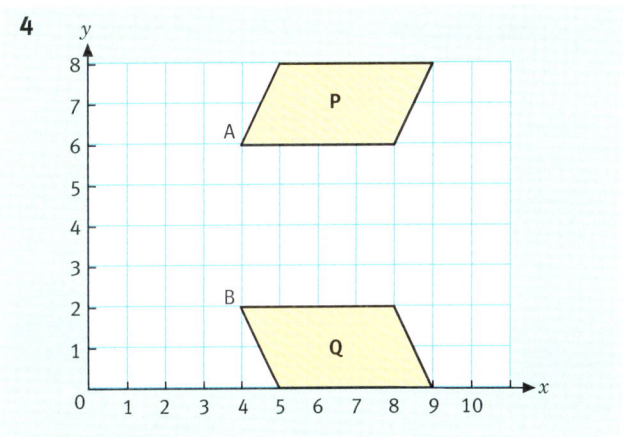

4

The parallelogram **P** is a reflection in a mirror line of the parallelogram **Q**.

a Copy the diagram and draw the mirror line on your copy.

A is a vertex of one parallelogram and B a vertex of the other.

b Join the points A and B on your copy.
  Write down the coordinates of the point where the line AB crosses the mirror line.
  Where is this point in relation to A and B?

23

E TRANSFORMATIONS
ROTATION AND TRANSLATION

1. Each shape has rotational symmetry. Copy each diagram and on it mark the centre of rotational symmetry with a cross.
   (You can use tracing paper if you wish.)

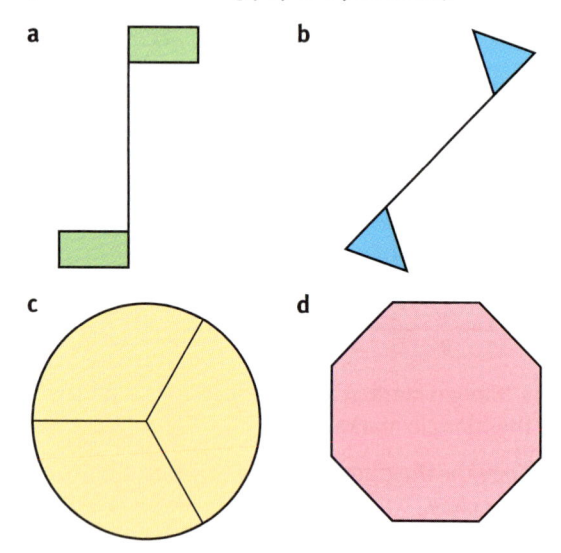

   a b c d

2. Copy each diagram.
   For each shape
   i write down the order of rotational symmetry
   ii mark the centre of rotational symmetry with a cross.

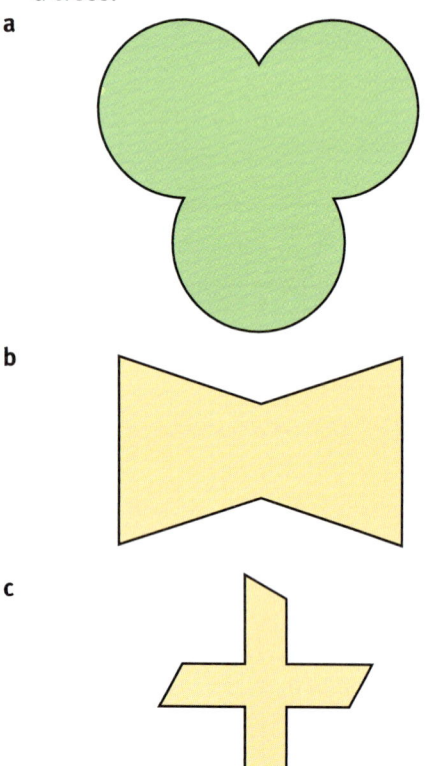

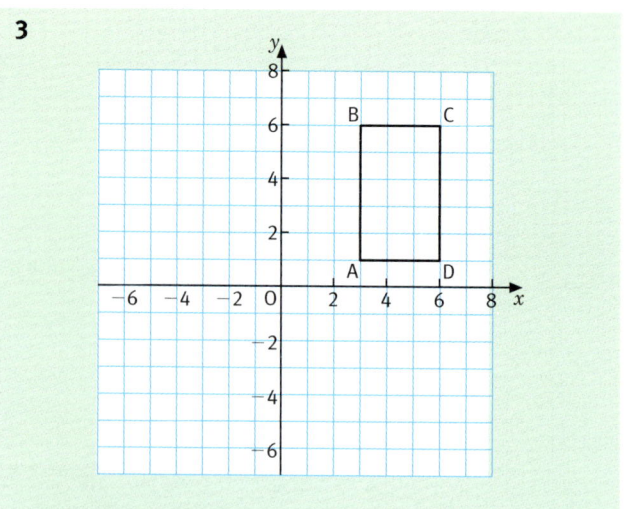

   a b c

3.

   Copy the diagram.

   a On your diagram draw the rectangle ABCD when it is translated 5 units to the left and 6 units down. Mark it **X**.
   Write down the coordinates of the point that C maps onto.

   b Draw the rectangle ABCD after it has been rotated through 90° anticlockwise about O. Mark it **Y**.

4.

   Which triangle on the diagram shows the new position of triangle **X** when it is

   a translated 6 units to the left

   b rotated through half a turn about O

   c rotated 90° clockwise about the point (3, 2).

E TRANSFORMATIONS
ENLARGEMENT

1

Copy the diagram onto squared paper.
a Enlarge the coloured shape using a scale factor of 3.
b How many times larger is the perimeter of the new shape than the perimeter of the original shape?
c How many times larger is the area of the enlarged shape than the original one?

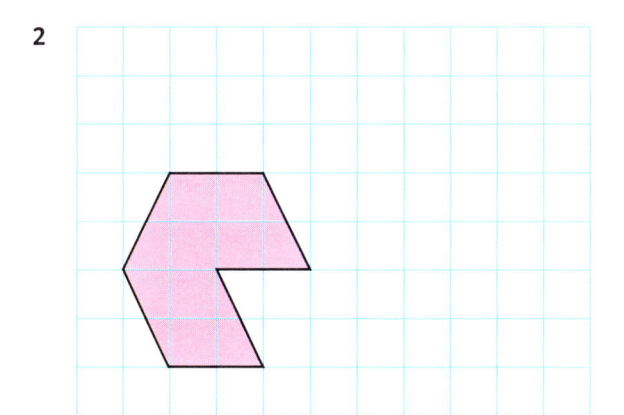

2

Copy this shape on a grid.
On your grid draw an enlargement, scale factor 2, of the coloured shape.

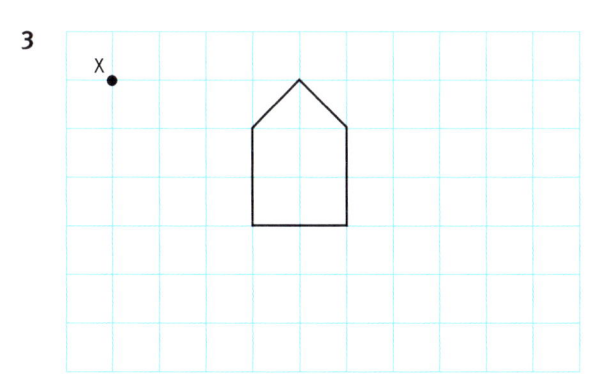

3

Copy this diagram.
On your grid, draw the enlargement of the pentagon, scale factor 2, centre X.

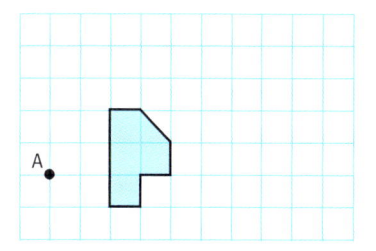

4

Copy the diagram.
On your grid draw an enlargement of the coloured figure using a scale factor of 2 and centre of enlargement A.

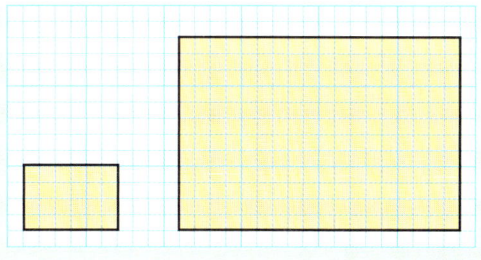

5

The diagram represent two sheets of paper.
Each small square represents a square of side 1 cm.
a Work out the area of the smaller sheet.
b The second sheet is an enlargement of the smaller sheet. What is the scale factor?
c Write down the measurements of the larger sheet.
d Work out the area of the larger sheet.
e Copy and complete this sentence:
The area of the larger sheet is .... times the area of the smaller sheet.

6

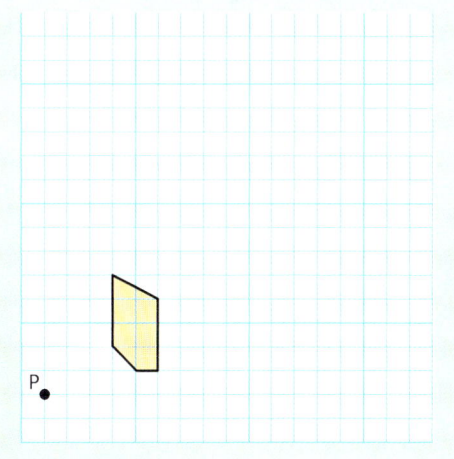

A pentagon is shown on a grid.
Copy the diagram.
On your grid, draw an enlargement of the pentagon, scale factor 3, centre P.

F SEQUENCES

CONTINUING A SEQUENCE

1. 5, 9, 13, 17, ...
   Each term is four more than the previous term.
   Write down the next three terms.

2. 99, 94, 89, 84, ...
   Each term is five less than the previous term.
   Write down the next three terms.

3. 5, 15, 45, 135, ...
   Each term is three times the previous term.
   Write down the next three terms.

4. 96, 48, 24, ...
   Each term is half the previous term.
   Write down the next three terms.

5. 2, 3, 5, 8, ...
   Each term is the sum of the previous two terms.
   Write down the next three terms.

6. ..., ..., 47, 43, ..., ...
   The rule for continuing this sequence is
   'take 4 from the previous term'.
   a Write down the next two terms after 43.
   b Write down the previous two terms before 47.

7. Write down the next two terms: 1, 3, 5, 7, ...
   What is name of all the numbers in this sequence?

8. Write down the next two terms: 3, 7, 11, 15, ...

9. Write down the next two terms: 20, 17, 14, 11, ...

10. Write down the next two terms: 2, 4, 8, 16, ...
    Copy and complete this sentence:
    Each term is a multiple of ....

11. Write down the next two terms: 2, 6, 18, 54, ...

12. Write down the next two terms: 1, 4, 9, 16, ...
    What is the name of every term in this sequence?

13. ..., ..., 19, 39, ..., ...
    The rule for continuing this sequence is
    'double the previous term and add 1'.
    a Write down the next two terms.
    b Write down the term before 19.

14. ..., ..., 8, 12, ..., ...
    The rule for continuing this sequence is
    'add the previous two terms'.
    a Write down the next two terms after 12.
    b Write down the two terms before 8.

15. Write down the next two terms: 2, 3, 5, 7, 11, ...
    What type of number is every term in this sequence?

16. Write down the next two terms: 128, 64, 32, 16, ...

17. These patterns of squares are made by joining rods.

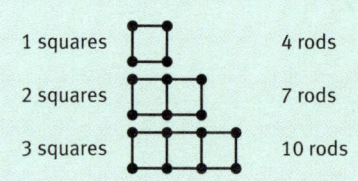

    1 squares   4 rods
    2 squares   7 rods
    3 squares   10 rods

    How many rods are needed to make
    a 4 squares   b 6 squares?

18. These patterns are made from squares.

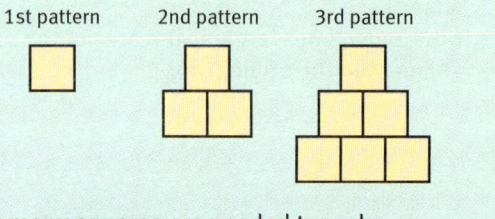

    1st pattern   2nd pattern   3rd pattern

    How many squares are needed to make
    a the 4th pattern   b the 8th pattern?

19. A fence is made by joining posts and rails.

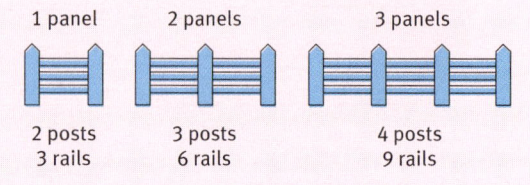

    1 panel   2 panels   3 panels

    2 posts   3 posts   4 posts
    3 rails   6 rails   9 rails

    a To make a fence with 4 panels,
        i how many posts are needed
        ii how many rails are needed?
    b To make a fence with 20 panels,
        i how many posts are needed
        ii how many rails are needed?

20. This is the rule for continuing a sequence.
    'If the previous term is odd, multiply it by 5 and then
    subtract 1, but if the previous term is even divide it
    by 2.'
    Use the rule to write down the next five terms of the
    sequence: 20, 10, 5, 24, 12, ...

21. Write down the next two terms of this sequence:
    ..., 3, 3, 6, 9, 15, ...
    What is the term before the first 3?

F SEQUENCES
FINDING THE PATTERN

1. Write down the next term of this sequence.

    2, 7, 12, 17, ...

    Explain how you found it.

2. Write down the rule for finding the next number in this sequence.

    5, 9, 13, 17, ...

3. What is the next number in this sequence?

    1, 2, 4, 8, ...

    Describe how you found it.

4. Write down the rule for finding the next term in this sequence.

    1, 5, 25, 125, ...

5. Find the next term in this sequence.

    100, 90, 80, 70, ...

    Describe how you found it.

6. These patterns are made from rods.

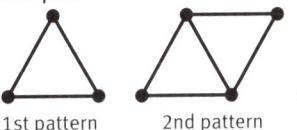

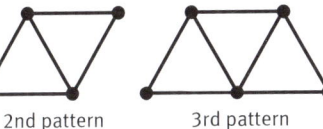

    1st pattern   2nd pattern   3rd pattern

    a Copy and complete this table.

	1st pattern	2nd pattern	3rd pattern	4th pattern	5th pattern
Number of rods	3	5	7		

    b Without working it out, explain how you can find the number of rods needed to make the 10th pattern.

7. These patterns are made with squares.

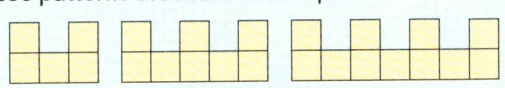

    1st pattern   2nd pattern   3rd pattern

    a Copy and complete this table.

	1st pattern	2nd pattern	3rd pattern	4th pattern	5th pattern
Number of squares	5	8	11		

    b Work out the number of squares needed to make the 12th pattern.
    Explain how you got your answer.

8. Look at these patterns of blue squares.

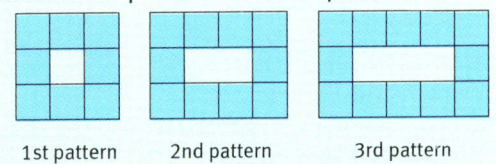

    1st pattern   2nd pattern   3rd pattern

    a How many squares do you need to make the 4th pattern?
    b How many squares do you need to make the 8th pattern?
    c How many squares do you need to make the 20th pattern?
    Explain how you obtained your answer.

9. Look at this sequence of numbers.

    4, 7, 10, 13, 16, ...

    a Write down the next term of this sequence.
    b Copy and complete this table.

1st term	2nd term	3rd term	4th term	5th term	6th term	7th term	8th term
4	7	10	13	16			

    c Explain how you can find the 20th term.

10. Look at this sequence of numbers.

    6, 12, 18, 24, ...

    a Write down the next term of this sequence.
    b Copy and complete this table.

1st term	2nd term	3rd term	4th term	5th term	6th term	7th term	8th term
6	12	18	24				

    c Find the 12th term.
    Explain how you got your answer.

11. a Write down the 5th term of this sequence.

    1, 4, 9, 16, ...

    b Write down the 10th term of this sequence.
    c Without working it out, explain how you can find the 17th term of the sequence.

12. Fences are made from posts and rails.
    A one panel fence has 2 posts and 4 rails,
    a two panel fence has 3 posts and 8 rails.

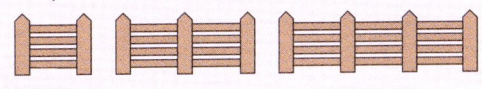

    1st pattern   2nd pattern   3rd pattern

    How many posts and how many rails are needed to make a 20 panel fence?

F SEQUENCES

DESCRIBING THE PATTERN

1 Look at this sequence:

21, 19, 17, 15, ...

   a Write down the 5th term.
   b Work out the 8th term.
   c Explain how you can get any term in the sequence from the term before it.

2 Look at this sequence:

6, 9, 12, 15, 18, ...

Explain how you can continue the sequence.

3 Look at this sequence:

6, 18, 54, 162, ...

Explain how you can continue the sequence.

4 Write down the next two terms in this sequence:

1, 1, 2, 3, 5, 8, ...

What is the rule for continuing the sequence?

5 Find the next two terms in the sequence

128, 64, 32, ...

What is the rule for continuing the sequence?

6 Look at this sequence:

7, 9, 11, 13, ...

   a Copy and complete this table.

1st term	2nd term	3rd term	4th term	5th term	6th term	...	12th term
5+2×1	5+2×2	5+2×3	5+2×4				

   b Write down the 50th term.
   c Explain how to work out any term.

7 Look at this sequence:

3, 6, 12, 24, ...

   a Copy and complete this table.

1st term	2nd term	3rd term	4th term	5th term	6th term	...	10th term
3	3×2^1	3×2^2	3×2^3				

   b Write down the 20th term.
   c Write down an expression for finding any term.

8 Look at this sequence:

3, 7, 11, 15, ...

   a Write down the 5th term.
   b Work out the 10th term.
   c Explain how to work out the 50th term.
   d Explain how to work out any term when you know the term number.

9 Look at this sequence:

2, 5, 8, 11, ...

   a Copy and complete this table.

1st term	2nd term	3rd term	4th term	5th term	...	8th term
2+3×0	2+3×1	2+3×2	2+3×3			

   b Write down the 15th term.
   c Write down the nth term where n is the term number.

10 Look at the sequence given in question **6** again. Write down the nth term.

11 Look at the sequence given in question **7** again. Write down the nth term.

12 Look at the sequence given in question **8** again. Write down the nth term.

13 Look at the sequence given in question **2** again. Write down the nth term.

14 Write down the nth term of the sequence:

4, 9, 14, 19, ...

15 Write down the nth term of the sequence:

10, 14, 18, 22, ...

Which term of this sequence is equal to 46?

16 These patterns are made from rods and joints.

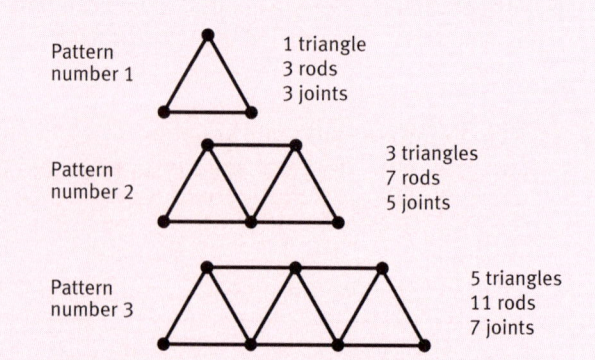

Pattern number 1: 1 triangle, 3 rods, 3 joints

Pattern number 2: 3 triangles, 7 rods, 5 joints

Pattern number 3: 5 triangles, 11 rods, 7 joints

   a Write down the number of rods in pattern number 6.
   b Write down an expression, in terms of n, for
      i the number of triangles in pattern number n
      ii the number of rods in pattern number n
      iii the number of joints in pattern number n.

28

F SEQUENCES

INVESTIGATION

Roof frames are made from wood beams.
Roof frames of different sizes need different numbers of beams.
You have to investigate the connection between the size of the frame and the number of beams needed to make it.

1. This is a two-span frame.
   How many beams are used to make the two-span frame?

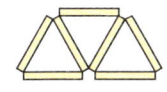

2. This is a five-span frame.
   How many beams are used to make the five-span frame?

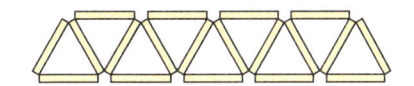

3. Draw a one-span frame.
   How many beams are used to make the one-span frame?

4. Draw a three-span frame and a four-span frame.
   Now copy and complete this table. Look for a pattern connecting the number of beams to the number of spans — draw more frames if you need to.

Number of spans	1	2	3	4	5	...	20	...	45
Number of beams									

5. Find a relationship between the number of spans and the number of beams needed to make the frame.
   Now copy and complete this sentence: A roof frame with n spans needs ...... beams.

Roofs can be made with two or more layers.
This is a three-span roof frame with two layers.

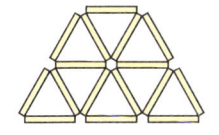

6. How many beams are needed to make this frame?

7. What happens if you try to make a one-span frame with two layers?

8. a Draw frames with two layers and with   i 2 spans   ii 4 spans   iii 5 spans.
   b Write down the number of beams needed to make each frame.
   c Make a table for frames with two layers like the table for question 4.
   d Find a relationship between the number of spans and the number of beams needed to make frames with two layers. Check your answer by drawing an eight-span frame with two layers.

9. a Draw a three-span frame with **three** layers.
   b What is the smallest number of spans that a frame with three layers can have?
      Explain your answer.
   c Draw some three-layer frames with different numbers of spans. Put your results in a table like that for question 4. Now find the relationship between the number of spans and the number of beams needed to make frames with three layers.

10. Investigate frames with four layers. Use the same reasoning as you did for question 9.

11. Copy this table. Use all your results to complete the table.

Number of layers	1	2	3	4	...	10	...
Number of beams needed for n spans							
Smallest number of spans possible							

Now look for a pattern connecting the number of beams needed for n spans with the number of layers.

G FRACTIONS
MEANING OF FRACTIONS

1 What fraction of each square is shaded?
  a   b   c

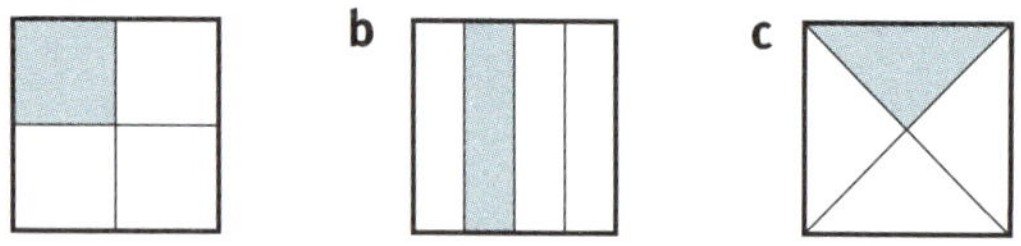

2 Is it true that half this circle is shaded? Give a reason for your answer.

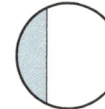

3 What fraction of this rectangle is shaded?

4 What fraction of this rectangle is shaded?

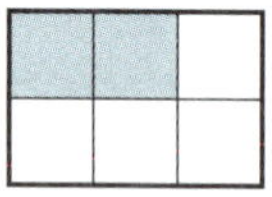

5 What fraction of this rectangle is shaded?

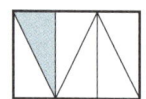

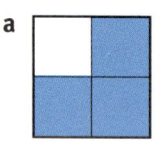

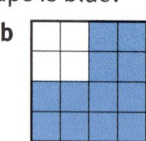

6 What fraction of each shape is blue?
  a   b
  c What number does the star stand for?
  $\frac{3}{4} = \frac{\star}{16}$

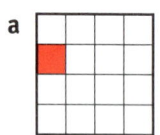

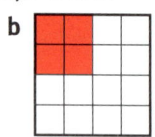

7 What fraction of each shape is red?
  a   b
  c Write down the number that the star stands for.
  $\frac{4}{16} = \frac{1}{\star}$

8 Is it true that half this square is shaded? Give a reason for your answer.

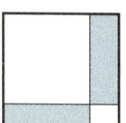

9 a What fraction of this square is red?
  b How many more squares need to be coloured red so that $\frac{3}{4}$ of the square is red?

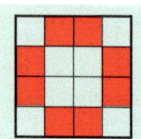

10 Two of these rectangles have the same fraction coloured green. Which two are they?
  A   B   C

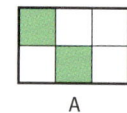

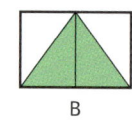

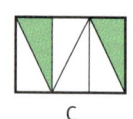

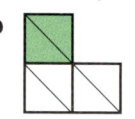

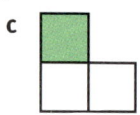

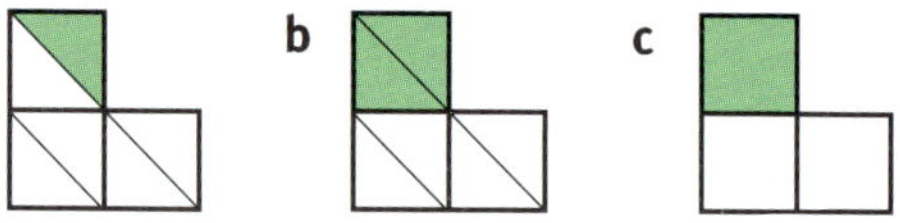

11 What fraction of each shape is green?
  a   b   c
  d Write down the number that the star stands for.
  $\frac{2}{6} = \frac{\star}{3}$
  e How many sixths are needed to make the whole shape?

12 Write down the fraction that is shaded.
  a   b
  c   d
  e   f

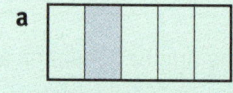

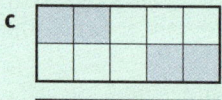

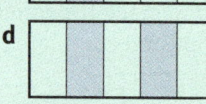

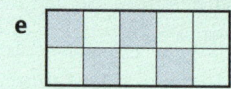

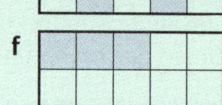

13 Write down the number that the star stands for.
  a $\frac{1}{5} = \frac{\star}{10}$ **b** $\frac{2}{5} = \frac{\star}{10}$ **c** $\frac{4}{10} = \frac{2}{\star}$

14 a What fraction of this circle is blue?
  b How many more squares need to be coloured blue so that $\frac{5}{8}$ of the circle is blue?

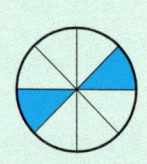

15 How many squares of this shape need to be shaded so that
  a $\frac{1}{12}$ is shaded
  b $\frac{1}{2}$ is shaded
  c $\frac{1}{3}$ is shaded
  d $\frac{1}{4}$ is shaded
  e $\frac{5}{6}$ is shaded
  f all of it is shaded?

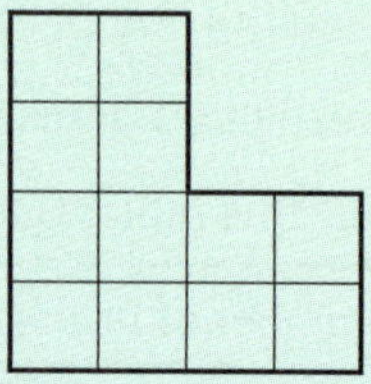

16 Give a reason why there is no whole number that can replace the star in $\frac{3}{10} = \frac{\star}{5}$

G FRACTIONS
EQUIVALENT FRACTIONS

> To simplify a fraction, divide top and bottom by the same number.

> To find an equivalent fraction multiply top and bottom by the same number.

1 Simplify
  a $\frac{2}{4}$ b $\frac{3}{6}$ c $\frac{5}{10}$ d $\frac{20}{40}$

2 Simplify
  a $\frac{3}{9}$ b $\frac{3}{12}$ c $\frac{2}{20}$ d $\frac{4}{16}$

3 Simplify
  a $\frac{6}{9}$ b $\frac{4}{6}$ c $\frac{10}{15}$ d $\frac{3}{3}$

4 Simplify
  a $\frac{6}{8}$ b $\frac{9}{12}$ c $\frac{12}{16}$ d $\frac{10}{10}$

5 Simplify
  a $\frac{10}{100}$ b $\frac{50}{100}$ c $\frac{30}{100}$ d $\frac{100}{100}$

6 What fraction of each shape is red?
Give your answer in its simplest form.
  a   b   c    d

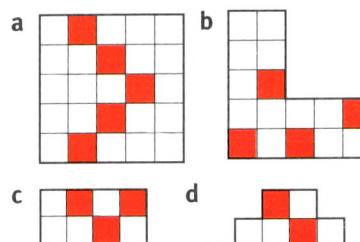

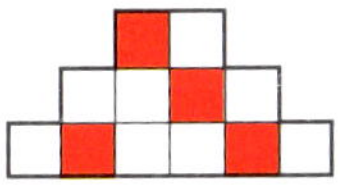

7 Simplify
  a $\frac{9}{24}$ b $\frac{8}{12}$ c $\frac{20}{100}$

8 Simplify
  a $\frac{8}{24}$ b $\frac{24}{100}$ c $\frac{20}{25}$

9 Simplify
  a $\frac{15}{30}$ b $\frac{12}{30}$ c $\frac{40}{200}$

10 Simplify
  a $\frac{40}{100}$ b $\frac{28}{100}$ c $\frac{75}{100}$

11 What fraction of the shape is blue?
Give your answer in its simplest form.

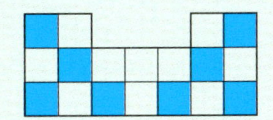

Example
Complete $\frac{1}{5} = \frac{\star}{15}$

$15 = 5 \times 3$

$\frac{1}{5} = \frac{1 \times 3}{5 \times 3} = \frac{3}{15}$

Copy and complete

12 a $\frac{1}{2} = \frac{\star}{4}$ b $\frac{1}{3} = \frac{\star}{6}$

13 a $\frac{1}{3} = \frac{\star}{9}$ b $\frac{1}{2} = \frac{\star}{8}$

14 a $\frac{1}{5} = \frac{\star}{10}$ b $\frac{1}{4} = \frac{\star}{12}$

15 a $\frac{1}{4} = \frac{\star}{20}$ b $\frac{1}{10} = \frac{\star}{20}$

16 Write $\frac{1}{2}$ as twelfths.

17 Write $\frac{1}{5}$ as twentieths.

18 Write $\frac{1}{10}$ as hundredths.

Copy and complete

19 a $\frac{2}{3} = \frac{\star}{6}$ b $\frac{3}{4} = \frac{\star}{8}$

20 a $\frac{3}{5} = \frac{\star}{10}$ b $\frac{3}{8} = \frac{\star}{16}$

21 a $\frac{2}{5} = \frac{\star}{20}$ b $\frac{3}{10} = \frac{\star}{100}$

22 a $\frac{1}{2} = \frac{4}{\star}$ b $\frac{2}{5} = \frac{6}{\star}$

23 a $\frac{3}{4} = \frac{9}{\star}$ b $\frac{3}{8} = \frac{9}{\star}$

24 Write 1 as quarters.

25 Write $\frac{2}{3}$ as twelfths.

26 Write $\frac{3}{5}$ as tenths.

27 How many squares need to be coloured blue so that $\frac{3}{5}$ of the diagram is blue?

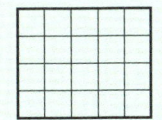

28 How many squares need to be coloured red so that $\frac{1}{4}$ of the diagram is red?

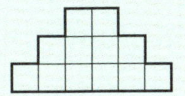

29 The fraction $\frac{1}{2}$ has been marked on the number line. Mark these fractions on a copy of this line.
  a $\frac{1}{4}$ b $\frac{1}{3}$ c $\frac{1}{8}$ d $\frac{2}{3}$ e $\frac{3}{4}$

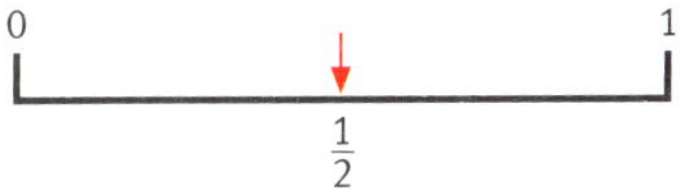

30 Which is smaller, $\frac{1}{3}$ or $\frac{1}{2}$?

31 Which is larger, $\frac{1}{5}$ or $\frac{1}{4}$?

Example
Which is larger, $\frac{2}{3}$ or $\frac{3}{5}$?

Change $\frac{2}{3}$ and $\frac{3}{5}$ to equivalent fractions with the **same** denominator: this is a number that is a multiple of both 3 and 5; 15 will do the job.

$\frac{2}{3} = \frac{10}{15}$
$\frac{3}{5} = \frac{9}{15}$
$\frac{10}{15} > \frac{9}{15}$ so $\frac{2}{3} > \frac{3}{5}$

32 Which is larger, $\frac{2}{3}$ or $\frac{3}{4}$?

33 Which is smaller, $\frac{1}{2}$ or $\frac{5}{8}$?

34 Which is smaller, $\frac{3}{10}$ or $\frac{2}{5}$?

35 Which is larger, $\frac{3}{4}$ or $\frac{4}{5}$?

36 Which is larger, $\frac{1}{3}$ or $\frac{3}{8}$?

37 Arrange these fractions in order with the smallest first.
$\frac{1}{2}, \frac{2}{5}, \frac{3}{10}$

38 Arrange these fractions in order with the smallest first.
$\frac{1}{3}, \frac{3}{4}, \frac{5}{6}$

39 Arrange these fractions in order with the largest first.
$\frac{2}{3}, \frac{1}{2}, \frac{5}{6}, \frac{3}{4}$

40 What fraction is halfway between 0 and $\frac{1}{2}$?

41 What fraction is halfway between $\frac{1}{2}$ and $\frac{3}{4}$? Use a number line like the one above.

G FRACTIONS
ADDING AND SUBTRACTING FRACTIONS

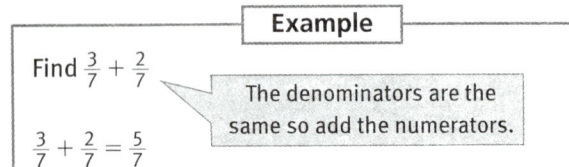

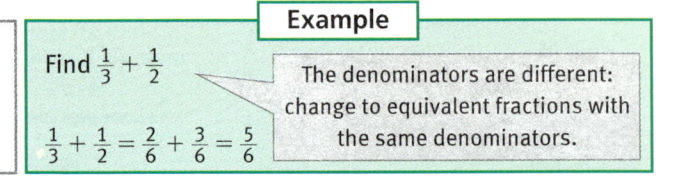

Example

Find $\frac{3}{7} + \frac{2}{7}$

The denominators are the same so add the numerators.

$\frac{3}{7} + \frac{2}{7} = \frac{5}{7}$

Example

Find $\frac{1}{3} + \frac{1}{2}$

The denominators are different: change to equivalent fractions with the same denominators.

$\frac{1}{3} + \frac{1}{2} = \frac{2}{6} + \frac{3}{6} = \frac{5}{6}$

Find

1 a $\frac{1}{5} + \frac{2}{5}$ b $\frac{1}{7} + \frac{3}{7}$

2 a $\frac{2}{9} + \frac{5}{9}$ b $\frac{1}{6} + \frac{4}{6}$

Example

Find $\frac{4}{7} - \frac{2}{7}$

The denominators are the same so subtract the numerators.

$\frac{4}{7} - \frac{2}{7} = \frac{2}{7}$

Find

3 a $\frac{3}{5} - \frac{1}{5}$ b $\frac{4}{9} - \frac{2}{9}$

4 a $\frac{5}{12} - \frac{4}{12}$ b $\frac{7}{10} - \frac{4}{10}$

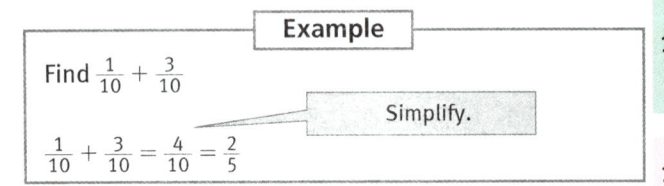

Example

Find $\frac{1}{10} + \frac{3}{10}$

Simplify.

$\frac{1}{10} + \frac{3}{10} = \frac{4}{10} = \frac{2}{5}$

Find

5 a $\frac{1}{9} + \frac{2}{9}$ b $\frac{3}{8} + \frac{3}{8}$

6 a $\frac{5}{6} - \frac{1}{6}$ b $\frac{5}{8} - \frac{3}{8}$

7 a $\frac{2}{9} + \frac{4}{9}$ b $\frac{7}{10} - \frac{3}{10}$

8 a $\frac{1}{3} + \frac{2}{3}$ b $\frac{3}{5} + \frac{2}{5}$

Have you remembered to simplify?

Find

9 a $\frac{1}{2} + \frac{1}{4}$ b $\frac{1}{4} + \frac{1}{8}$

10 a $\frac{1}{5} + \frac{1}{10}$ b $\frac{2}{3} + \frac{1}{6}$

11 a $\frac{5}{9} + \frac{1}{3}$ b $\frac{1}{3} - \frac{1}{6}$

12 a $\frac{1}{2} + \frac{1}{3}$ b $\frac{2}{3} - \frac{1}{2}$

Example

Find $1 - \frac{5}{9}$

Change 1 to ninths.

$1 - \frac{5}{9} = \frac{9}{9} - \frac{5}{9} = \frac{4}{9}$

13 Find
   a $1 - \frac{5}{8}$ b $1 - \frac{7}{20}$ c $1 - \frac{39}{100}$

14 Find
   a $\frac{3}{5} + \frac{2}{5}$ b $\frac{9}{20} + \frac{11}{20}$ c $\frac{27}{100} + \frac{63}{100}$

15 Find a $\frac{1}{6} + \frac{1}{4}$ b $\frac{1}{6} - \frac{1}{9}$

16 Find a $\frac{3}{4} + \frac{1}{10}$ b $\frac{3}{5} - \frac{2}{15}$

17 Find the missing fraction
   a $\frac{1}{2} + ? = \frac{3}{4}$
   b $\frac{2}{3} - ? = \frac{1}{2}$

18 $\frac{2}{5}$ of the heat output from a boiler is wasted. What fraction of the heat output is not wasted?

---

19 Ann eats $\frac{1}{2}$ of this bar. Pete eats $\frac{1}{3}$ of this bar.
   a What fraction of the bar is eaten?
   b What fraction of the bar is left?

20 Look at this number: 3792.
   a Choose two different digits from this number to make a fraction that fits on this number line.
   b How many of these fractions can you make?
   c Mark your fractions on a copy of the line.
   d Subtract the smallest fraction from the largest fraction.

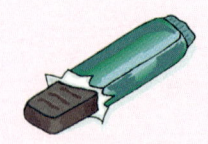

32

H DECIMALS
MEANING OF DECIMALS

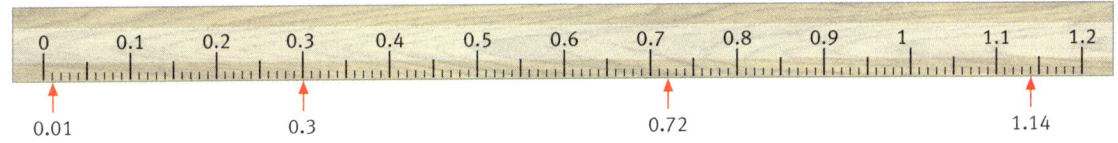

1. Which is bigger, 0.09 or 0.1?
2. Which is smaller, 1.1 or 1.01?
3. Which is bigger, 1.03 or 1.12?
4. Which is smaller, 5.5 or 6.1?
5. Which is larger, 10.9 or 10.05?

$0.1 = \frac{1}{10}$, $0.01 = \frac{1}{100}$

Example

Write $\frac{3}{10}$ as a decimal.

$\frac{3}{10} = 0.3$

Put 0 before the decimal point to show that there are no units.

6. Write as a decimal a $\frac{7}{10}$ b $\frac{3}{100}$ c $\frac{13}{100}$
7. What is the value of the digit
   a 3 in 1.35   b 7 in 5.07   c 2 in 2.56
8. Look at the number 24.035. Write down the digit
   a giving the number of units
   b in the second decimal place
   c in the first decimal place.
9. Look at the number 209.107 What digit gives
   a the number of tenths
   b the second decimal place
   c the number of tens?

Example

Write 0.2 as a fraction.

1 decimal place: 1 with one zero on bottom.

$0.2 = \frac{2}{10} = \frac{1}{5}$

Write as a fraction

10. 0.5   11. 0.4   12. 0.8   13. 0.7

Example

Write 0.35 as a fraction.

2 decimal places: 1 with two zeros on bottom.

$0.35 = \frac{35}{100}$ Simplify
$= \frac{7}{20}$

Write as a fraction

14. 0.25   15. 0.08   16. 0.75
17. 0.05   18. 0.1   19. 0.45

Write as a fraction

20. 0.375 21. 0.875 22. 0.005
23. 1.5   24. 3.5   25. 2.05

Example

Give 12.78 to the nearest whole number.

2 units   0.78 is nearer 1 than 0 so round up

12.78 = 13 to the nearest whole number.

Write to the nearest whole number.

26. 25.26   27. 8.58   28. 13.03
29. 15.95   30. 19.72 31. 29.56

Example

Give 35.322 correct to 1 decimal place.

3 tenths   under 5 so don't add 1 to 3

35.322 = 35.3 correct to 1 d.p.

Write these numbers correct to 1 decimal place.

32. 4.79   33. 18.449   34. 25.088
35. 147.216 36. 50.023   37. 0.507

Write these numbers correct to 2 decimal places.

38. 0.158   39. 5.262   40. 18.1033
41. 0.0198 42. 0.0477   43. 20.2099

44. Write 15.73 to the nearest ten.
45. Write 37.055 correct to 1 d.p.
46. Write 0.0799 correct to 2 d.p.
47. Write 569.702 to the nearest whole number.
48. Find the difference between the value of the digit 5 and the value of the digit 4 in the number 25.46.
49. What is the difference in value between the two figures 3 in the number 23.03?
50. Write these numbers in order of size with the smallest first.

0.3, $\frac{2}{5}$, 0.8, $\frac{1}{2}$

H DECIMALS

ADDING AND SUBTRACTING DECIMALS

Find

1. 2.1 + 4.6
2. 5.3 + 4.9
3. 10.7 + 3.1
4. 3.3 + 4.2

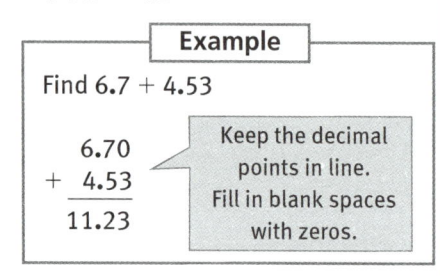

Example

Find 6.7 + 4.53

```
  6.70
+ 4.53
-----
 11.23
```

Keep the decimal points in line. Fill in blank spaces with zeros.

Find

5. 3.21 + 4.5
6. 4 + 3.8
7. 5.03 + 7
8. 1.56 + 3.2
9. 0.125 + 0.18
10. 1.5 + 2.56 + 1.62

Estimate

11. 25.7 + 18.4
12. 0.293 + 0.748
13. 2.16 + 0.94
14. 0.147 + 1.055
15. 126 + 59.66

Estimate, then find exactly

16. 27.9 + 8.82
17. 0.527 + 1.072
18. 151.2 + 59.37
19. 0.029 + 0.194
20. 3.82 + 0.756
21. 1.27 + 3.82 + 5.19
22. 2.66 + 1.18 + 2.4 + 5.03

Example

Find 3 − 0.6

```
  3.0
− 0.6
-----
  2.4
```

Keep the decimal points in line. Fill in blank spaces with zeros.

Find

23. 1.7 − 0.5
24. 0.6 − 0.3
25. 1 − 0.2
26. 5 − 0.7
27. 1 − 0.25
28. 3 − 2.5
29. 1.8 − 0.9
30. 2.6 − 1.1
31. 3.7 − 0.02
32. 4.45 − 2.6

Estimate

33. 56.7 − 21.4
34. 5.17 - 3.82
35. 25.5 − 4.72
36. 36.17 − 0.94
37. 80.193 − 0.027

Estimate, then find exactly

38. 56.21 − 18.4
39. 3.27 − 0.58
40. 16.1 − 2.5

Estimate, then find exactly

41. 38.7 + 2.9 − 20.6
42. 7.8 − 8.8 + 2.5
43. 5 − (1.36 + 2.52)
44. 10.5 − (3.7 + 1.15)

What number does the ★ stand for?

45. 25.1 + ★ = 30.7
46. 0.2 + ★ = 1
47. 4.8 − ★ = 2.3
48. 5.6 − ★ = 0.7
49. 2.5 + ★ − 3.6 = 4.2
50. 0.2 − ★ = 0.05

---

51. Anna buys a plant costing £7.64 and a bag of peat costing £3.52.
She pays with a £20 note. How much change does she get?

52. Pete needed to buy edging strip for a flower bed.
The edges of the bed are 2.4 m long in total.
An extra 0.4 m is needed for joins.
What length is 0.4 m more than 2.4 m?

53. A bag of damp sand weighed 12.7 kg.
After it had dried out, it weighed 0.2 kg less.
What was the weight then?

54. Harvey bought four different paving stones.
Their lengths were 1.12 m, 1.16 m, 0.95 m and 1.63 m.
He laid them end to end to make a path. How long was the path?

55. The sum of the weights of two sacks of soil is 25.7 kg.
One sack is 7.9 kg heavier than the other.
What is the weight of each sack?

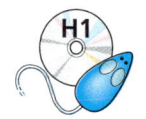

34

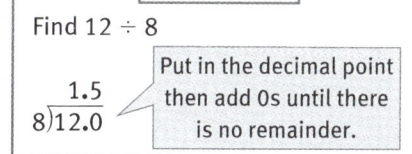

H DECIMALS
MULTIPLYING AND DIVIDING BY WHOLE NUMBERS

Work out
1. 2.76×10
2. 24.7×100
3. 0.0269×10^2
4. 83.27×10^3
5. 5.7×1000

Work out
6. $7.12 \div 10$
7. $0.25 \div 10$
8. $5.3 \div 10^2$
9. $246 \div 100$
10. $12 \div 10^3$

Work out
11. 1.2×3
12. 0.6×4
13. 5×2.5
14. 1.2×5
15. 3.5×6

Example
Find $4.6 \div 5$

$$5)\overline{4.60} \quad 0.92$$

Add 0s until there is no remainder.

Find
16. $3.6 \div 2$
17. $1.7 \div 4$
18. $5.6 \div 5$
19. $0.96 \div 3$
20. $24.1 \div 4$

Example
Find $12 \div 8$

$$8)\overline{12.0} \quad 1.5$$

Put in the decimal point then add 0s until there is no remainder.

Find
21. $6 \div 4$
22. $8 \div 5$
23. $7 \div 4$
24. $20 \div 8$
25. $9 \div 6$

Example
Find 3.5×200

Multiply by 2: $3.5 \times 2 = 7.0$
Then by 100: $7.0 \times 100 = 700$

$3.5 \times 200 = 700$

Find
26. 5.2×20
27. 0.8×40
28. 200×1.4
29. 1.8×3000
30. 0.06×600

Example
Find $6.24 \div 300$
$6.24 \div 300 = 0.0624 \div 3$

Divide by 100: $6.24 \div 100 = 0.0624$
Then divide by 3: $0.0624 \div 3$

$$3)\overline{0.0624} \quad 0.0208$$

Work out
31. $0.8 \div 20$
32. $1.2 \div 300$
33. $0.16 \div 40$
34. $12.2 \div 200$
35. $4.2 \div 6000$

Example
Estimate 12.4×32
Is your estimate larger or smaller than the accurate answer?

$12.4 \times 32 \approx 12 \times 30 = 360$
Smaller because both numbers are estimated as smaller.

36. Estimate
  a 21.5×42 b 59×450.4
  Are your estimates larger or smaller than the accurate answer? Give a reason.

37. Estimate
  a $266.5 \div 28$ b $0.059 \div 42$

Estimate, then work out exactly
38. a 85×5.3 b 356×1.8
39. a 27.5×15 b 95.5×250
40. a $19.5 \div 15$ b $3.68 \div 23$
41. a $0.434 \div 31$ b $21.875 \div 35$

Example
Work out $24.6 \div 7$ correct to 2 decimal places.

Carry on dividing until you have found the third decimal place.

$$7)\overline{24.600} \quad 3.514$$

$24.6 \div 7 = 3.51$ to 2 d.p.

Work out
42. $2.57 \div 5$ correct to 1 d.p.
43. $392.7 \div 6$ correct to 1 d.p.
44. $0.773 \div 3$ correct to 2 d.p.
45. $1.954 \div 7$ correct to 2 d.p.
46. $2.9 \div 8$ correct to 2 d.p.

---

47. One sheet of paper is 0.012 cm thick.
    How thick is a stack of 150 of these sheets?

48. A pile of 300 sheets of paper is 2.46 cm thick.
    What is the thickness of one sheet of paper?

49. The price of one text book is £6.95.
    Find the cost of 87 of these text books.

50. A publisher offers a pack of 25 books for £122.60.
    What is the cost of one book? Give your answer correct to the nearest penny.

H DECIMALS
CHANGING FRACTIONS TO DECIMALS

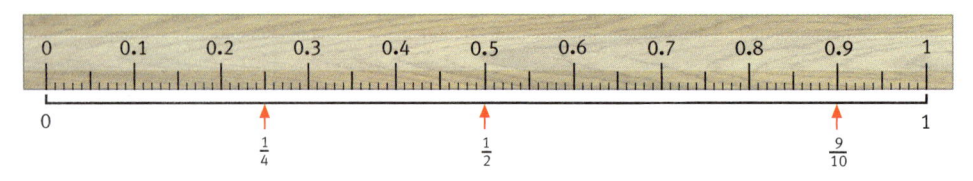

1 The ruler shows that $\frac{1}{2} = 0.5$.

Use the ruler to write these fractions as decimals.

a $\frac{1}{4}$ **b** $\frac{3}{4}$ **c** $\frac{3}{10}$ **d** $\frac{2}{5}$ **e** $\frac{4}{5}$

Example

Change $3\frac{1}{2}$ to a decimal.

$3\frac{1}{2}$ means $3 + \frac{1}{2}$ and $\frac{1}{2} = 0.5$

$3\frac{1}{2} = 3.5$

2 Write as a decimal

a $1\frac{1}{4}$ **b** $6\frac{1}{2}$ **c** $2\frac{3}{4}$ **d** $3\frac{1}{5}$ **e** $5\frac{7}{10}$

3 Write these numbers in order with the smallest first.

0.6, $\frac{1}{2}$, $\frac{2}{5}$, 0.3

4 Write these numbers in order with the largest first.

1.5, $2\frac{1}{4}$, $1\frac{1}{5}$, 2.3

5 Write these numbers in order with the smallest first.

$3\frac{1}{4}$, 2.75, $1\frac{9}{10}$, 3.4

Example

Write $\frac{3}{8}$ as a decimal.

$\frac{3}{8}$ means $3 \div 8$

$$8 \overline{)3.000} \quad 0.375$$

Put in the decimal point and then add 0s.

$\frac{3}{8} = 0.375$

Change to a decimal

6 a $\frac{5}{8}$ **b** $\frac{3}{20}$ **c** $\frac{1}{25}$ **d** $\frac{1}{8}$ **e** $\frac{5}{16}$

Example

Give $\frac{1}{3}$ as a decimal correct to 2 decimal places.

$$3 \overline{)1.000} \quad 0.333$$

Find the 3rd decimal place.

$\frac{1}{3} = 0.33$ to 2 d.p.

Write as a decimal correct to two decimal places.

7 a $\frac{2}{3}$ **b** $\frac{5}{6}$ **c** $\frac{2}{9}$ **d** $\frac{1}{6}$ **e** $\frac{5}{12}$

8 a $2\frac{2}{3}$ **b** $1\frac{4}{9}$ **c** $4\frac{1}{3}$ **d** $2\frac{1}{9}$ **e** $5\frac{3}{11}$

9 Copy this table and fill in the missing numbers:

Fractions	Decimal
	0.15
$\frac{4}{30}$	
	1.75
$1\frac{5}{8}$	

10 Show, with an arrow, where these numbers fit on a copy of this number line.

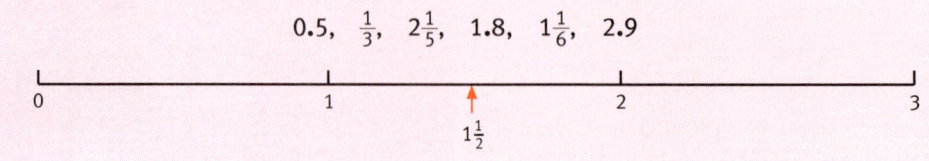

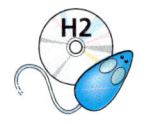

0.5, $\frac{1}{3}$, $2\frac{1}{5}$, 1.8, $1\frac{1}{6}$, 2.9

H DECIMALS
MULTIPLYING AND DIVIDING BY DECIMALS

Example

Find 0.2×1.61

$161 \times 2 = 322$

$0.2 \times 1.61 = 0.322$

1 d.p.   2 d.p.   3 d.p.

Find
1. 0.4×0.3
2. 1.4×0.2
3. 1.2×0.5
4. 0.15×0.3
5. 0.27×0.1
6. 0.4×0.5
7. 12.8×0.1
8. 0.6×0.5
9. 0.01×0.1
10. 0.2^2
11. 0.01^2

Example

Estimate 2.29×0.67

$2.29 \times 0.67 \approx 2 \times 0.7$
$= 1.4$

Estimate
12. 3.82×21.7
13. 150.9×3.07
14. 0.144×0.699
15. 146.5×0.0232
16. 84.9^2

Division can be written as a fraction. To divide by a decimal make an equivalent fraction with a whole number on the bottom.

Example

Find $0.12 \div 0.5$

$0.12 \div 0.5 = \dfrac{0.12}{0.5} = \dfrac{1.2}{5}$

$5\overline{)1.20}$ → 0.24

Multiply top and bottom by 10.

$0.12 \div 0.5 = 0.24$

Find
17. $1.5 \div 0.3$
18. $0.26 \div 0.2$
19. $54.6 \div 0.02$
20. $2.8 \div 0.07$
21. $0.45 \div 0.5$

Find
22. $3 \div 0.2$
23. $12 \div 0.8$
24. $1.7 \div 0.4$
25. $5 \div 0.4$
26. $30 \div 1.5$

Find correct to 2 decimal places
27. $1.4 \div 0.3$
28. $0.4 \div 0.03$
29. $7.3 \div 0.6$
30. $26 \div 0.12$
31. $0.047 \div 0.6$

Estimate
32. $1.79 \div 4.36$
33. $0.657 \div 0.205$
34. $15.82 \div 0.19$
35. $0.57 \div 5.26$
36. $240.32 \div 39.95$

Remember BODMAS.

Find
37. $1.2 \times 3 - 0.36$
38. $4.3 + 5 \times 1.2$
39. $6.5 - 1.2 \times 0.2$
40. $(3.6 + 4.2) \div 0.3$
41. $7.8 - 1.3 \div 0.5$

Example

Estimate $\dfrac{4.82 + 7.53}{0.29}$

$\dfrac{4.82 + 7.53}{0.29} \approx \dfrac{5 + 8}{0.3}$

$= \dfrac{13}{0.3} = \dfrac{130}{3} \approx 43$

Estimate
42. $\dfrac{5.8 - 0.9}{3.7}$
43. $\dfrac{0.84 \times 1.29}{0.37}$
44. $\dfrac{6.8}{1.2 + 3.5}$
45. $\dfrac{2.86 - 0.75}{0.94 + 0.27}$
46. $\dfrac{(0.104)^2}{0.057 + 0.194}$

H DECIMALS

USING A CALCULATOR

1. Sam is making new curtains.
   Sam used her calculator to work out how many metres of material she needs.
   The display showed 26.7897
   How many metres should she buy?

2. Doug used a calculator to work out the VAT in pounds on a television set.
   The display showed 17.5
   How much is the VAT?

3. Amin bought a box of 36 envelopes that cost £8.24.
   He worked out the cost of one envelope on a calculator. He entered 8.24 ÷ 36 =
   The calculator display showed 0.2288888
   How much did one envelope cost?

4. Vera used her calculator to change a fraction to a decimal.
   The display showed 0.33333333
   What fraction did Vera change?

5. Debra used her calculator to work out
   $$2.51 + 3.6 \times 1.7$$
   a Estimate her answer.
   She keyed
   [2][.][5][1][+][3][.][6][=][×][1][.][7][=]
   The display showed 10.387
   b i Explain why this is the wrong answer.
     ii Write down the sum for which this is the correct answer.
   c Write down the correct answer to the given calculation.

6. Tom used his calculator to work out
   $$\frac{2}{7} + \frac{5}{11}$$
   a Two of these keying sequences give the correct answer. Which are they?

   A [(][2][+][5][)][÷][(][7][+][1][1][)][=]
   B [(][2][÷][7][)][+][(][5][÷][1][1][)][=]
   C [2][+][5][÷][7][÷][1][1][=]
   D [2][÷][7][+][5][÷][1][1][=]

   b Explain why the other two keying sequences give a wrong answer.

Example
Estimate $\sqrt{19}$
$\sqrt{16} < \sqrt{19} < \sqrt{25}$
so $\sqrt{19}$ is between 4 and 5.

First estimate then use your calculator to find each square root correct to 2 decimal places.

7. $\sqrt{5}$ 8. $\sqrt{40}$ 9. $\sqrt{96}$ 10. $\sqrt{137}$

11. First estimate then use your calculator to find each square correct to 1 decimal place.
    a 1.91^2 b 23.7^2 c 3.01^2 d 0.37^2

12. First find an estimate then use your calculator to find, correct to 1 decimal place, the value of
    a $25.2 \times 8.2 - 12.2$ b $25.2 + 8.2 \times 12.2$

13. First estimate, then find correct to 1 decimal place
    a $\dfrac{24.1 \times 36.4}{182}$ b $\dfrac{58.3 + 12.2}{46.3}$

14. To calculate $\dfrac{2428.4}{12.3 \times 8.25}$, Lily entered

    [2][4][2][8][.][4][÷][1][2][.][3][×][8][.][2][5][=]

    a Why does this give the wrong answer?
    b Which key stroke is wrong?
    c Find the right answer rounded to the nearest whole number.

15. Use your calculator to change these fractions to decimals.
    a $\frac{1}{6}$ b $\frac{1}{9}$ c $\frac{1}{12}$ d $\frac{1}{15}$

    What do you notice about your answers?

16. John bought a box of 250 paper clips.
    The box cost £3.26.
    How much does one paper clip cost?
    Make sure that your answer is sensible.

17. Estimate the value of
    $$\sqrt{13.5 + 9.4}$$
    Describe how you could use your calculator to find the value correct to 1 decimal place.

18. Emily had to find $\dfrac{12.1 + 27.26}{4.13 - 3.21}$ correct to 1 d.p.

    She wrote down $\dfrac{12.1 + 27.26}{4.13 - 3.21} = \dfrac{39.4}{0.9} = 43.8$

    This is wrong. Why?

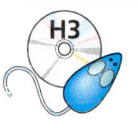

1 USING NUMBERS
UNITS OF LENGTH, MASS, CAPACITY

1 cm = 10 mm
1 m = 1000 cm
1 km = 1000 m

1 Write down the length of the orange strip in
   a centimetres   **b** millimetres
2 How many millimetres is   **a** 5 cm   **b** 12.5 cm?
3 How many centimetres is   **a** 2 m   **b** 0.8 m?
4 How many metres is   **a** 3 km   **b** 1.25 km?
5 How many metres is   **a** 2000 cm   **b** 52 cm?
6 How many kilometres is   **a** 5000 m   **b** 500 m?

1 kg = 1000 g
1 tonne = 1000 kg

7 There is a small packet on the scale. What does it weigh
   a in grams   **b** in kg?
8 How many grams is
   a 3 kg   **b** 1.5 kg   **c** 0.7 kg?
9 How many kilograms is
   a 4 t   **b** 1.4 t   **c** 0.15 t?
10 How many kilograms is
   a 2000 g   **b** 4500 g   **c** 500 g?
11 How many tonnes is
   a 5400 kg   **b** 550 kg?

1 litre = 1000 ml
1 cl = 10 ml

12 How much liquid is in this sprayer
   a in millilitres   **b** in litres?
13 How many millilitres is
   a 3 litres   **b** 0.3 litres   **c** 0.15 cl?
14 How many litres is
   a 2500 ml   **b** 500 ml   **c** 50 ml?
15 Write down the unit you would use to measure
   a the weight of a bread roll
   b the length of your classroom
   c a spoonful of water
   d the distance between London and Dover
   e the weight of a sackful of potatoes
   f the weight of a lorry
   g the length of your arm
   h the length of an eyelash
   i the amount of water in a bucket.

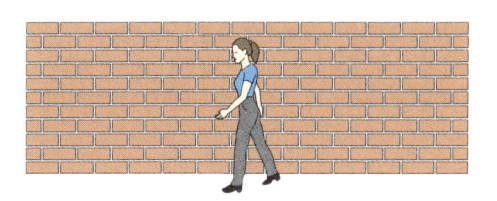

16 Estimate **a** the height of this wall
              b the length of this wall.
17 Estimate the height of this elephant.

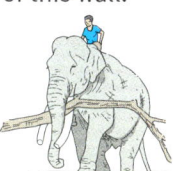

1 km ≈ $\frac{5}{8}$ mile and 1 mile ≈ 1.6 km
1 m ≈ 3 feet
1 kg ≈ 2.2 lb (pounds)
1 litre ≈ 1.75 pints
1 litre ≈ 0.22 gallons

Example

Approximately, how many miles is 50 km?
50 km ≈ 50 × $\frac{5}{8}$ miles
      = (50 × 5) ÷ 8 miles
      = 250 ÷ 8 miles
      = 31 miles to the nearest mile

18 About how many miles is   **a** 80 km   **b** 500 km?
19 About how many pounds is   **a** 5 kg   **b** 15 kg?
20 About how many pints is   **a** 5 litres   **b** 2 litres?
21 About how many gallons is   **a** 10 litres   **b** 50 litres?
22 About how many feet is   **a** 3 m   **b** 10 m   **c** 50 m?
23 Which is greater, a distance of 40 miles or a distance of 80 km?
24 Blackadder is 170 cm tall. How tall is Blackadder in
   a metres   **b** roughly in feet? (use 1 m ≈ 3.3 ft)
25 The table gives the depth of water in a pond.

December	2.5 m
August	1.9 m

Find the difference in the depth between December and August. Give your answer in centimetres.
26 Betty posts 120 letters. Each letter weighs 50 g. Find the weight of the 120 letters in kilograms.
27 A jug holds 1.5 litres. A glass holds 125 ml. How many glasses can be filled from a full jug?

1 USING NUMBERS
TIME AND SPEED

1. In the year 2030, June 1st is a Saturday.
   a What day of the week is June 16th?
   b What day of the week is the last day of June?

2. The summer term ends on 21 July.
   The autumn term starts on 31 August.
   How many days is the summer holiday?

3. Otis goes on holiday on 9th July.
   He is away for nine nights.
   On what date does he return?

> 1 day = 24 hours
> 1 hour = 60 minutes
> 1 minute = 60 seconds

4. Write these times in order, with the shortest time first.
   a 1 hour 10 minutes, 90 minutes, $1\frac{1}{3}$ hours.
   b $1\frac{1}{2}$ minutes, 150 seconds, 1 minute 50 seconds.

5. The diagram shows the dial on a timer.
   a What is the time shown by the pointer?
   b Kyle wants to set a time of 2 hours 15 minutes. Where should the pointer be?

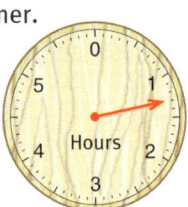

6. The first lesson of a school day starts at 0900.
   Each lesson is 50 minutes long,
   There are three lessons before morning break.
   What time does break start?

7. Parking costs 20 p for 20 minutes.
   The time on the ticket machine is 1236.
   Martin puts two 20 p coins into the machine.
   What is the expiry time shown on the ticket?

Use this rail timetable to answer questions **8** to **11**.

London Waterloo	0953	1023	1027	1053	1123	1153	1227	1253	1327	1353
Ashford International	1053	—	—	—	1223	1253	1327	—	—	1453
Calais Fréthun	—	—	—	—	—	1431	—	—	—	—
Lille Europe	—	—	1324	—	1426	—	1529	—	—	—
Brussels Midi	—	—	1405	—	1507	—	1610	—	—	—
Paris Nord	1353	1417	—	1453	—	1559	—	1653	1720	1753

8. Anna catches the 0953 train to Paris.
   a What time should this train arrive in Paris?
      Give your answer in twelve-hour clock time.
   b How long should the journey take?
   c The train was delayed and the journey actually took 4 hours and 25 minutes.
      What time did the train arrive in Paris?

9. Dale needs to go to Brussels.
   He wants to catch the first train to leave Waterloo after midday.
   a What time should this train leave Waterloo?
   b What time should this train arrive in Brussels?
   c How long should the journey take?

10. Emile caught a train from Ashford to Brussels.
    He arrived in Brussels just after 4 p.m.
    What time did he leave Ashford?

11. Jean wants to go to Brussels on the first train leaving Lille after 3 p.m.
    a Which train should he catch?
    b How many minutes should the journey take?

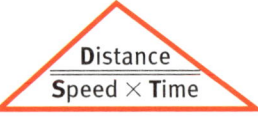

$$\frac{\text{Distance}}{\text{Speed} \times \text{Time}}$$

12. Find the distance covered when travelling at
    a 20 mph for 3 hours   b 45 mph for 3 hours.

13. Find the time taken to travel
    a 5 miles at 2 mph   b 400 miles at 50 mph.

14. Find the average speed for a journey of
    a 8 miles in 2 hours   b 650 miles in 5 hours.

15. Find the distance covered when travelling at
    a 20 mph for $1\frac{1}{2}$ hours   b 10 mph for 30 minutes.

16. Find the time taken to travel
    a 58 miles at 12 mph   b 400 km at 80 km/h.

17. Find the average speed for a journey of
    a 8 miles in 15 minutes
    b 65 kilometres in 1 hour 15 minutes.

18. Mike travelled 80 miles by car.
    The journey took him $2\frac{1}{4}$ hours.
    What was his average speed?
    Give your answer correct to 1 decimal place.

19. Naeem travels by coach from his home to Brighton.
    He uses this timetable.   DEPART: 1307 1724
    ARRIVE: 1516 2010
    a How long does the journey take on the earlier coach?
    b Naeem gets the later coach one day.
       It arrives 46 minutes late. What time does it arrive?
    c The coach journey is 56 miles.
       When both journeys are on time, find
       i the average speed of the earlier coach
       ii the average speed of the later coach.

1 USING NUMBERS
TRAVEL GRAPHS

$$\frac{\text{Distance}}{\text{Speed} \times \text{Time}}$$

These travel graphs show different journeys.
For each journey find
a the distance travelled
b the time taken
c the distance travelled in 1 hour
d the speed.

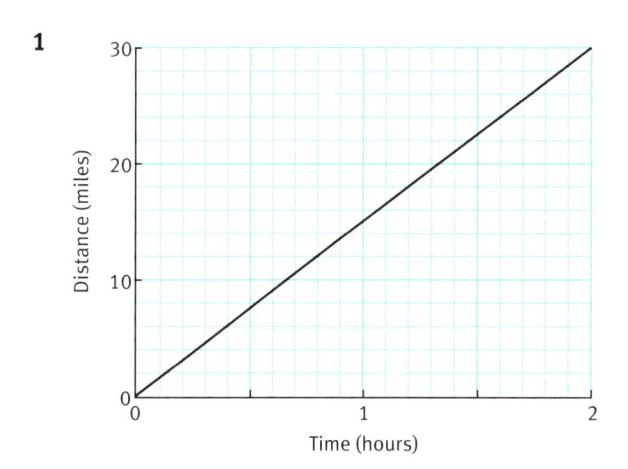

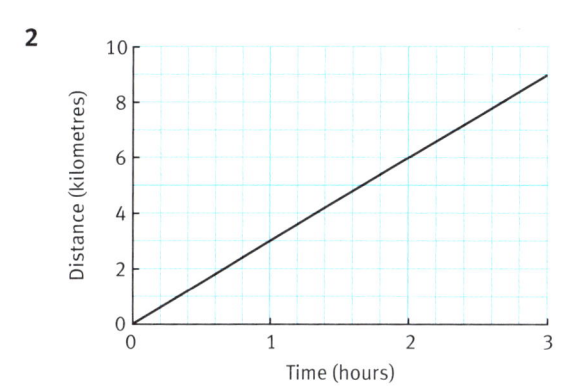

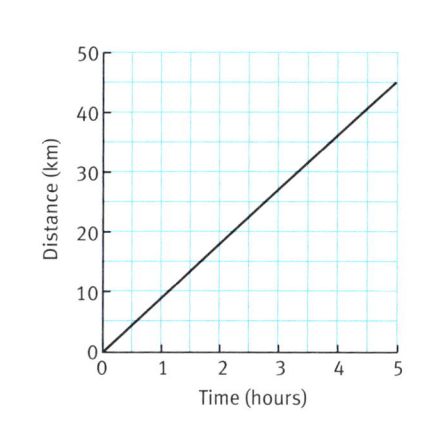

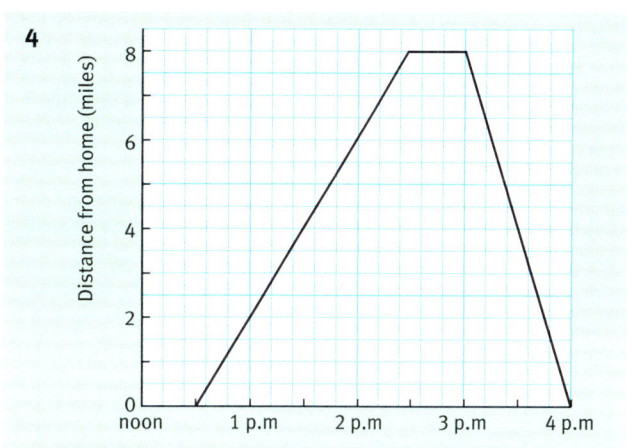

1 *(Graph: Distance (miles) vs Time (hours), line from (0,0) to (2,30))*

2 *(Graph: Distance (kilometres) vs Time (hours), line from (0,0) to (3,9))*

3 *(Graph: Distance (km) vs Time (hours), line from (0,0) to (5,45))*

4 *(Graph: Distance from home (miles) vs Time, from noon(0) rising to 8 miles at 2:30pm, flat until 3pm, down to 0 at 4pm)*

The graph shows Colin's journey. He goes from home to Eaton. He stops for a while at Eaton. Then he goes straight home.
a How far is Eaton from Colin's home?
b How long did he stay at Eaton?
c How long was Colin away from home?
d What was his average speed from home to Eaton?
e On the outward journey was he most likely to be walking, jogging or cycling?
Give a reason for your answer.
f Was the journey home faster or slower than the journey to Eaton? Give a reason.

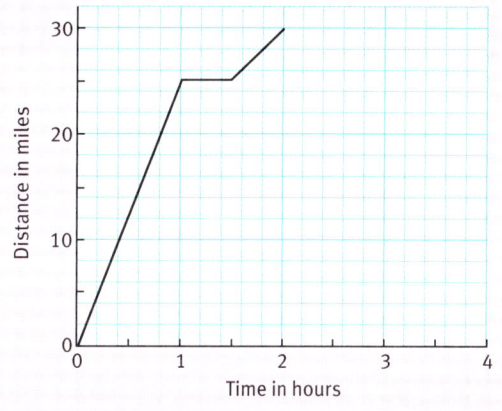

5 Mr White is a commercial traveller. This graph shows his journey one morning as far as his second stop.

(Graph: Distance in miles vs Time in hours, rising from (0,0) to (1,25), flat to (1.5,25), then rising to (2,30))

a How long was he getting to his first stop?
b Find his average speed from home to his first stop.
c How long did he stay at his first stop?
d How long did he take from the time he left his first stop until he reached his second stop?

He stayed at his second stop for 1 hour.
He then travelled home at a steady 30 miles per hour.
e Copy and complete the graph to show this information.
f How far did he travel altogether that morning?

1 USING NUMBERS

MONEY

1. Ellie is paid £5 an hour.
   How much does she earn for
   a 5 hours work   b working 35 hours a week?

2. Carl is paid £6.50 an hour.
   a How much does he earn for working a 6-hour shift?
   b What is he paid for a week in which he works 40 hours?

3. Rajiv earns a salary of £18 600 a year.
   How much is he paid each calendar month?

4. Liz earns £260 a week. £62 is deducted from her pay for tax, NI, and pension contributions.
   What is her net pay?

5. Martin is paid a weekly wage of £175.
   He works 35 hours a week.
   a How much is he paid an hour?

   Martin is paid £10 an hour for every hour he works overtime.
   b How much extra does he earn for working 6 hours overtime?
   c What does he earn in a week in which he works 3 hours overtime?

6. Steve is paid a car allowance of £4 for every 10 miles.
   Find the allowance for a journey of
   a 50 miles   b 260 miles.

7. The cost of hiring a car is £25 a day or £160 a week.
   a How much does it cost to hire a car for 6 days?
   b How much more does it cost to hire the car for a week?

8. Viv buys a secondhand car.
   She pays a deposit of £250 and twelve monthly instalments of £315.
   Find the total amount that Viv pays for the car.

9. Jan earns £5.50 an hour.
   On Monday she clocked in at 0905 and clocked out at 1717.
   She had an hour for lunch for which she is not paid.
   How much does she earn on Monday?

10. A car-hire company charges a fee of £50 plus £14 a day. Kate's bill came to £190.
    For how many days did Kate hire a car?

This list was shown at the foreign currency counter.
It shows what £1 would buy of some other currencies.

Euros (€)	1.66
Mexican pesos	12.70
Swiss francs	2.52
Turkish lira (l)	942 807
US dollars ($)	1.60

11. How many Swiss francs did £50 buy?
12. How many Turkish lira did £200 buy?
13. How many US dollars did £150 buy?
14. How many Euros did £500 buy?
15. How many Mexican pesos did £700 buy?

Example

Joe changed 400 Swiss francs into pounds when the exchange rate was 2.60 francs for £1.
How many pounds and pence did he get?

2.60 francs = £1

1 franc = £$\frac{1}{2.6}$ *Divide to change back to £.*

400 francs = £$\frac{400}{2.6}$ = £153.85 (nearest penny)

Use the table above question 11 to find how many pounds and pence you would have got for

16. 50 US dollars
17. 10 000 000 Turkish lira
18. 500 Euros
19. 800 Mexican pesos.
20. Jon changed £500 into Japanese yen. How many yen did he get when the exchange rate was 160 yen for £1?
21. The exchange rate for changing pounds to Australian dollars is £1 = $2.5
    a How many Australian dollars can be bought for £250?
    b Find the price in pounds of a bowl marked $500.
    c Ed came home with 50 Australian dollars and changed them back into pounds. How many pounds did he get?
22. Sam changed £450 into Indian rupees.
    He got 27 720 rupees.
    What was the exchange rate?
23. A bottle of water cost 75 p in London.
    The same bottle of water cost 2.20 New Zealand dollars in Auckland when the exchange rate was $3.20 to the pound.
    In which city was the bottle of water cheaper?

1 USING NUMBERS

NEGATIVE NUMBERS

1. Write down the temperatures shown on these thermometers.
   a   b   c

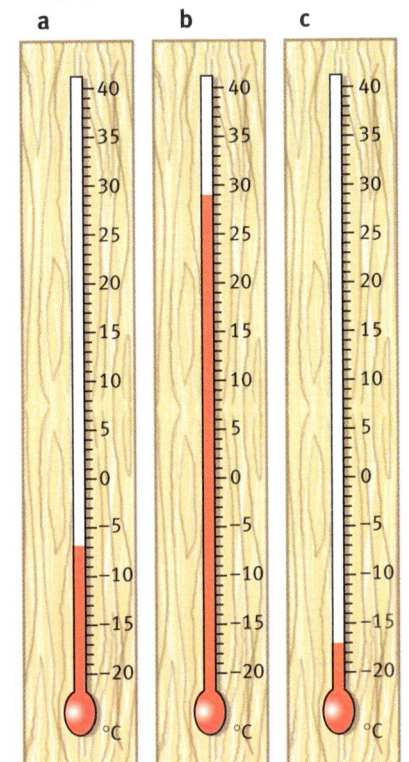

2. Write these temperatures in order, coldest first.
   a −2 °C, 5 °C, −18 °C
   b 25 °C, −10 °C, 0 °C.

3. Find the difference in temperature between
   a 2 °C and −3 °C
   b −2 °C and 5 °C
   c 20 °C and −10 °C
   d −2 °C and −5 °C.

4. Find the change when the temperature goes from
   a −6 °C to 5 °C
   b 6 °C to −5 °C
   c 10 °C to −2 °C
   d −6 °C to −5 °C.

   (Remember to say if the temperature rises or falls.)

5. The diagram shows the control panel in a lift. Write down which button to press when you start at 
   a floor 1 and go up 2 floors
   b floor 3 and go down 5 floors
   c floor −1 and go up 3 floors
   d floor −1 and go down 2 floors
   e floor −3 and go up 6 floors.

6. 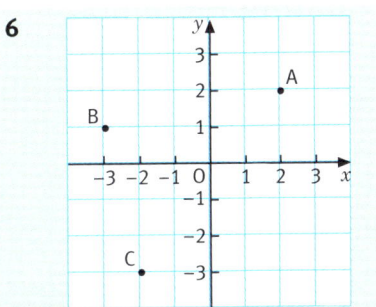
   a Write down the coordinates of the points i A ii B iii C.
   b The point B is moved two squares down and four squares to the right. What are the coordinates of its new position?

7. Copy this grid. 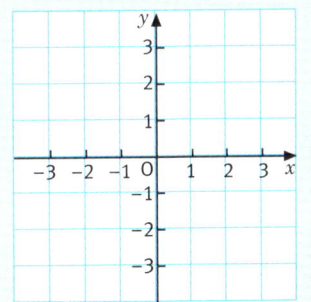
   a On your copy, mark the points A(1, 3), B(1, −2), C(−2, −2) and D(−2, 3).
   b Join the points in alphabetical order. What is the name of the shape ABCD?
   c What is the difference between the y-coordinate of A and the y-coordinate of B?
   d Describe how, starting with the x-coordinate of B, you can get the x-coordinate of C.

8. The marks for questions in a multiple choice test are
   2 for a correct answer
   −1 for a wrong answer
   0 for no answer.
   There were five questions.
   a Lucy got two questions correct, two questions wrong and didn't answer one. What was her mark?
   b Brian got four questions right and one wrong. What did he score?
   c Tina got one question correct but still managed to score −2. How did she answer the other questions?

9. The marks in a quiz are
   5 for a correct answer
   −2 for a wrong answer
   −1 for passing.
   a In round 1, team A got two questions correct, two questions wrong and passed on one question. What did team A score?
   b In round 2, team B got two questions correct and three questions wrong. What did team B score?
   c At the end of round 3, team A had scored 15 and team B had scored 18.
   Round 4 is the last and Team A scored 12 in this round. What must Team B score in this round so that they win the quiz?

10. This display shows that the temperature in a freezer is 2 °C above normal.

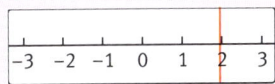

    The normal temperature is −18 °C.
    a What is the temperature in the freezer when the red line is over
      i 1   ii −2?
    b Where is the red line when the temperature is
      i −21 °C   ii −16 °C?

43

J USING FRACTIONS
FINDING A FRACTION OF A QUANTITY

Example

Find $\frac{1}{3}$ of £12.

$\frac{1}{3}$ of £12 = £12 ÷ 3
       = £4

Find
1. $\frac{1}{2}$ of £8
2. $\frac{1}{4}$ of £12
3. $\frac{1}{8}$ of £64
4. $\frac{1}{5}$ of £120

Example

Find $\frac{2}{3}$ of £60.

$\frac{2}{3}$ of £60 = (£60 ÷ 3) × 2
       = £20 × 2 = £40

Find
5. $\frac{2}{5}$ of £40
6. $\frac{3}{4}$ of £100
7. $\frac{3}{7}$ of £14
8. $\frac{5}{9}$ of £27

Find
9. $\frac{3}{20}$ of 360°
10. $\frac{5}{12}$ of 144 apples
11. $\frac{7}{10}$ of 500 metres
12. $\frac{7}{8}$ of 64 litres

Example

Estimate $\frac{3}{20}$ of 485 tonnes.

$\frac{3}{20}$ of 485 t ≈ (500 t ÷ 20) × 3
       = 25 t × 3 = 75 t

Estimate
13. $\frac{1}{5}$ of £48
14. $\frac{2}{3}$ of £92
15. $\frac{3}{4}$ of 207 metres
16. $\frac{3}{8}$ of £671

First estimate and then find to the nearest penny
17. $\frac{2}{3}$ of £56
18. $\frac{1}{4}$ of £8.57
19. $\frac{3}{5}$ of £12.82
20. $\frac{5}{8}$ of £127

21. An apple weighs 100 g. What does $\frac{1}{2}$ the apple weigh?

22. A full tank holds 500 litres. How many litres is in half a full tank?

23. A rod is 260 cm long. How long is $\frac{1}{4}$ of the rod?

24. There are 280 peaches in a box. $\frac{3}{4}$ of these have gone bad. How many are bad?

25. Harry buys a bike costing £270 on credit. He makes a down payment of $\frac{1}{3}$ of this price. What amount is the down payment?

$4\frac{1}{2}$ means $4 + \frac{1}{2}$

Example

1 loaf weighs 250 g.
What do $4\frac{1}{2}$ loaves weigh?

4 loaves weigh 250 g × 4
       = 1000 g

$\frac{1}{2}$ a loaf weighs 250 g ÷ 2
       = 125 g

$4\frac{1}{2}$ loaves weigh 1000 g + 125 g
       = 1125 g

26. 1 tray holds 24 eggs. How many eggs fit in $2\frac{1}{2}$ trays?

27. 1 ream of paper is 500 sheets. How many sheets is $3\frac{1}{2}$ reams?

28. 1 bag of sand weighs 20 kg. What do $2\frac{1}{4}$ bags weigh?

29. Anna is paid £4 an hour. She is paid $1\frac{1}{4}$ times this when she works on Sunday. What is she paid for an hour's work on Sunday?

This recipe makes 24 biscuits.

500 g flour
100 g margarine
250 g sugar
20 ml milk
2 eggs

30. David makes $2\frac{1}{2}$ times this amount.
    a How many biscuits does this make?
    b How much sugar does this use?

31. Yasmin makes $\frac{3}{4}$ of this amount.
    a How many biscuits does Yasmin make?
    b How much flour does Yasmin use?

32. Sam wants to make the full amount but spills $\frac{1}{5}$ of the milk she needed. How much milk does Sam have left?

J USING FRACTIONS
FRACTIONAL CHANGE

Example

£20 is increased by $\frac{1}{4}$. Find the increase.

Increase = $\frac{1}{4}$ of £20
= £20 ÷ 4
= £5

Find the increase when

1. £40 is increased by $\frac{1}{5}$
2. £120 is increased by $\frac{1}{3}$
3. 48 kg is increased by $\frac{1}{8}$
4. 60 metres is increased by $\frac{1}{12}$

Find the decrease when

5. £30 is decreased by $\frac{1}{3}$
6. £45 is decreased by $\frac{1}{9}$
7. 50 litres is decreased by $\frac{1}{5}$
8. 200 grams is decreased by $\frac{1}{4}$

Find the change when

9. £80 is decreased by $\frac{2}{5}$
10. £64 is increased by $\frac{5}{8}$
11. £27 is decreased by $\frac{4}{9}$
12. 900 m is increased by $\frac{2}{3}$

Example

Phil earns £4.50 an hour. He gets a rise of $\frac{1}{10}$.

How much extra does he get?

Increase = $\frac{1}{10}$ of £4.50
= £4.50 ÷ 10
= £0.45 = 45 p

13. Buns are sold in packs of 12.
    A special offer gives a quarter more buns.
    How many more buns are in the new pack?

14. The price of a CD has fallen by $\frac{1}{3}$.
    It used to cost £9.
    How many £s has the price fallen by?

15. In March, 8 000 people were looking for work.
    This number is expected to fall by $\frac{1}{20}$ next month.
    How many fewer people is this?

16. The number of orchids on Barrow Down is 450.
    This number is expected to increase by $\frac{2}{5}$ in the next five years.
    How many more orchids is this?

17. Emma bought oranges at 20 p each.
    She added $\frac{1}{4}$ of this price for her profit.
    a How much profit did Emma make on one orange?
    b What price did she charge for an orange?

Example

The price of a shirt is reduced by $\frac{1}{3}$ in a sale.

The normal price is £24.60.

What is the sale price?

Reduction is $\frac{1}{3}$ of £24.60
= £24.60 ÷ 3 = £8.20

First find the reduction.

Sale price = £24.60 − £8.20
= £16.40

Full price − reduction

18. The share price of Internet.com increased by $\frac{7}{8}$ in one week.
    One share cost £1.60 at the beginning of the week.
    What did a share cost at the end of the week?

19. The price of a new car was £8500.
    The value of the car fell by $\frac{2}{5}$ in the first year.
    What was the car worth at the end of that year?

20. A new 'improved' bottle of shampoo contains $\frac{1}{5}$ more shampoo.
    The old bottle contained 125 ml.
    a How much shampoo does the new bottle hold?

    The old bottle cost £1.35.
    The new bottle costs $1\frac{1}{3}$ times the old one.
    b How much more does the new bottle cost?

J USING FRACTIONS
ONE QUANTITY AS A FRACTION OF ANOTHER

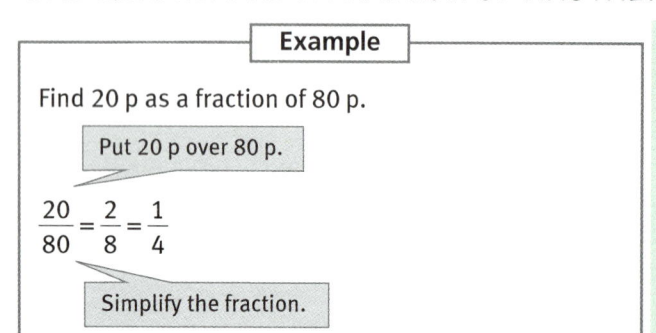

Example

Find 20 p as a fraction of 80 p.

Put 20 p over 80 p.

$$\frac{20}{80} = \frac{2}{8} = \frac{1}{4}$$

Simplify the fraction.

Find

1. 50 p as a fraction of 100 p
2. 10 p as a fraction of 30 p
3. 4 cm as a fraction of 16 cm
4. 10 g as a fraction of 20 g
5. £2 as a fraction of £6
6. £2 as a fraction of £20
7. 9 nails as a fraction of 36 nails
8. 2 seeds as a fraction of 24 seeds
9. 20° as a fraction of 180°
10. 15 ml as a fraction of 100 ml.

Example

Find £1.20 as a fraction of £4.

£1.20 = 120 p
£4 = 400 p

Change both to pence.

$$\frac{120}{400} = \frac{12}{40} = \frac{3}{10}$$

Find

11. £1.50 as a fraction of £3
    (Did you remember to change to pence?)
12. £1.10 as a fraction of £22
13. 50 p as a fraction of £2.

Find

14. 80 p as a fraction of £5
15. £1.50 as a fraction of £100
16. 20 cm as a fraction of 1 m
    (Did you remember to change 1 m to cm?)
17. 200 g as a fraction of 1 kg
    (Did you remember to change 1 kg to g?)
18. 400 ml as a fraction of 1 litre
19. 5 mm as a fraction of 2 cm
20. 1.5 cm as a fraction of 5 cm.
21. The water level in my pond was 60 cm.
    It has risen by 10 cm.
    Find the fractional rise.

Example

My bus fare has increased from 60 p to 70 p.
Find the fractional increase.

The increase is 10 p. ← First find the increase.

Fractional increase = $\frac{10}{60} = \frac{1}{6}$ ← Increase over original fare

22. The interest on a loan of £8000 increases the amount owed to £9000.
    Find the interest as a fraction of the loan.
23. A bar of chocolate weighs 75 g.
    The weight is increased by $\frac{1}{3}$.
    Find the new weight as a fraction of the old weight.
24. The price of a computer is £540. This includes a sum of £80 for VAT.
    Find the VAT as a fraction of the price.
25. The density of new houses is reduced from 15 houses per acre to 12 houses per acre. By what fraction has the density been reduced?

26. *The Record* is a daily newspaper.
    The daily sales in November averaged 360 000 copies.
    The daily sales in the following May averaged 480 000 copies.

    a What was the fractional change in sales?

    In November the price of the paper was 25 p.
    Next May the price was 20 p.
    b How much money came from sales in November?
    c How much money came from sales in May?
    d What was the fractional change in the value of sales between November and May?

J USING FRACTIONS

RATIO

1. Find the ratio of 2 eggs to 5 eggs.
2. Find the ratio of 3 cm to 2 cm.
3. Find the ratio of 3 minutes to 1 minute.
4. Find the ratio of £1 to £5.
5. Find the ratio of 7 kg to 9 kg.

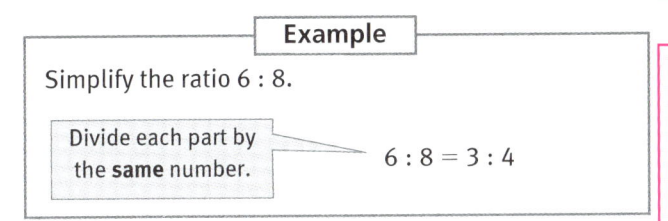

> **Example**
> Simplify the ratio 6 : 8.
> Divide each part by the **same** number.
> 6 : 8 = 3 : 4

Simplify

6. 2 : 4
7. 3 : 9
8. 4 : 6
9. 6 : 10

> **Example**
> A pastry mix contains 200 g of flour and 100 g of butter. What is the ratio of flour to butter?
> 200 : 100 = 2 : 1

Find ratio of

10. 2 kg to 6 kg
11. 60 g to 150 g
12. £20 to £5
13. 75 cm to 90 cm
14. 5 m to 20 m
15. 12 hours to 3 hours
16. £1.50 to £2
    (Did you remember to change both sums to pence?)
17. 20 minutes to 1 hour
    (Did you remember to use minutes for both times?)
18. 2 cm to 5 mm
19. 80 p to £1.60
20. $1\frac{1}{4}$ hours to 2 hours

> **Example**
> Pastry is made by mixing 200 g of flour with 100 g of butter. What fraction of the mix is butter?
> The whole mix is 200 g + 100 g
> $\frac{100}{300} = \frac{1}{3}$

21. 3 buckets of sand are mixed with 2 buckets of gravel.
    a What is the ratio of sand to gravel?
    b What fraction of the mix is sand?
22. There are 4 women and 6 men on a committee.
    a What is the ratio of women to men?
    b What fraction of the committee are men?

23. A drink is made by mixing 20 ml cordial with 500 ml of water.
    a What is the ratio of cordial to water?
    b What fraction of the drink is water?
24. There are 30 pupils in Class 10A. 12 of them are boys. What is the ratio of boys to girls?

> **Example**
> The ratio of girls to boys in a class is 2 : 5.
> a What fraction of the class is girls?
> b There are 28 pupils in the class. How many of them are girls?
> 2 girls to 5 boys means 2 out of 7 pupils are girls.
> a $\frac{2}{7}$ of the class are girls.
> b Number of girls = $\frac{2}{7}$ of 28 = (28 ÷ 7) × 2 = 8

25. The ratio of men to women on the staff is 2 : 7.
    a What fraction of the staff are men?
    b There are 108 people on the staff. How many are men?
26. The number of red to yellow balloons in a bag is in the ratio 3 : 8.
    a What fraction of the balloons are red?
    b There are 33 ballons in the bag. How many are yellow?
27. A charity spends its money on staff and grants in the ratio 3 : 21. What fraction of its money is spent on staff?

> **Example**
> Divide £50 in the ratio 2 : 3.
> The two parts are in the ratio 2:3 so the smaller part is $\frac{2}{5}$ of £50.
> Smaller part = $\frac{2}{5}$ of £50
> = (£50 ÷ 5) × 2 = £20
> Other part = £50 − £20 = £30

28. Divide £80 in the ratio 1 : 3.
29. Divide £120 in the ratio 2 : 3.
30. Divide 150 cm in the ratio 7 : 8.
31. Divide £2000 in the ratio 5 : 9. Give your answers correct to the nearest penny.
32. A coat is a made from a mixture of cotton and acrylic in the ratio 4 : 1.
    The coat weighs 1.5 kg.
    What is the weight of cotton in the coat?

47

J USING FRACTIONS
RATIO AND PROPORTION

1

a Count the number of teeth on the smaller gear wheel.
b Count the number of teeth on the larger gear wheel.
c What is the ratio of the number of teeth on the smaller wheel to the number of teeth on the larger wheel?
d The larger wheel is turned round once. How many turns does the smaller wheel make?

2

a Find the ratio of the number of teeth on the little gear wheel to the number of teeth on the big gear wheel.
b The big wheel turns once. How many turns does the little wheel make?
c The big wheel turns twice. How many turns does the little wheel make?

3

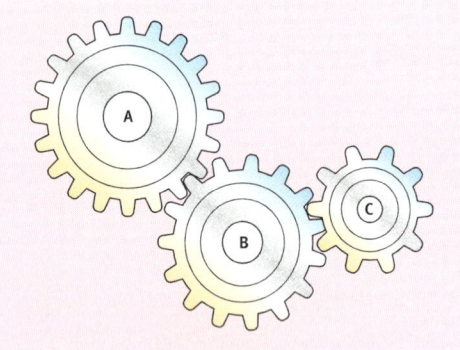

a How many teeth are there on
  i wheel A   ii wheel B   iii wheel C?
b Find the ratio of the number of teeth on A to the number of teeth on B.
c Find the ratio of the number of teeth on B to the number of teeth on C.
d What happens to wheel C when A turns once?

> **Example**
>
> You need 150 g of chocolate to make 12 muffins.
> How much chocolate do you need to make
> a 4 muffins   b 20 muffins? 
>
> a $\frac{1}{3}$ of 150 g = 50 g
>
> 4 muffins is a third of 12 muffins so you need a third of the chocolate.
>
> b 1 muffin needs (150 ÷ 12) g of chocolate.
>   = 12.5 g
>   20 muffins need 12.5 g × 20
>   = 250 g

4 20 bags of sand are needed to lay 100 paving stones. How many bags are needed to lay 5 paving stones?

5 4 packets of powder are needed to make 6 gallons of wallpaper paste.
How many packets are needed to make
a 3 gallons of paste
b 18 gallons of paste?

6 This recipe makes 40 biscuits.

> Flour: 250 g
> Butter: 120 g
> Eggs: 2
> Sugar: 100 g

How much do you need of each ingredient to make 60 biscuits?

7 A pile of 150 sheets of paper is 1.4 cm thick.
How thick is a pile of 500 sheets of the same paper?
Give your answer correct to 1 decimal place.

8 Susan changed £80 into US dollars. She got $185.
a Geri changed £20 into dollars at the same exchange rate. How many dollars did she get?
b Andy changed £55 into dollars at the same exchange rate. How many dollars did he get?

J USING FRACTIONS

SCALE DRAWING

1. This map has been drawn using a scale of 1 cm to represent 20 miles.
   a. About how many miles is Portsmouth from London?
   b. Estimate the distance between Reading and Brighton.
   c. Find the bearing of Chelmsford from London.

2. This is a scale drawing of a garden. The scale is 1 cm to 2 metres.
   a. How long is the whole garden?
   b. How wide is the patio?
   c. What is the name of the shape of the flower bed?
   d. There is a tap in the corner of the garden at A. A hose needs to reach from the tap to the opposite corner of the garden at B. How long must the hose be?

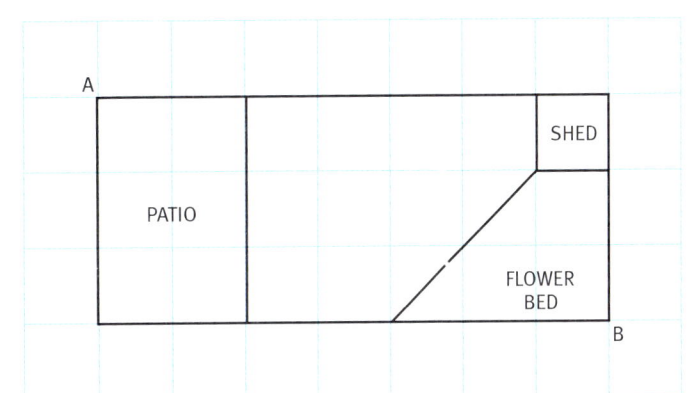

3. This is a scale drawing of the floor plan of a living room. The scale is 1 : 100.
   a. How many metres is represented by 1 cm on the diagram?
   b. How long is the longest wall of the living room?
   c. How far is it from the wall with the window to the wall with the door?

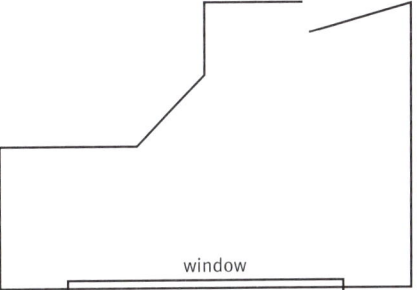

4. This is a sketch of a building plot. It is not drawn to scale.
   a. What is the shape of this plot called?

   You have to make a scale drawing. The scale you must use is 1 cm to represent 2 m.

   b. How long must you draw the line
      i. BC   ii. AB   iii. AD?
   c. Make a scale drawing of this plot on 1 cm square paper. (You may need to use a pair of compasses.)
   d. Use your drawing to measure the angle ADC.

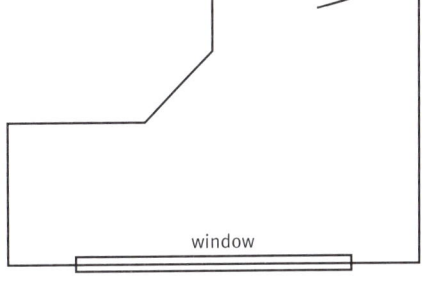

5. This is a sketch of the floor plan of a bathroom.
   a. Make a scale drawing of this plan on 1 cm square paper. Use a scale of 1 : 20.
   b. Use your plan to find the distance from the corner A to the corner B in the actual bathroom.

J USING FRACTIONS

PIE CHARTS

1

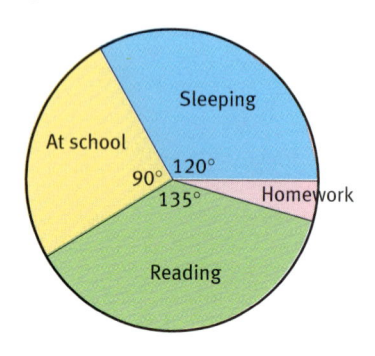

This pie chart shows how Ernie spends his time on a school day.

a How many hours are there in a day?

b What does the blue sector represent?

c What colour is the sector representing the time that Ernie is at school?

d What fraction of the chart represents the time that Ernie is at school?

e What fraction of the day does Ernie spend at school?

f How many hours a day does Ernie spend at school?

g Work out the angle for the pink sector.

h What fraction of the chart is the pink sector?

i How many hours does Ernie spend doing homework?

j How many hours does Ernie spend sleeping?

2 Thirty-six people kept taking their driving test until they passed.
Half passed first time and one-third passed at the second attempt.

a How many people passed at their first attempt?

b How many people passed at their second attempt?

The rest passed at their third attempt.

c i How many passed at their third attempt?
  ii What fraction is this number of the 36 people?

Lisa wants to show this information on a pie chart. She needs to know what size to make the sector representing those who passed on their second attempt.

d i What fraction of the circle must this sector be?
  ii What size angle should the sector have?

e Copy and complete this table.

	Passed first time	Passed second time	Passed third time
Fraction of total	$\frac{1}{2}$	$\frac{1}{3}$	
Angle	180°		
Number			

f Draw a pie chart to represent the data. (Have you remembered to label your chart?)

3 Twenty-four pupils were asked how many upstairs rooms they had at home.
The replies are represented in the pie chart.

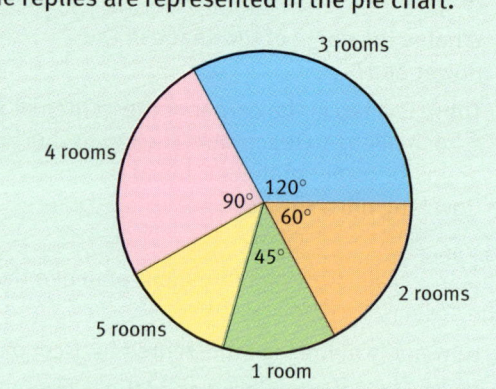

a i Find the missing angle on the pie chart.
  ii What fraction of the pie chart is yellow?
  iii How many pupils are represented by the yellow sector?

b Copy and complete the following table.

Number of upstairs rooms	Angle of sector	Fraction of whole	Number of pupils
1	45°		
2	60°		
3	120°		
4	90°	$\frac{1}{4}$	6
5			

c How many pupils live in homes with three or more upstairs rooms?

d How many upstairs rooms are there altogether in all the houses?

4 Forty-five students were asked how many books they had borrowed last month from the library.
The table shows some of this information.

Number of books	Frequency
0 to 2	30
3 to 5	5
6 to 10	9
more than 10	

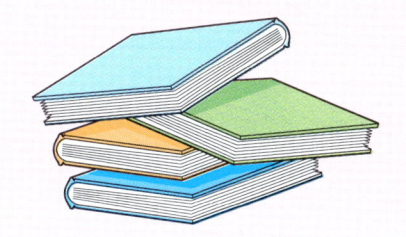

a How many students borrowed more than 10 books?

b Construct a pie chart for this data.

c What fraction of the 45 students borrowed fewer than 6 books?

5 Harry counted the number of animals at a livestock market.
They were: sheep 80, cows 104, pigs 20, poultry 36.
He wants to show this information on a pie chart.

a How many animals are there altogether?

b What fraction of these are sheep?

c Explain why the angle at the centre of the sector for sheep is 120°.

d Copy and complete the following table.

	Sheep	Cows	Pigs	Poultry
Number				
Fraction of total				
Angle	120°			

e Draw a pie chart for this data.

6 Cathy collected details about how two charities spent the money they collected.
The information is given in the tables.

Charity A

Office costs	Advertising	Aid
£50 000	£60 000	£250 000

Charity B

Office costs	Advertising	Aid
£40 000	£35 000	£105 000

a Make a table like the one for question 5 for Charity A.
Now draw a pie chart to illustrate the information.

b Make another table, this time for Charity B and draw a pie chart.

c Compare your two charts and write a sentence describing what you notice.

K PERCENTAGES
MEANING OF PERCENTAGE

1. This 'L' shape is divided into 100 squares.

   > 1 square = $\frac{1}{100}$ th of the 'L' = 1% of the 'L'

   a. How many squares are black?
   b. What fraction of the 'L' is black?
   c. What percentage of the 'L' is black?

2. This disc is divided into 100 slices.

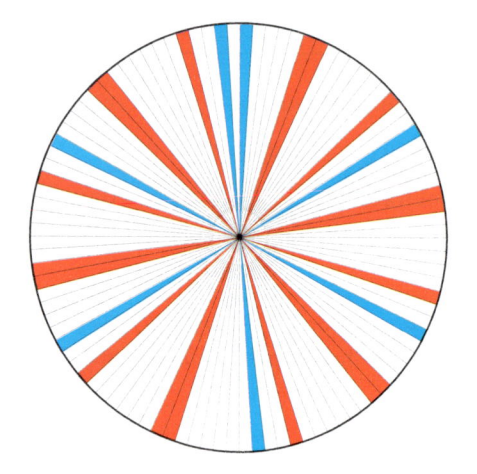

   > 1 slice = $\frac{1}{100}$ th of the disc = 1% of the disc

   a. How many red slices are there?
   b. What percentage of the disc is red?
   c. What fraction of the disc is red?
   d. What percentage of the disc is not red?
   e. What fraction of the disc is not red?
   f. What percentage of the disc is blue?
   g. What fraction of the disc is blue?

3.
   > 100 p = £1, 1 p = $\frac{1}{100}$ th of £1 = 1% of £1

   a. What amount is 50% of £1?
   b. What fraction of £1 is 50% of £1?
   c. How many pence is $\frac{1}{4}$ of £1?
   d. What percentage is $\frac{1}{4}$ of £1?
   e. What is the value of 20% of £1?

4. There are 20 biscuits in this box. 
   a. 50% of these biscuits are chocolate. How many biscuits are chocolate?
   b. 10% of the biscuits are broken. What percentage of the biscuits are not broken?

5. 40 people went on a coach trip to Calais. 25% were stopped at customs on their return to the UK. 
   a. What percentage were not stopped?
   b. How many people were stopped?

52

K PERCENTAGES
PERCENTAGES AS FRACTIONS

Example

Find 20% as a fraction.

20% means 20 out of 100.

$20\% = \frac{20}{100} = \frac{2}{10} = \frac{1}{5}$

Write as fractions

1. 10%
2. 50%
3. 25%
4. 40%
5. 30%
6. 45%
7. 75%
8. 84%
9. 5%
10. 3%
11. 28%
12. 15%
13. 6%
14. 36%
15. 8%

(Did you remember to cancel?)

Example

Find 150% as a fraction.

150% means 150 out of 100.

$150\% = \frac{150}{100} = \frac{15}{10} = \frac{3}{2} = 1\frac{1}{2}$

Write as fractions

16. 110%
17. 200%
18. 180%
19. 105%
20. 250%
21. 160%
22. 125%
23. 108%
24. 375%
25. 400%
26. 125%
27. 205%

Example

Find $17\frac{1}{2}$% as a fraction.

$17\frac{1}{2}$% means $17\frac{1}{2}$ out of 100.

$17\frac{1}{2}\% = \frac{17\frac{1}{2}}{100} = \frac{35}{200} = \frac{7}{40}$

Multiply top and bottom by 2.

Write as fractions

28. $12\frac{1}{2}$%
29. $33\frac{1}{3}$%
30. $2\frac{1}{2}$%
31. $112\frac{1}{2}$%
32. $117\frac{1}{2}$%
33. $62\frac{1}{2}$%

Write as fractions

34. 42%
35. 115%
36. 58%
37. 120%
38. 26%
39. 550%
40. 67%
41. 230%
42. 4%
43. 37%
44. 18%
45. 130%

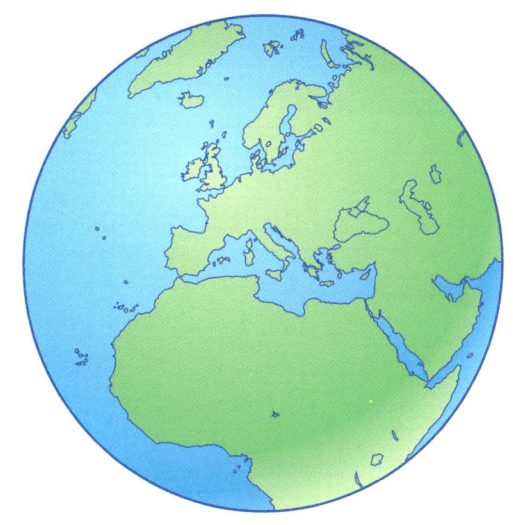

46. 70% of the Earth's surface is covered in water.
    a What fraction of the Earth's surface is covered in water?
    b What fraction of the Earth's surface is **not** covered with water?

47. 33% of the land on Earth is desert.
    What fraction of the land on Earth is desert?

48. 23% of humans on Earth live in China.
    What fraction of humans on Earth live in China?

49. 78% of the atmosphere is nitrogen.
    What fraction of the atmosphere is nitrogen?

50. Europe is 8% of the land mass of the Earth.
    What fraction of the land mass is Europe?

51. By 2010 it is expected that the population of the United Kingdom will be roughly 60 million.
    a 84% will live in England.
    What fraction is this?
    b 8% will live in Scotland.
    What fraction is this?
    c The remaining population will be equally divided between Wales and Northern Ireland.
    What fraction of the population of the United Kingdom will live in Wales?

K PERCENTAGES

PERCENTAGES, FRACTIONS AND DECIMALS

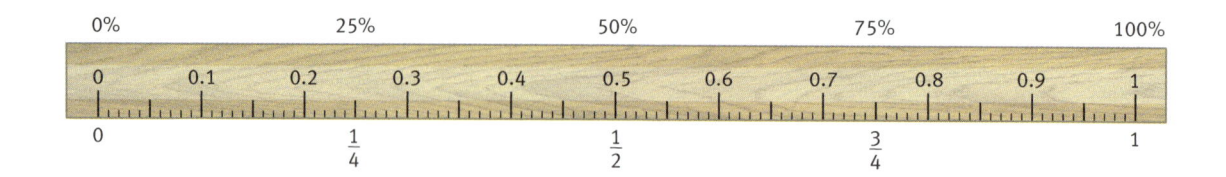

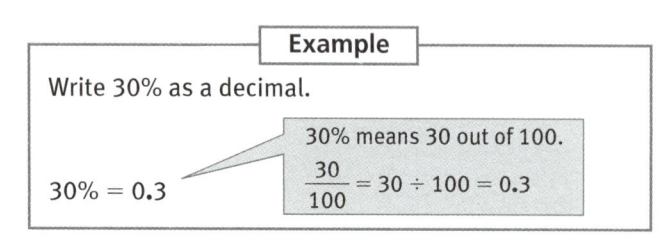

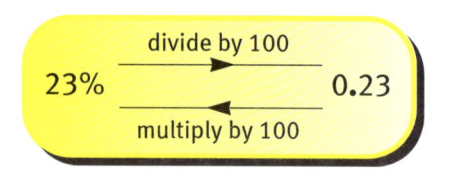

Example

Write 30% as a decimal.

30% means 30 out of 100.
$\frac{30}{100} = 30 \div 100 = 0.3$

30% = 0.3

23% $\xrightarrow{\text{divide by 100}}$ 0.23
0.23 $\xrightarrow{\text{multiply by 100}}$ 23%

Write as a decimal
1. 40%
2. 36%
3. 15%
4. 50%
5. 24%
6. 85%
7. 110%
8. 215%
9. 157%
10. 125%
11. 350%
12. 233%
13. 10.5%
14. 15.5%
15. 3.8%
16. 26.5%
17. 8.6%
18. 125.5%

19. **a** 20% of the weight of this hamburger is bread. What decimal part of the weight is bread?
   b $17\frac{1}{2}$% of the cost of this hamburger is added as VAT. What decimal fraction of the cost is added as VAT?

20. Write 50%   **a** as a fraction   **b** as a decimal.
21. Write $\frac{1}{4}$ **a** as a decimal   **b** as a percentage.
22. Write 0.6   **a** as a fraction   **b** as a percentage.

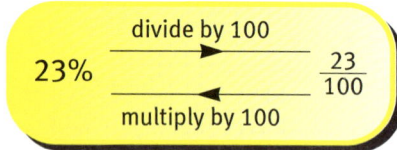

23% $\xrightarrow{\text{divide by 100}}$ $\frac{23}{100}$
$\frac{23}{100}$ $\xrightarrow{\text{multiply by 100}}$ 23%

Write as a fraction
23. 28%
24. 66%
25. 15%
26. 4%

Write as a percentage
27. $\frac{2}{5}$
28. $\frac{7}{10}$
29. $2\frac{1}{2}$
30. $\frac{1}{8}$
31. $\frac{3}{4}$
32. $\frac{1}{10}$
33. $\frac{5}{8}$
34. $\frac{4}{5}$

Write as a decimal
35. 54%
36. 61%
37. 8%
38. 110%

Write as a percentage
39. 0.45
40. 0.12
41. 0.28
42. 1.25
43. 0.4
44. 1.5
45. 0.883
46. 0.175

47. Copy and complete this table.

Percentage	Decimal	Fraction
12.5		
	1.25	
		$\frac{6}{25}$
140		

48. Write the numbers in order of size with the smallest first.
    a $\frac{3}{4}$, 70%, 0.8
    b 0.3, $\frac{1}{4}$, 20%

49. **a** One drawer of this filing cabinet holds $2\frac{1}{2}$ times its empty weight. Write $2\frac{1}{2}$ as a decimal.
    b The cost of a set of keys is 0.2 times the cost of the cabinet. What fraction is the cost of the keys of the cost of the cabinet?
    c The value added tax is 17.5% of the cost of the cabinet. Write 17.5% as a decimal.
    d One drawer is 70% full. What fraction of the drawer is empty?

L PROBABILITY
PROBABILITY SCALE

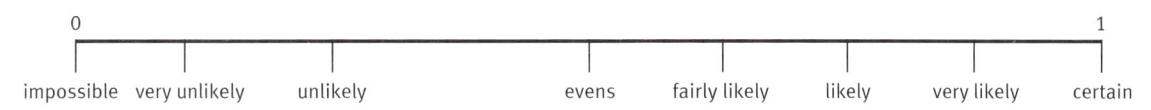

0 —— impossible — very unlikely — unlikely — evens — fairly likely — likely — very likely — certain —— 1

1 Choose words from the scale above to describe the probability that
   a you will get a score of 10 when you roll a dice
   b you will get a head when you flip a fair coin
   c you will score less than 11 on a test marked out of 10
   d you will score 5 or 6 when you roll a six-sided fair dice.

2 The pointer is spun. Choose words from the scale above to describe the probability that
   a it stops on red
   b it stops on green.

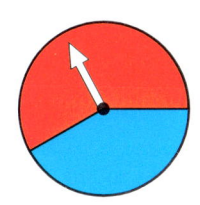

3 Copy this probability scale.

   0 —————————— 1

   Write each letter on the line to show the probability that the event will happen.
   a **A**: When I flip a coin it will come down tails.
   b **B**: It will rain in the desert tomorrow.
   c **C**: I buy one ticket for the national lottery and win the jackpot.
   d **D**: I score more than one when I roll a fair six-sided dice.

4 A six-sided dice is rolled.
   Write down all the possible scores.

5 This spinner is spun once.
   Write down all the possible outcomes.

6 This spinner is spun once.
   a Which colour is it most likely to come to rest on? Give a reason for your answer.
   b How many chances does it have of landing on red?
   c What words would you use to describe the chance that it lands on blue?

$$\text{Probability} = \frac{\text{Number of outcomes you want}}{\text{Total number of possible outcomes}}$$

Example

One sweet is chosen at random from the sweets in this bag. Find the probability that it is a green sweet.

The possible outcomes (colours of sweet) are:
green, green, red, red, red, red, red.
There are 7 of these, 2 of which are green.

Probability that sweet is green = $\frac{2}{7}$

7 A fair six-sided dice is rolled once.
   a Find the probability of scoring 6.
   b Find the probability of scoring 5 or 6.

8 A fair six-sided dice is rolled once.
   a What is the probability that the score is 1?
   b What is the probability that the score is 2?
   c What is the probability that the score is more than 2?

9 A bag contains 3 red discs, 4 green discs and 5 blue discs. One disc is taken out of the bag at random.
   a What is the probability that it is a blue disc?
   b What is the probability that it is a white disc?

10 One hundred tickets are sold for a raffle. The tickets are numbered 1 to 100.
   a Mehta buys one ticket. What is the probability that he wins first prize?
   b What it the probability that the number on the winning ticket is less than 20?

11 There are 20 red grapes and 21 green grapes on a tray. One grape is removed at random.
   Is it true that it is equally likely that the grape is red or green? Give a reason.

12 There are two chocolate muffins and three blueberry muffins on the table. John chooses one. Why is it not true that the probability that he takes a chocolate muffin is $\frac{2}{5}$?

L PROBABILITY

FINDING AND USING PROBABILITY

1. The bar chart shows the test marks of some pupils.

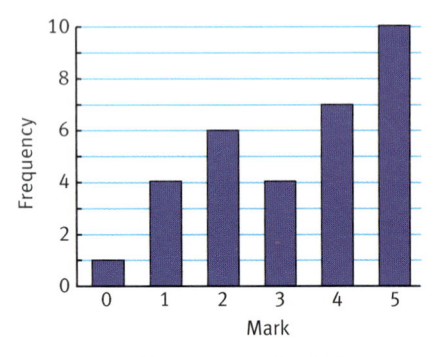

   a How many pupils got a mark of 4?

   b How many pupils took the test?

   c One of these pupils is chosen at random. What is the probability that the pupil's mark was 4?

2. Eggs are packed in boxes.
   Each box in a crate was examined for broken eggs. The bar chart shows the numbers of broken eggs in the boxes.

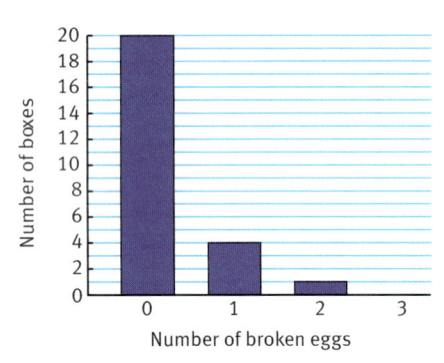

   a How many boxes were in the crate?

   b How many boxes had at least one broken egg in them?

   c One of these boxes is chosen at random. What is the probability that there is at least one broken egg in it?

3. A coin is biased. It is flipped 50 times.
   It came down showing a head 15 times.
   The coin is flipped once more.

   a What is the probability that it lands head up?

   b What is the probability that it lands tail up?

4. Roger flips a coin 50 times.
   He gets 40 heads and 10 tails.
   Is the coin fair?
   Give a reason for your answer.

5. A fair coin is flipped once.

   a What is the probability that it lands head up?

   A fair coin is flipped 20 times.

   b About how many heads would you expect?

6. There are 20 sweets in a bag:
   8 red ones, 5 yellow ones and 7 orange ones.
   One sweet is taken out of the bag at random.

   a What is the probability that it is red?

   b What is the probability that it is not red?

7. A fair six-sided dice is rolled 12 times.

   a About how many sixes would you expect?

   No sixes were scored.

   b Jo said 'The next roll will be a six.'
   Why might she be wrong?

8. Seema and Bryn play a game.
   They roll a fair dice.

   a What is the probability of scoring 3 or more?

   b What is the probability of scoring less than 3?

   c Seema said 'If the score is 3 or more, I win.'
   Why is this not fair?

9. 200 people are expected to play this game at a school fête. An ordinary pack of 52 playing cards is used.

   a What is probability of cutting an ace?

   b About how many prizes are needed?

   Cut an ace to win a prize.

10. This pointer is spun once.

    a Pat said
    'If it stops on blue I win,
    if it stops on green you win,
    if it stops on red we have another go.'
    Why is this not fair?

    b Explain in words how you can work out the probability that the pointer stops on red.

L PROBABILITY
SUMS OF PROBABILITIES

1 There are only red beads and white beads in a bag. One bead is taken out at random.

   a What is the probability that the bead is red or white?

   b What is the probability that the bead is yellow?

   c The probability that this bead is red is $\frac{1}{10}$. What is the probability that the bead is white?

2 The probability of winning a prize in a raffle is 0.002.
What is the probability of not winning a prize?

3 This spinner is spun once.

   a What is the probability that it lands on a yellow side?

   b What is the probability that it lands on a red, blue or green side?

   The probability that it lands on a red or blue side is 0.7.

   c What is the probability that it lands on the green side?

   d The spinner is spun 20 times. About how many times will it land on the green side?

4 John, Bill and Kate play a game. It involves rolling a ball to knock over a target numbered 1, 2 or 3. If the ball hits 1, John scores a point. If the ball hits 2, Bill scores a point and if the ball hits 3, Kate scores a point.

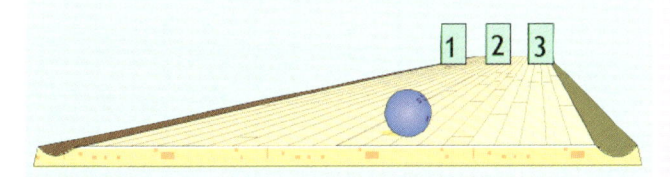

   They play 40 times. John wins 10 times, Bill wins 5 times and Kate wins the rest.

   a They play the game once more. Esimate the probability that Kate wins.

   b Is this a game of chance or a game of skill? Give a reason.

5 The pointer is spun once.

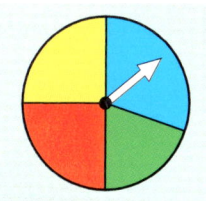

   a Which two colours is the pointer equally likely to stop on?

   b The probability that the pointer stops on yellow is 0.25.
What is the probability that the pointer stops on red?

   c The probability that the pointer stops on blue is 0.35.
What is the probability that the pointer stops on green?

6 Flowers grown from a packet of seeds are different colours. The table gives the probability of each colour.

Colour	Red	Yellow	Pink	Blue
Probability	$\frac{1}{10}$	$\frac{3}{10}$		$\frac{1}{5}$

   a What is the probability that the flower will be red, yellow or blue?

   b What is the probability that the flower will be pink?

   100 plants are grown.

   c How many of these should have red flowers?

7 A coin is rolled onto a squared board.
The squares are coloured red, blue or green.
If the coin lands completely inside a square, the player wins a prize.
The table gives the probabilities that the coin lands inside a square.

Square colour	Red	Blue	Green
Probability	0.03	0.02	0.04

What is the probability that the coin does not land completely inside a square?

57

L PROBABILITY
TWO EVENTS

1 Each of these spinners is spun once.

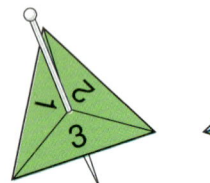

a Copy and fill in this table to show all the possible outcomes.

	Red	Blue	Yellow
1	1, Red		
2			
3			

b What is the probability that the result is (2, yellow)?

c What is the probability that the result is (1, red)?

2 Bill takes one card from the red set and one card from the green set without seeing the numbers on them.

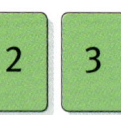

a Copy and complete this table to show all the possible choices.

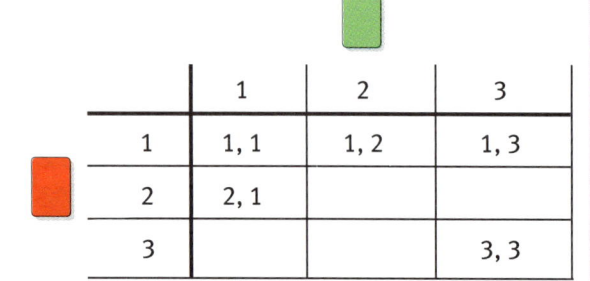

	1	2	3
1	1, 1	1, 2	1, 3
2	2, 1		
3			3, 3

b What is the probability that Bill takes 2 twos?

c What is the probability that both cards have the same number?

The numbers on the two cards taken are added together.

d What is the probability that the sum is 5?

If this sum is 5 or 6, Bill wins a prize.

e What is the probability that he wins a prize?

3 Two fair dice are rolled and the scores are added.

a Copy and complete this table to show all the possible outcomes.

	1	2	3	4	5	6
1	2					
2	3	4				
3						
4				7		
5						
6						

b What is the probability that the sum will be **i** 6 **ii** 10?

c What is the probability of getting a sum of **i** 10 or more **ii** less than 6?

4 Jill takes one card from the blue set and one card from the yellow set without seeing the numbers on them.

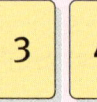

This diagram shows all the possible outcomes when the numbers on the cards are added together.

		Blue		
		1	2	2
Yellow	2	X	X	X
	3	X	X	X
	4	X	X	X

a What is the outcome represented by the cross in the grey square?

b What is the probability that the total on the two cards is **i** 6 **ii** 5?

c An extra yellow card with the number 1 is added to the yellow set.
Explain why the number of outcomes with total 6 is not changed but the probability that the total is 6 is changed.

58

L PROBABILITY
INVESTIGATION

This is a fair dice.
Can you do better than chance by predicting what the score will be next time this dice is rolled?
If you can, you have special powers!

1. Suppose that you have no special powers.
   a. If you predict that the score will be 4 next time this dice is rolled, what is the probability that you will be right?
   b. If you predict that the score will be 2 next time this dice is rolled, what is the probability that you are right?
   c. If you predict that the score will be 6 next time this dice is rolled, what is the probability that you are right?
   d. Does the score that you predict affect the probability that you will be right?
      Give a reason for your answer.
      Write a sentence like this one:
      Whatever score I predict, the probability that I am right is .... because ....
   e. If you predict the score several times, about how often will you be right by chance?

2. Now you need to test whether you can do better than chance.
   To do this, you must plan an experiment to collect some information about your powers of prediction. You can do this by writing down your prediction, then rolling the dice and then writing down whether or not you are correct.
   a. Write down a sentence about the advantages of collecting the information this way.
   b. Write down a sentence about the disadvantages of collecting the information this way.
   c. Can you think of a way to improve the experiment so that you get rid of possible bias?
      Write a sentence to describe how you can do this.

3. Write down a description of the experiment you have decided to do.
   Include
   a. a design of a data collection sheet
   b. the number of times you need to repeat the experiment to give worthwhile results, with reasons.
      For example, are 6 predictions enough, are 60 enough, are 600 enough – what is a practical number?)

4. Now perform your experiment.

5. You need to use the data from your experiment to work out the probability that you can predict the right score. How will you do this? Will a frequency table help?
   Will a bar chart or a pie chart help to give a summary of the data?
   a. Draw any tables or diagrams that you have decided will help.
   b. Now work out the probability that you can predict the right score from your data.

6. You can now decide how you have performed. Have you done better than chance – if you have, is it a little better or much better? Have you done worse than chance?
   Write a sentence to describe how you have done, with reasons.

7. Now look again at your investigation. Can you use the information to work out if you are better at predicting some scores than others?
   Write a short description of how you can do this with the information you have collected.
   If you cannot use the information already collected, say how you could change the way you recorded the results so that you could work this out.

M TRIANGLES, QUADRILATERALS AND POLYGONS
ANGLES OF A TRIANGLE

1

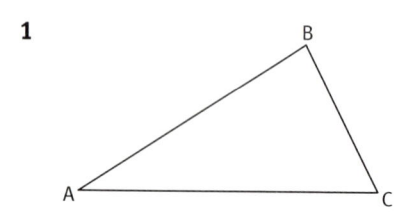

On a copy this diagram
a put a × in the angle BAC
b put a ● on the midpoint of BC
c draw a line through B that is perpendicular to AC.

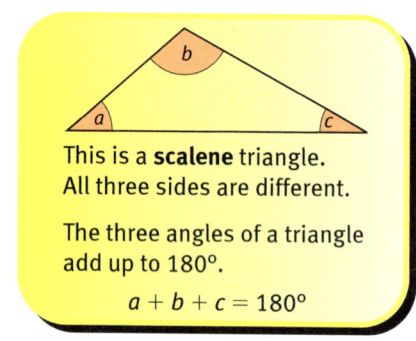

This is a **scalene** triangle.
All three sides are different.

The three angles of a triangle add up to 180°.

$$a + b + c = 180°$$

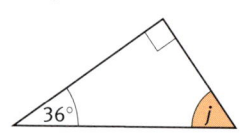

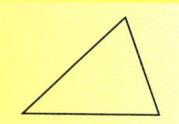

This is an **acute-angled** triangle.
All three angles are acute.

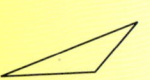

This is an **obtuse-angled** triangle.
One of the angles is obtuse.

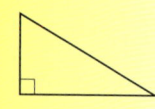

This is a **right-angled** triangle.
One of the angles is 90°.

Find the angle marked with a letter.

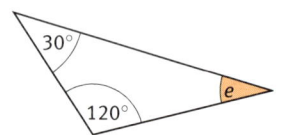

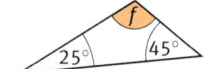

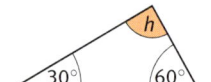

2 50°, 70°, d

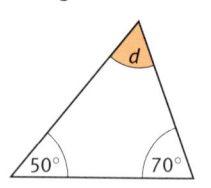

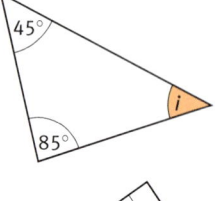

3 30°, 120°, e

4 25°, 45°, f

5 30°, 60°, h

6 45°, 85°, i

7 36°, j (right angle)

8 Which triangles from questions 2 to 7 are acute-angled triangles?

9 Which triangles from questions 2 to 7 are obtuse-angled triangles?

10 Which triangles from questions 2 to 7 are right-angled triangles?

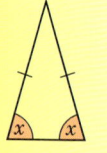

This is an **isosceles** triangle.
Two sides are equal and two angles are equal.

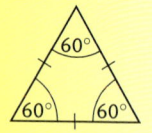

This is an **equilateral** triangle.
All three sides are equal.
All three angles are 60°.

In questions **11** to **14** say which triangle is isosceles, which is equilateral, which is right-angled and which is none of these.

11 60°, 60°

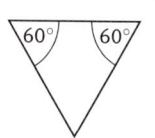

12 30°, 75°

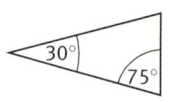

13 60°, 30°

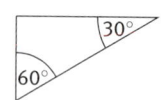

14 70°, 50°

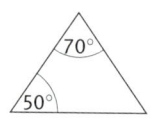

Find each angle marked with a letter.

15 50° at apex, d and e at base (isosceles)

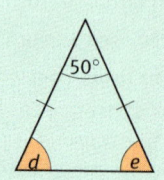

16 g at apex, f at base (equilateral marks)

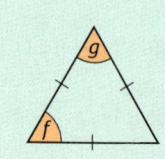

17

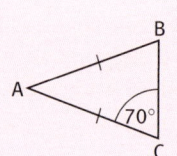

Find a angle ABC
      b angle BAC.

(Triangle with AB = BC marked, angle at C = 70°)

18

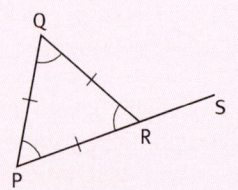

Find a angle PQR
      b angle QRS.

(Triangle PQR with PQ = PR marked, R extended to S)

> An exterior angle of a triangle is equal to the sum of the two interior opposite angles.
> $c = a + b$

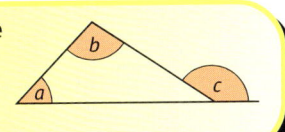

In questions **19** to **26** find the marked angles.

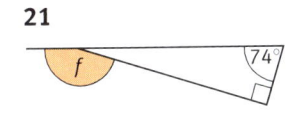

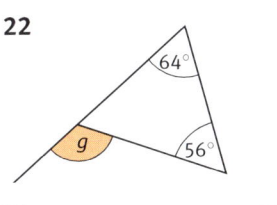

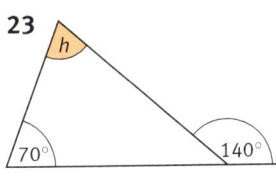

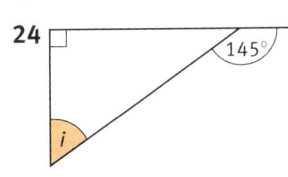

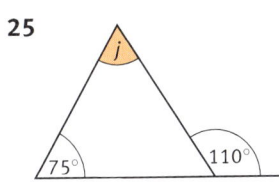

19 70°, 60°, d

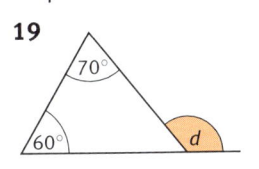

20 65°, 65°, e

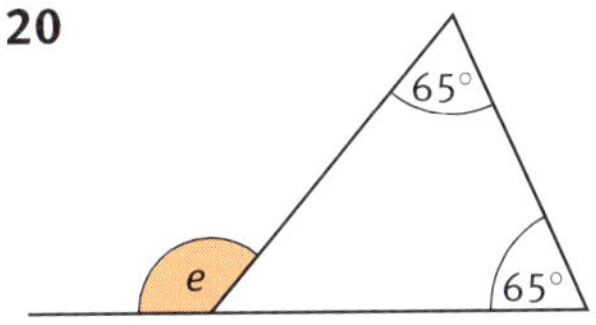

21 74°, right angle, f

22 64°, 56°, g

23 70°, 140°, h

24 right angle, 145°, i

25 75°, 110°, j

26 155°, 75°, k

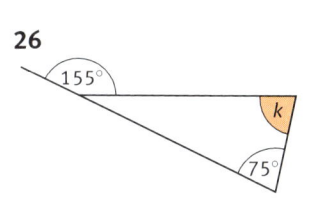

27 Copy the statements and fill in the blanks.

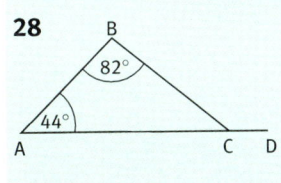

a 50°, d, e
$d + e + \square = \square$

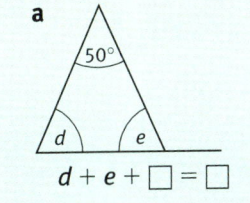

b 55°, f, g, h
$55° + \square = \square$

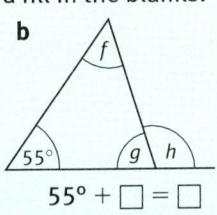

28 B 82°, A 44°, C, D
Find angle BCD.

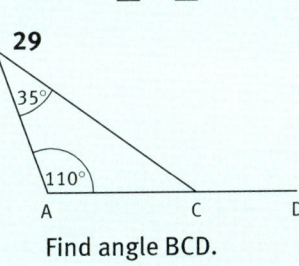

29 B 35°, A 110°, C, D
Find angle BCD.

30 Q, P 44°, R 85°, S
Find **a** angle PQR **b** angle QRP.

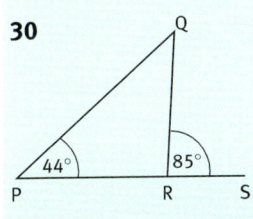

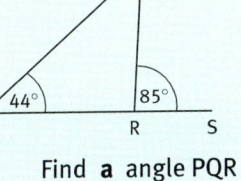

31 E, D 95°, F 150°, G
Find **a** angle DEF **b** angle EFD.

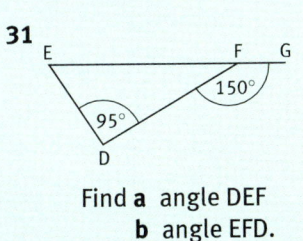

32 Copy the statements and fill in the blanks.

B, D, C, A

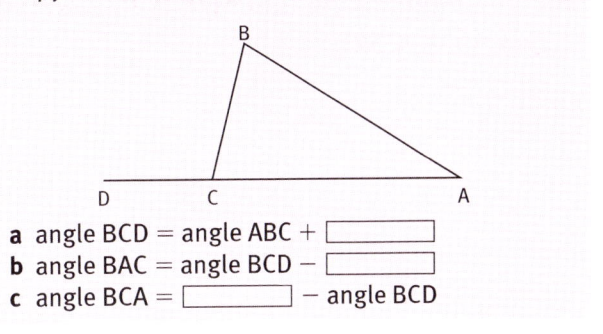

a angle BCD = angle ABC + ☐
b angle BAC = angle BCD − ☐
c angle BCA = ☐ − angle BCD

Construct the following triangles. You will need a ruler, a protractor and a pair of compasses.

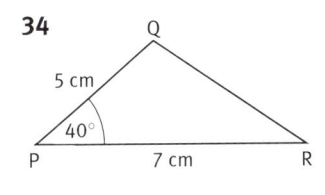

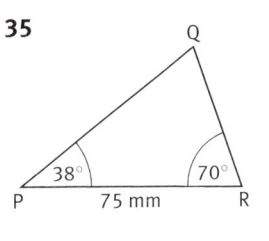

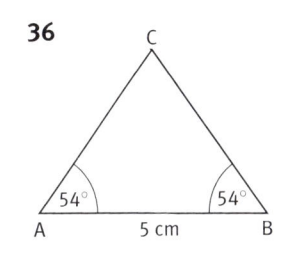

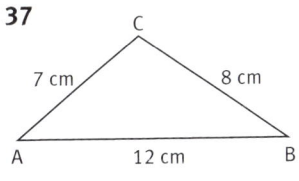

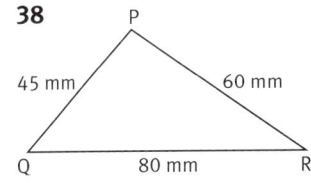

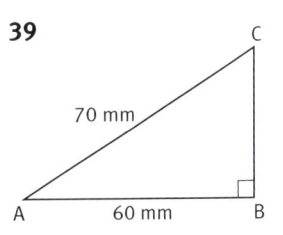

33 A, 4 cm, B, 6 cm, C (right angle at B)

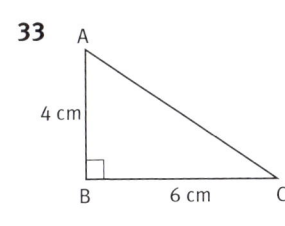

34 Q, 5 cm, P 40°, 7 cm, R

35 Q, P 38°, 75 mm, R 70°

36 C, A 54°, 5 cm, B 54°

37 C, A 7 cm, 12 cm, 8 cm B

38 P, Q 45 mm, 80 mm, 60 mm R

39 C, A, 70 mm, 60 mm, B (right angle at B)

40 F (right angle), 6 cm, D, 10 cm, E

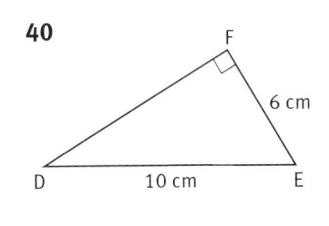

41 Construct an equilateral triangle with sides of length 6 cm.

42 Show that two triangles can be drawn with these measurements.

a Q, 5.5 cm, 6 cm, R 60° P

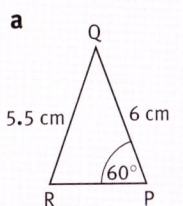

b B, 7 cm, 5 cm, A 40°, C

61

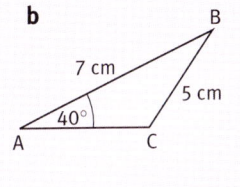

M TRIANGLES, QUADRILATERALS AND POLYGONS
QUADRILATERALS

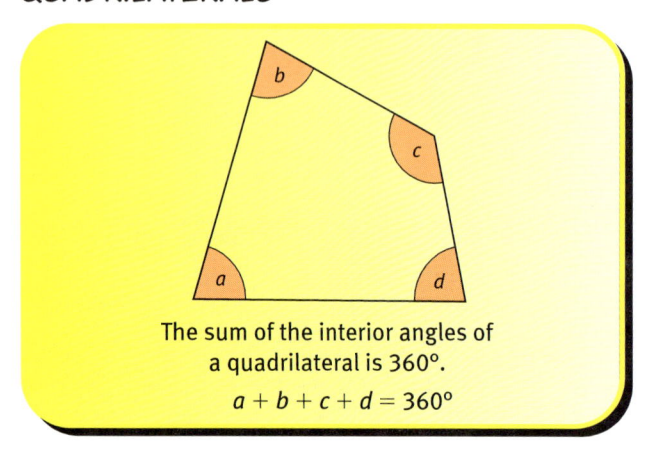

The sum of the interior angles of a quadrilateral is 360°.

$a + b + c + d = 360°$

In questions **1** to **8** find the angles marked with letters.

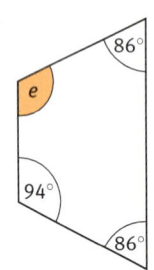

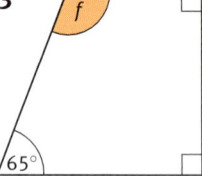

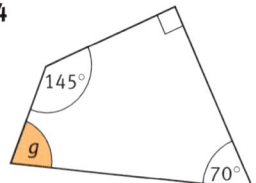

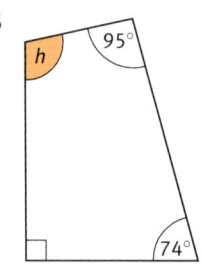

1 95°, 120°, 70°, d

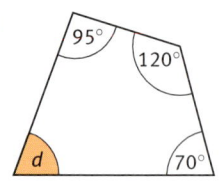

2 86°, e, 94°, 86°

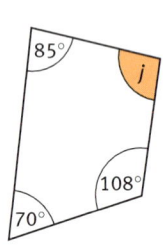

3 f, 65°, (two right angles)

4 145°, g, 70°, (right angle)

5 h, 95°, 74°, (right angle)

6 75°, 64°, 136°, i

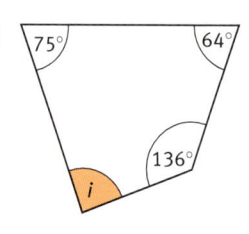

7 85°, j, 108°, 70°

8 66°, k, 58°, k

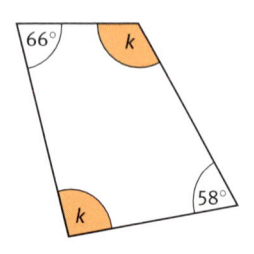

9 In ABCD, angle BAD = 95°, angle BCD = 85° and angle CDA = 64°. Draw your own diagram and mark the values of the three given angles. Find angle ABC.

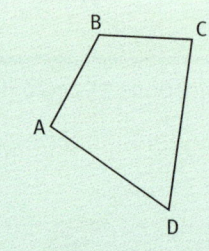

10 In quadrilateral ABCD, angle ABC = 90°, angle ADC = 90° and angle DAB = 105°. Draw your own diagram and mark the values of the three given angles. Work out the value of angle BCD.

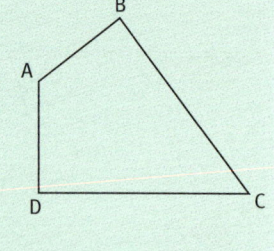

11 In quadrilateral DEFG, angle EDG = 45°, angle DEF = 150° and angle DGF = 105°. Find angle EFG.

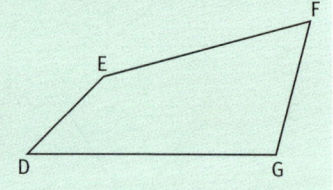

12

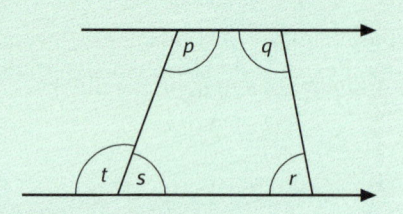

a What is the sum of *p*, *q*, *r* and *s*?
b *p* = 115°. Work out the size of *t*.
c *r* = 85°. Work out the size of *q*.

13 a Find the size of the angle marked *p*.

b Find the size of the angle marked *q*.

c Find the size of the angle marked *r*.

d What is the value of *p* + *q* + *r*?

e What is special about the lines AD and BC?

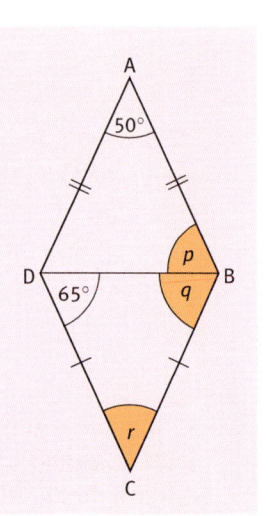

62

M TRIANGLES, QUADRILATERALS AND POLYGONS
SPECIAL QUADRILATERALS

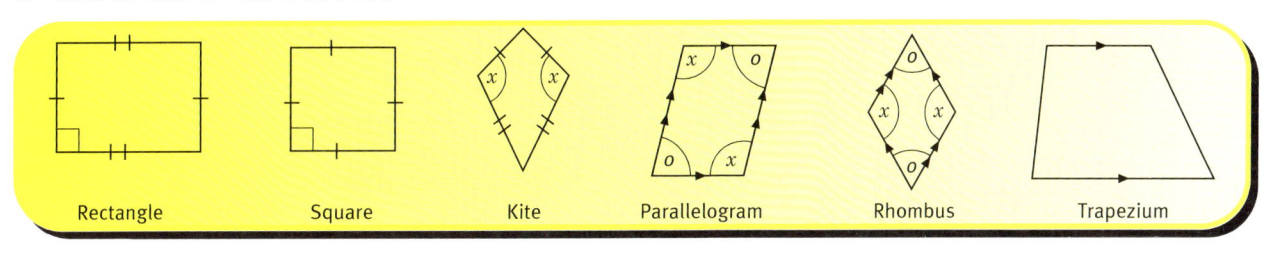

Rectangle Square Kite Parallelogram Rhombus Trapezium

1 a What special name do we give to this shape?
b Copy the shape and put a cross in an acute angle.

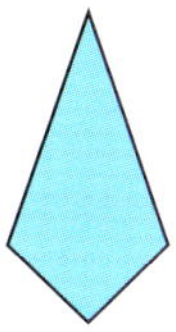

2
a What name do we give to this shape? 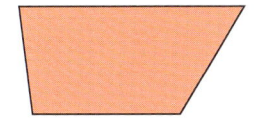
b Copy this shape and put a cross in an obtuse angle.

3 Draw a parallelogram like this one.
a On your diagram add arrows to show any lines that are parallel.
b Mark any sides that are equal.
c Put crosses in two angles that are equal.
d Are the two unmarked angles equal? Give a reason for your answer.

4 What special name do we give
a to quadrilateral ABCD
b to quadrilateral ABCE?

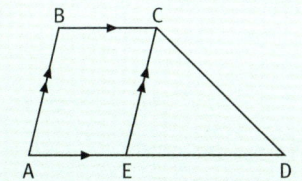

5 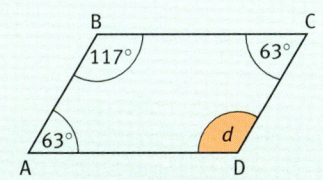
a Find the angle marked d.
b What name do we give to this type of quadrilateral?
c Name any lines that are parallel.

6 ABCD is a rhombus. Work out
a the size of angle ADC
b the size of angle BAD.

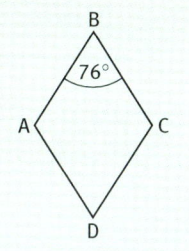

7 PQRS is a trapezium.
a Which sides are parallel?
b Find the size of the angle PSR.

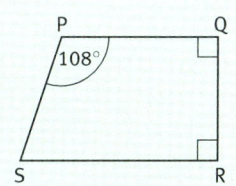

8 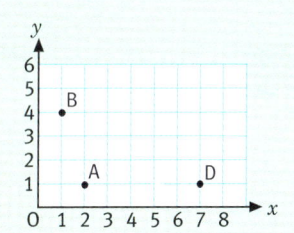 ABCD is a parallelogram. What are the coordinates of C?

9 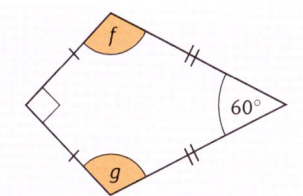
a What is the name of this shape?
b Work out the size of the angle marked f.

10 The sketch shows a bicycle frame. BE is parallel to CD and AB = AE.
a Work out the angle BAE.
b Work out the angle CDE.

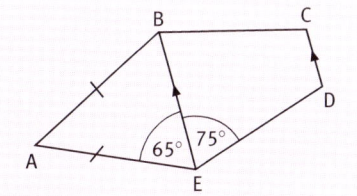

M TRIANGLES, QUADRILATERALS AND POLYGONS
POLYGONS

A regular polygon has all its sides equal and all its angles equal.

Regular pentagon (5 sides) Regular hexagon (6 sides) Regular octagon (8 sides)

The sum of the exterior angles of any polygon is 360°.

$a + b + c + d + e + f = 360°$

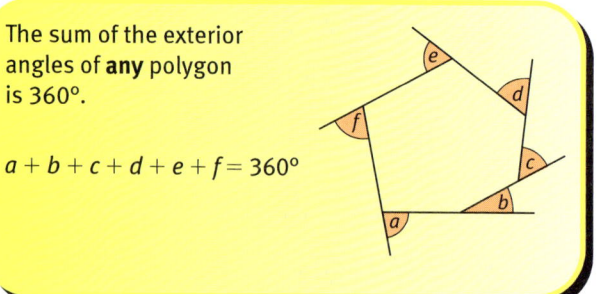

1. What name do we give to
   a a regular triangle
   b a regular quadrilateral?

2. 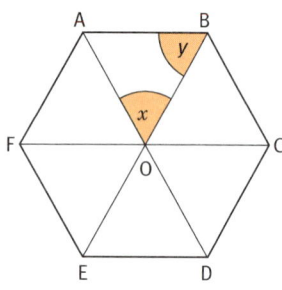
   a i How many angles are there at the centre of this regular hexagon?
     ii Are they equal? Give a reason.
   b Work out the value of the angle marked x.
   c Work out the value of the angle marked y.
   d What special name do we give to triangle OAB?

3. Draw a regular pentagon.

4. Draw a regular polygon with 10 sides.

5. O is the centre of a regular pentagon ABCDE.
   a Work out the size of the angle marked p.
   b What type of triangle is triangle OAB?
   c Work out the value of the angle marked q.
   d What is the order of rotational symmetry of ABCDE?
   e i How many lines of symmetry are there?
     ii Copy the diagram and draw these lines of symmetry.

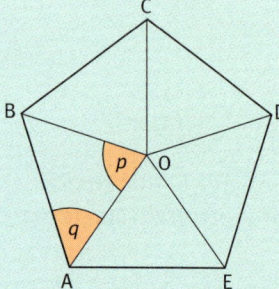

In questions **6** to **9** find the angles marked with letters.

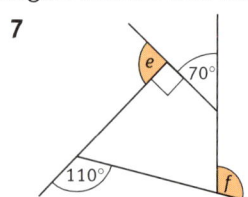

6. (angles 160°, 140°, d)

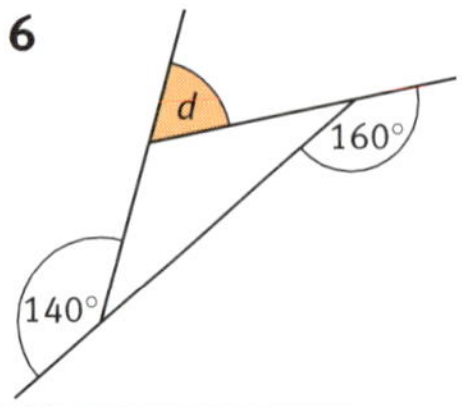

7. (angles 70°, 110°, e, f, with right angle)

8. (angles 65°, 55°, 100°, 50°, g)

9. (angles 50°, 75°, 85°, 60°, 45°, h)

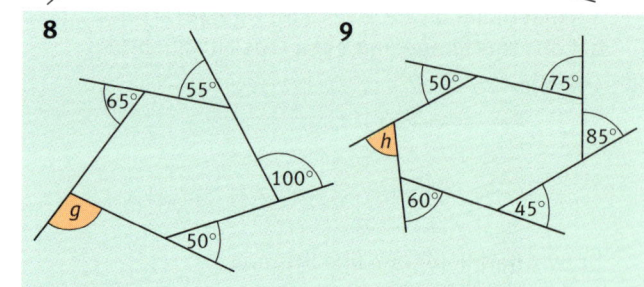

10. a What is the sum of the exterior angles of a regular octagon?
    b How many exterior angles does an octagon have?
    c Find the size of one exterior angle of a regular octagon.

11. a Draw a regular polygon with 7 sides.
    b Produce all the sides in order and mark the exterior angles.
    c Work out the size of one of these angles.

12. a i How many sides does the regular polygon ABCDEFGH have?
       ii What do you know about the lengths of these sides? 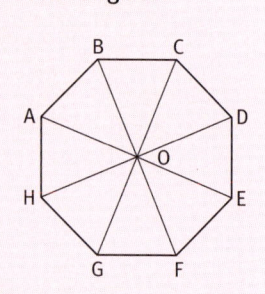
    O is the centre of the polygon.
    b Find the size of angle AOB.
    c What name do we give to triangle OAB?
    d Work out the size of angle ABO.
    e What is the size of angle ABC?
    f The side AB is extended to a point K. Work out the size of angle KBC.

M TRIANGLES, QUADRILATERALS AND POLYGONS
CONGRUENCE AND TESSELLATION

> Two identical shapes are congruent.

1 Are these two shapes congruent?
   a
   b
   c
   d

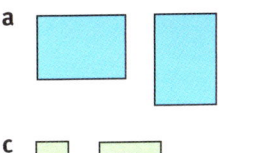

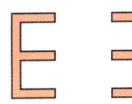

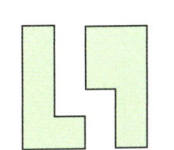

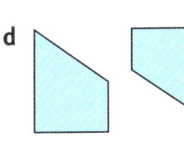

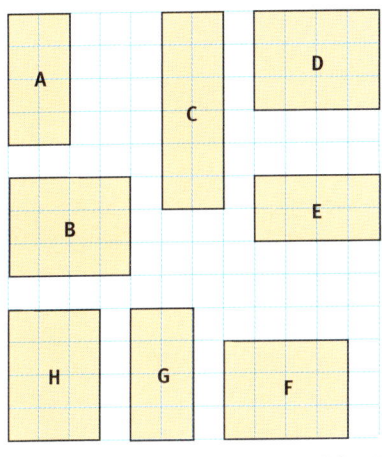

2
   a Which rectangles are congruent with B?
   b Name any rectangles congruent with A.
   c Name a rectangle that covers the same number of squares as F but is not congruent with F.

3 Ben draws a circle of radius 5 cm.
Diana draws a circle of diameter 10 cm.
Are these circles congruent?
Give a reason.

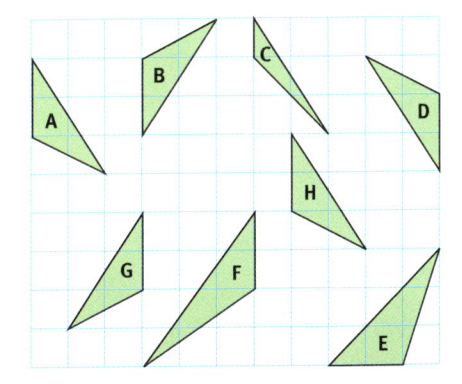

4
   a Which triangles are congruent with A?
   b Are triangles E and F congruent?
      Give a reason.

5

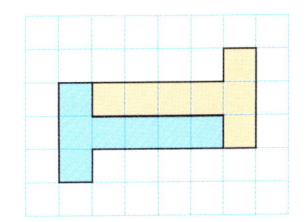

The diagram shows two 'T' shapes.
Copy them on to a grid.
On your grid show, by drawing at least six more Ts, that this shape tessellates.

6

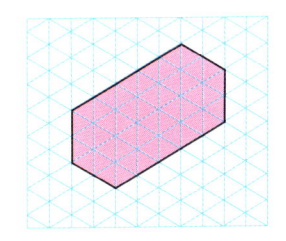

The diagram shows a hexagon.
Copy it onto a grid.
   a How many lines of symmetry does this hexagon have?
   b Show, on your grid, that this hexagon tessellates. You need to draw at least six more hexagons.

7

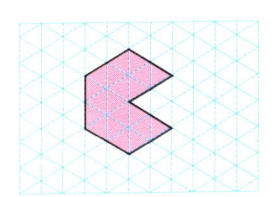

By drawing this shape at least eight times on your own grid show that it tessellates.

8

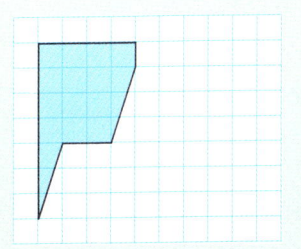

This shape is made by cutting off one corner of a square and putting it in a new position.
Copy it onto a grid.
   a Draw the shape at least another five times to show that it could be used to give a tiling pattern.
   b Do you think this design is ever likely to be used? Give a reason for your answer.

N PERIMETER AND AREA

PERIMETER

> The perimeter of a shape is the distance all round it.

Example

Find the perimeter of this postcard.

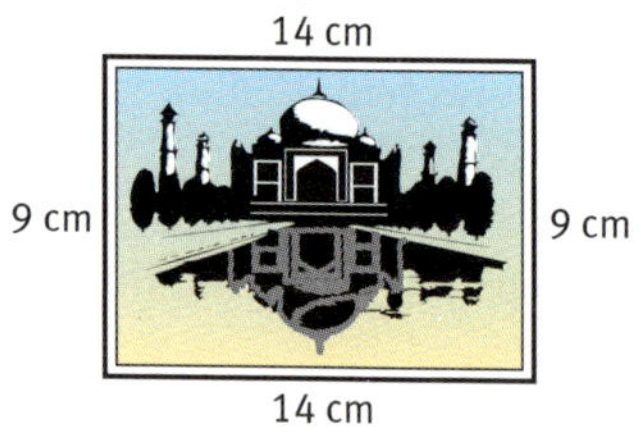

14 cm
9 cm   9 cm
14 cm

Perimeter = (14 + 9 + 14 + 9) cm = 46 cm

1 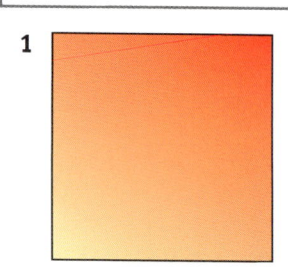
   a Measure, in millimetres, the length of an edge of this square.
   b Find the perimeter of the square.

2 
   a Measure, in millimetres,
      i the length of this rectangle   ii its width.
   b Find the perimeter of the rectangle.

3 Find the perimeter of this certificate.
   15 cm
   20 cm

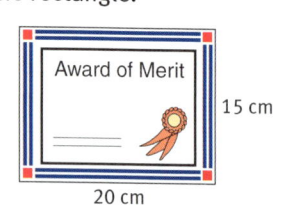

4 Find the perimeter of this carpet.
   3.5 m
   4 m

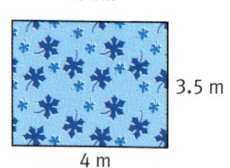

5 Peter walks around the edge of this garden centre. How far does he walk?
   40 m, 65 m, 65 m, 80 m, 50 m

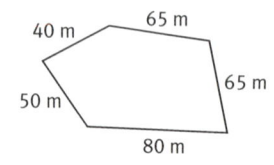

6 A soccer field is 120 yards long and 80 yards wide. How far is it all the way round?

7 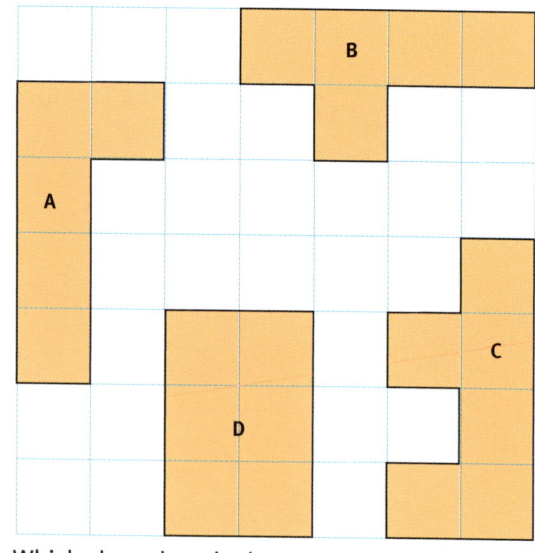
   a Which shape has the longest perimeter?
   b Which shape has the shortest perimeter?
   c Which two shapes have the same perimeter?
   d Measure, in millimetres, the length of D.
   e Measure, in millimetres, the width of D.

8 Work out the distance around the edge of this field.
   300 m
   1000 m
   300 m
   700 m

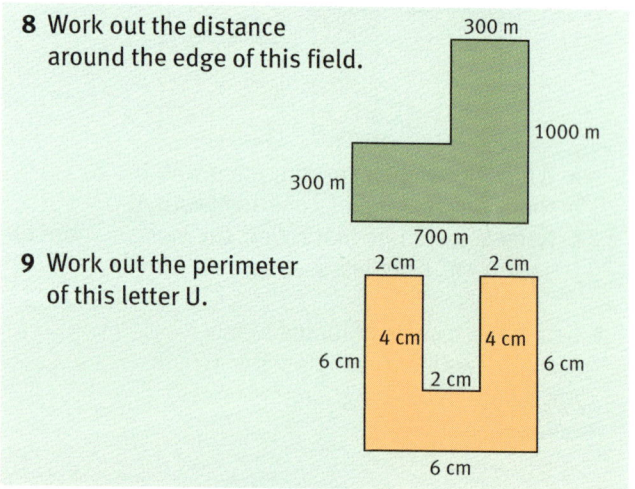

9 Work out the perimeter of this letter U.
   2 cm, 2 cm
   4 cm, 4 cm
   6 cm, 6 cm
   2 cm
   6 cm

10
   Side 6 cm
   Side, Side 7 cm
   Side
   11 cm

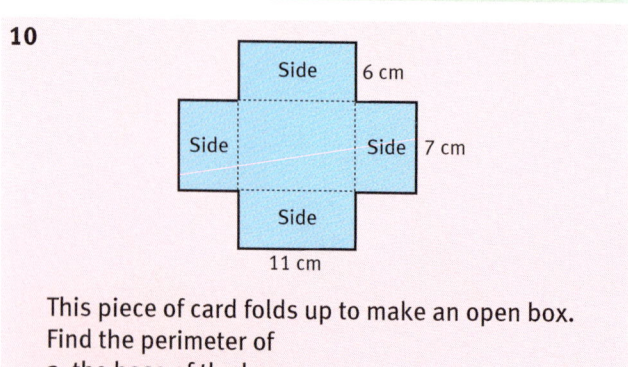

This piece of card folds up to make an open box. Find the perimeter of
   a the base of the box
   b a larger vertical face
   c a smaller vertical face.

N PERIMETER AND AREA
AREA BY COUNTING SQUARES

> The area of a shape is measured by finding the number of squares that cover the shape.

Example

Find the area of this metal plate by counting squares.

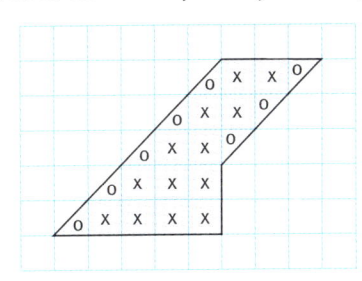

By counting

Area = 13 whole squares + 8 half-squares
     = 13 squares + 4 squares
     = 17 squares

Example

The diagram shows the outline of a forest on a map. Each square represents one square kilometre. By counting squares find the area of the forest.

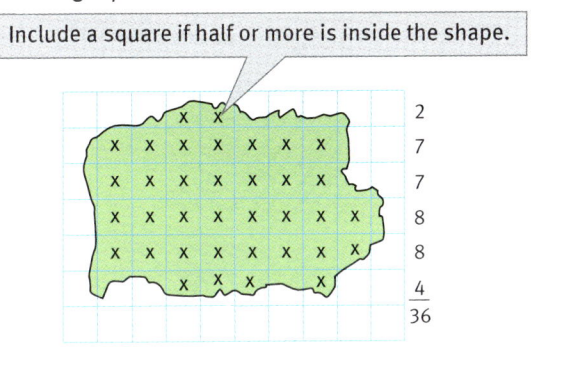

Include a square if half or more is inside the shape.

$$\begin{array}{r} 2 \\ 7 \\ 7 \\ 8 \\ 8 \\ \underline{4} \\ 36 \end{array}$$

The area of the forest is 36 sq km.

1 Count squares to find the area of this table.

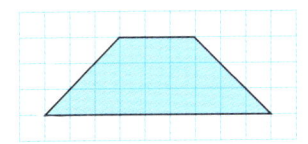

2 Count squares to find the area of this plot of land.

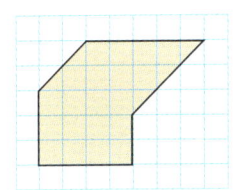

3 Count squares to find the area of this piece of metal.

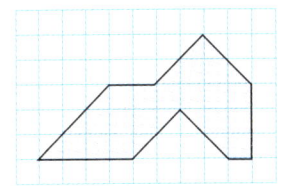

4 Count squares to find the area of this end wall of a building.

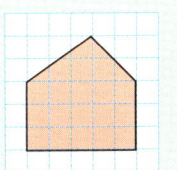

5

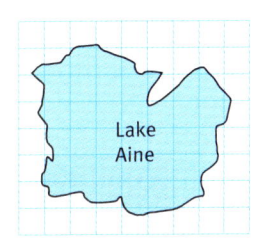

Each square represents 1 sq km.
Count squares to find the area of Lake Aine.

6

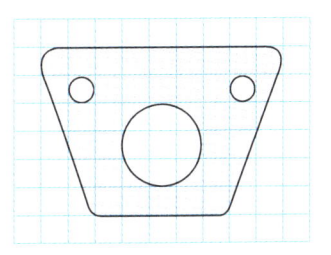

Each square represents 1 sq cm.
Count squares to find the area of this gasket.

7

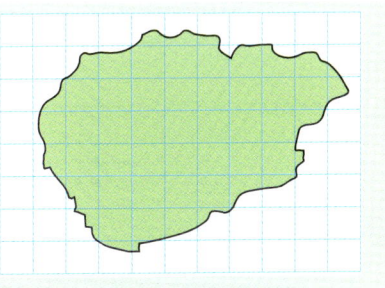

Each square represents 1 hectare of land.
Count squares to find the numbers of hectares of land on this island.

67

N PERIMETER AND AREA
AREAS OF SQUARES AND RECTANGLES

> Area of a rectangle = length × width
>
> Area of a square
> = length of side × length of side
> = (length of side)^2

Example

Find the area of this postcard.

9 cm
14 cm

Area of postcard = length × width
= 14 cm × 9 cm
= 126 cm^2

Find the area of this postage stamp.

2 cm

Area of square stamp = (length of side)^2
= 2 cm × 2 cm
= 4 cm^2

Find the area of each tile.

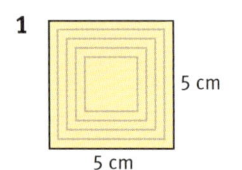

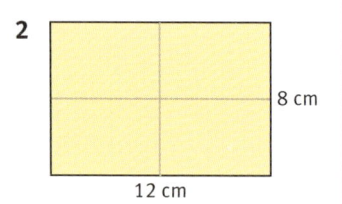

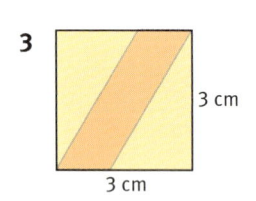

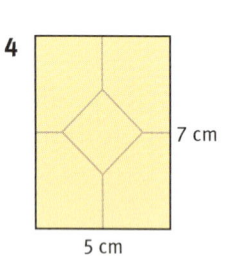

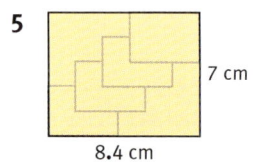

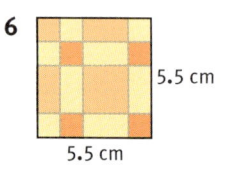

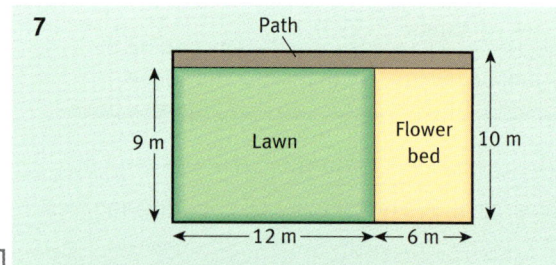

1 5 cm × 5 cm

2 12 cm × 8 cm

3 3 cm × 3 cm

4 7 cm, 5 cm

5 8.4 cm, 7 cm

6 5.5 cm × 5.5 cm

7

9 m, 12 m, 6 m, 10 m (Path, Lawn, Flower bed)

This is Jim's garden.
Find a the perimeter of the lawn
  b the area of the path
  c the area of the flower bed
  d the total area of the garden.

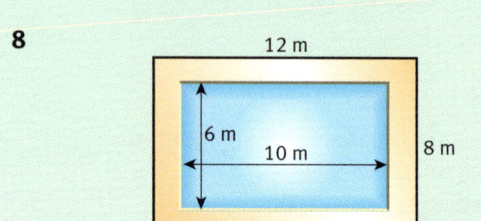

8

12 m, 6 m, 10 m, 8 m

This shows a swimming pool with a tiled area around the sides.
 a Find the area of the pool.
 b Find the total area of the pool and tiled area.
 c Use your answers to parts **a** and **b** to find the tiled area.

The diagram shows a tennis court marked for Doubles and Singles.

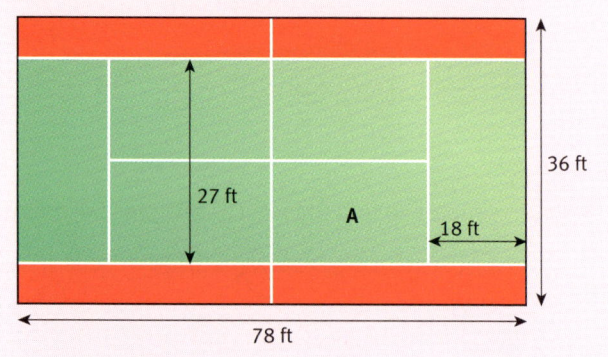

27 ft, 18 ft, 36 ft, 78 ft, A

9 Find, in square feet
 a the area of a Doubles court (the total area)
 b the area of a Singles court (shown green).

10 What additional area (shown red) is needed for a Singles court to become a Doubles court?

11 Find the area (marked **A**) into which a player must serve the ball.

N PERIMETER AND AREA
AREAS INVOLVING MIXED UNITS

Draw each rectangle and write both measurements in centimetres.

1 3 m, 50 cm
2 1.5 m, 20 cm
3 4 m, 1.4 m
4 250 cm, 0.8 m
5 60 cm, 2.5 m

Draw each rectangle and write both measurements in centimetres.

6 9 cm, 150 mm
7 20 mm, 1.2 cm
8 100 mm, 130 mm
9 120 mm, 250 mm

Example

This is one section of a Venetian blind.
Find its area in square centimetres (cm^2).

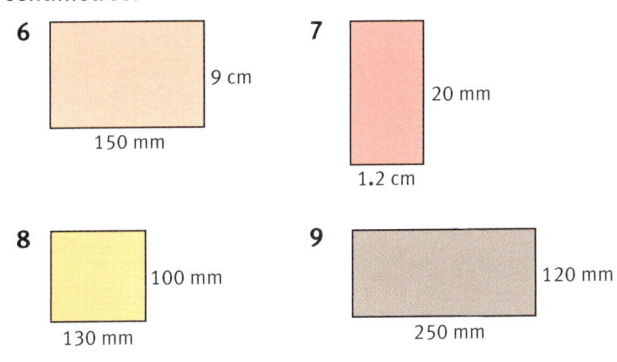

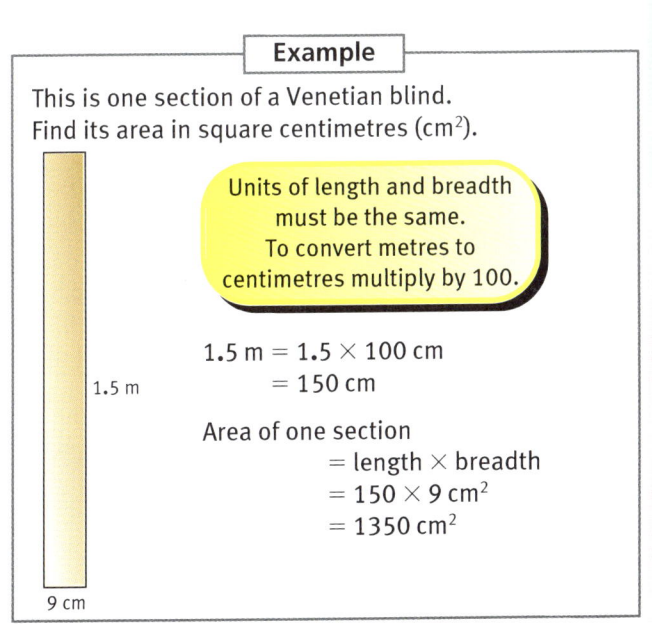

1.5 m, 9 cm

Units of length and breadth must be the same. To convert metres to centimetres multiply by 100.

$1.5\ m = 1.5 \times 100\ cm$
$\qquad = 150\ cm$

Area of one section
$\qquad = length \times breadth$
$\qquad = 150 \times 9\ cm^2$
$\qquad = 1350\ cm^2$

Find the area of each rectangle in square centimetres (cm^2).

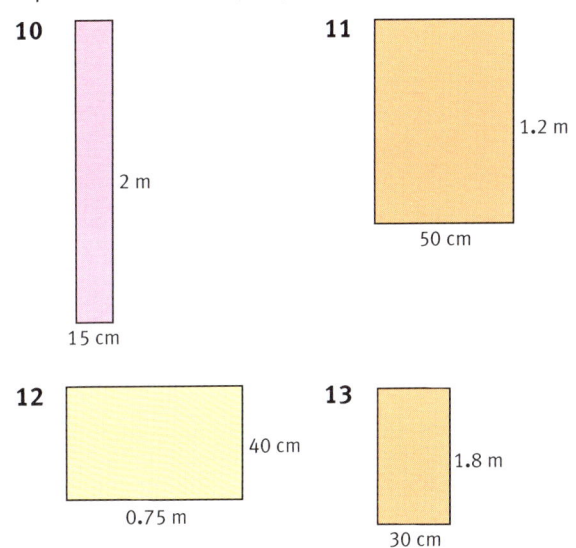

10 2 m, 15 cm
11 1.2 m, 50 cm
12 40 cm, 0.75 m
13 1.8 m, 30 cm

14 Find the area of each rectangle in square millimetres (mm^2).

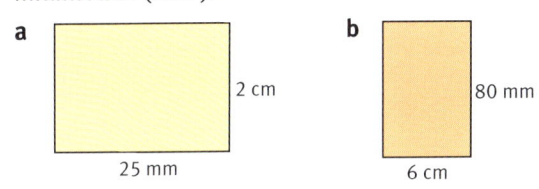

a 2 cm, 25 mm
b 80 mm, 6 cm

(Did you remember to convert cm to mm?)

15 A pavement is 340 metres long and 150 cm wide.
  a Write down 150 cm in metres.
  b Work out the area of the pavement in square metres (m^2).

16 My bedroom is a rectangle 3.5 m long and 250 cm wide.
Work out the floor area in square metres.

17 Len's drive is 35 m long and 3.2 m wide.
He lays blocks to cover it.
Each block is 20 cm by 10 cm.
All the blocks are laid longways across the drive starting with the first row at the front gate.
  a How many blocks are needed for one row?
  b How many rows are there altogether?
  c Work out the total number of blocks needed.

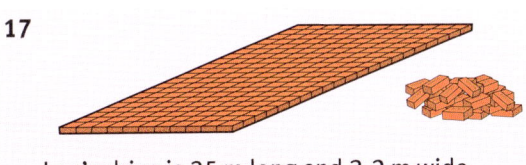

N PERIMETER AND AREA
AREAS OF COMPOUND SHAPES

Example

Find the area of this shop floor.

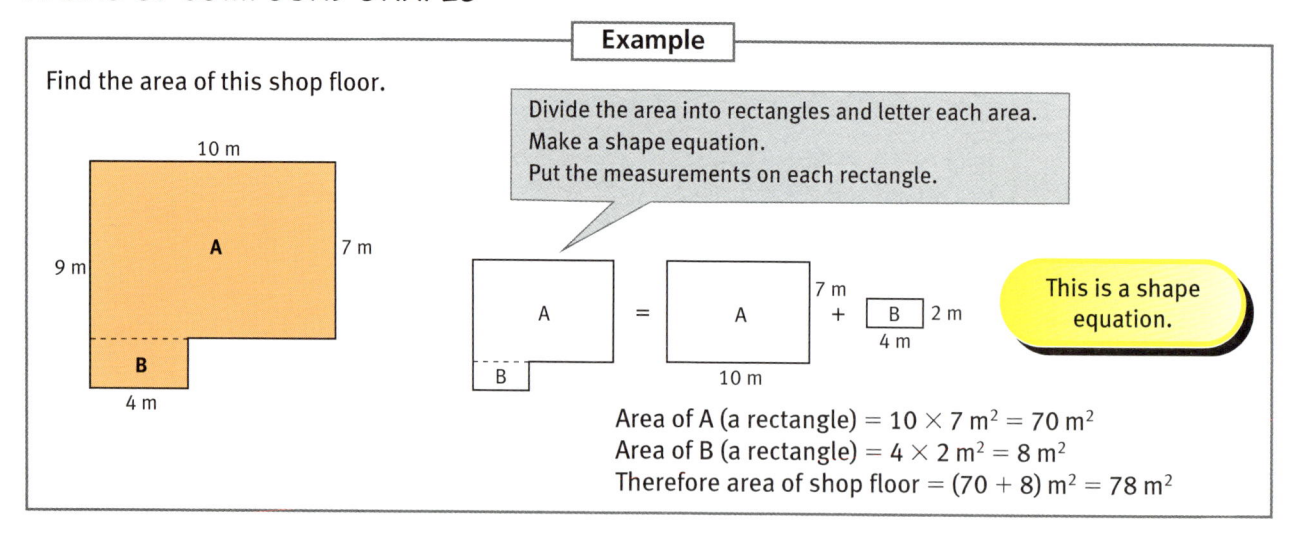

Divide the area into rectangles and letter each area.
Make a shape equation.
Put the measurements on each rectangle.

This is a shape equation.

Area of A (a rectangle) = 10×7 m² = 70 m²
Area of B (a rectangle) = 4×2 m² = 8 m²
Therefore area of shop floor = $(70 + 8)$ m² = 78 m²

In questions **1** to **4** various pieces of metal are shown.
All measurements are in centimetres.
For each shape
a draw a shape equation
b find the area of the shape.

1

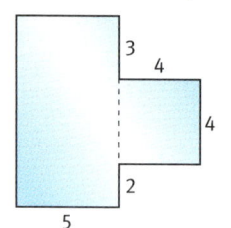

2

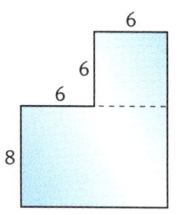

3

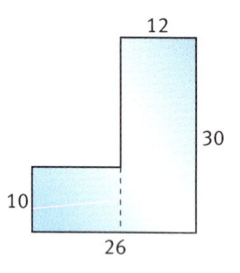

4

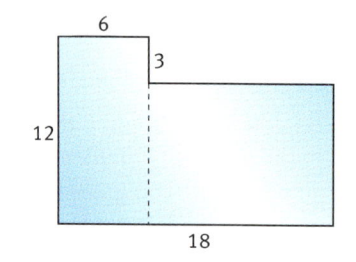

5

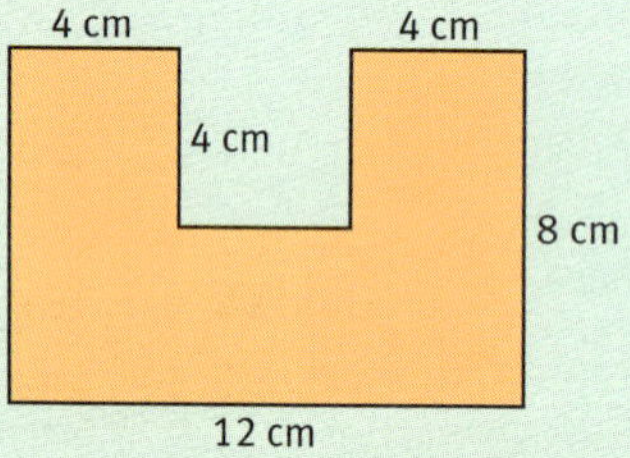

a Divide this shape into three rectangles.
Mark them A, B and C.
b Work out the area of this shape.

6 Find the floor area of this L-shaped room.

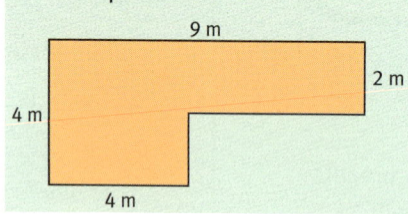

7

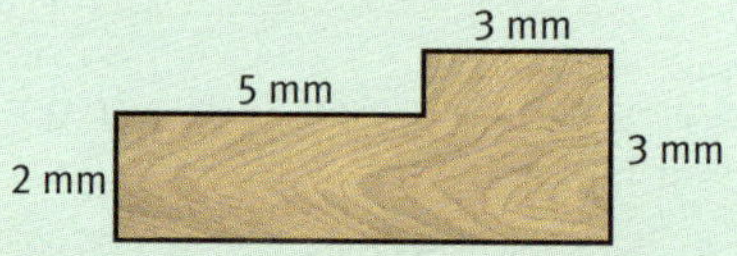

The diagram shows the end of a two-metre length of wooden moulding.
Find the area of the end in square millimetres.

8

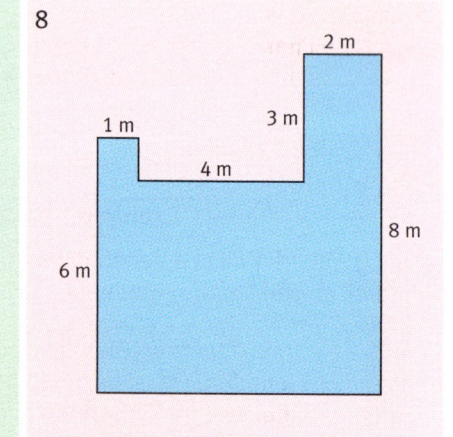

a Make a copy of this shape.
b Put all measurements on it.
c Work out the perimeter of the shape.
d Divide the shape into three rectangles. Work out its area in square metres.

N PERIMETER AND AREA

INVESTIGATION

Different shapes can be made with 1 cm squares.
For example these shapes can be made using four squares.

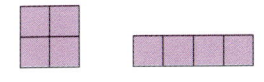

A shape that is a reflection or rotation of another shape is not a different shape. These two shapes are the same.

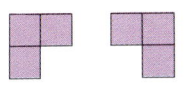

The squares must be arranged so that they touch along the whole of one side.
These shapes are not allowed.

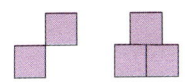

Investigate the relationship between the perimeters and the areas of the shapes you can make.

1 How many squares make a shape with an area of   **a** 20 sq cm   **b** 36 sq cm?

2 Start by looking at **different shapes with the same area** and investigate their perimeters.
   For example: How many different shapes can be made with an area of 4 sq cm?
              Which of these has the longest perimeter and which has the shortest?

3 You can answer this by using 4 squares to draw as many different shapes as you can.
   Then put your results in a table like this one.

Area = 4 sq cm				
Perimeter	10 cm			

4 Repeat questions **2** and **3** for shapes whose area is 5 sq cm,
   then 6 sq cm, 7 sq cm and 8 sq cm. What about 3 sq cm?

5 Look at all your results so far.
   Can you make a general observation about which arrangement gives the longest perimeter?
   Write a sentence similar to this one:

   The perimeter is always longest when the squares are arranged ....

   Can you do the same for the shortest perimeter?
   What do you notice about all your perimeters? What kind of numbers are they?

6 Now look at **different shapes with the same perimeter**.
   What is the smallest possible perimeter?
   How many shapes can you draw with this perimeter?
   What lengths are possible for the perimeter?
   Choose a length and draw as many shapes as you can with this perimeter.
   What are their areas? Repeat this for more perimeters.

   Put your results in a table like this one which is for shapes with a perimeter of 12 cm.

Perimeter = 12 cm 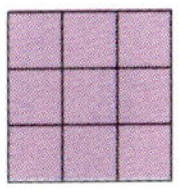 			
Area	9 sq cm	5 sq cm	

What is the smallest area with a perimeter of 12 cm?, 14 cm?, 16 cm?
Without drawing the shapes, can you say what the smallest area is to make a perimeter of 100 cm?
Give a reason for your answer.

O USING PERCENTAGES
PERCENTAGE OF A QUANTITY

> Remember that 'of' means '×'.

Example

Find 42% of £3.50

> Write 42% as a decimal then multiply.

42% of £3.50 = 0.42 × £3.50
            = £1.47

Find

1. 25% of £40
2. 10% of 20 p
3. 20% of £2.50
4. 50% of £96
5. 83% of £200
6. 15% of £40
7. 75% of £20
8. 60% of £210
9. 2% of £80
10. 5% of £250
11. 3% of £2500
12. 200% of £150
13. 400% of £82
14. 150% of £400
15. 4% of £82
16. 8% of £550

Example

Find $12\frac{1}{2}$% of 200 m.

$12\frac{1}{2}$% = 10% + half of 5%

10% is 20 m
5% (= $\frac{1}{2}$ of 10%) is 10 m
$2\frac{1}{2}$% (= $\frac{1}{2}$ of 5%) is 5 m
$12\frac{1}{2}$% of 200 m = 20 m + 5 m = 25 m

Find

17. $2\frac{1}{2}$% of 80 m
18. $7\frac{1}{2}$% of 260 litres
19. $12\frac{1}{2}$% of 80 tonnes
20. $22\frac{1}{2}$% of £1200
21. $17\frac{1}{2}$% of £120
22. $117\frac{1}{2}$% of £200
23. A builder quotes £2000, excluding VAT, for a job. He must add $17\frac{1}{2}$% of this quote to the bill for value added tax (VAT). Find $17\frac{1}{2}$% of £2000.

Example

Find, to the nearest £1, 5.8% of £2700.

5.8% = 0.058

5.8% of £2700 = 0.058 × £2700
              = £156.6 = £157 (nearest £1)

24. Find 2.4% of £500.
25. Find, to the nearest gram, 36.7% of 554 g.
26. Find, to the nearest metre, 16.7% of 81 m.
27. Find, to the nearest £1, 17.5% of £876.
28. In 1995, the population of the United Kingdom was 58 606 000.

   Give answers to the nearest 1000 people.

   a. 21% of the population was under 16. How many were under 16?
   b. 9% of the population lived in Scotland. How many lived in Scotland?
   c. 43% of the population were in work. How many were in work?
   d. The population of the UK in 2020 is expected to be 103% of the 1995 population. What is the expected population in 2020?

29. Viv pays income tax. This is 10% of the first £2000 of his taxable income. He then pays 22% on £15 000 which is the remainder of his taxable income.
    How much tax does Viv pay?

30. The annual rate of inflation in May was 3.1%. Peter's hourly pay was £4.
    His pay is increased by the rate of inflation.
    What is the increase?
    Give your answer correct to the nearest penny.

O USING PERCENTAGES
PERCENTAGE INCREASE

> An increase is calculated on the quantity **before** any change.

Example

£50 is increased by 15%.
Find the increase.

Increase = 15% × £50
= 0.15 × £50
= £7.50

Find the increase when

1 £8 is increased by 10%

2 £20 is increased by 40%

3 70 grams is increased by 15%

4 800 metres is increased by 12%

5 £56 is increased by 30%.

6 A jar of coffee costs £2.50.
   Next month the price will increase by 10%.
   How much will the price increase by?

7 Rolls are sold in packs of 4.
   For a promotion, this number is increased by 50%.
   How many extra rolls are in the promotion pack?

8 12 000 people lived in Hampton in 1999. This number is expected to grow by 20% in ten years. How many more people is this?

Example

Find the new quantity when £8.50 is increased by 30%.

First find the increase.

Increase = 30% of £8.50
= 0.3 × £8.50
= £2.55

Now add on the increase.

New quantity = £8.50 + £2.55 = £11.05

Find the new quantity when

9 £80 is increased by 40%

10 £2.50 is increased by 10%.

Find the new quantity when

11 900 litres is increased by 5%

12 600 seats are increased by 12%

13 £2.80 is increased by 25%.

Example

Jane's bus fare to work is 80 p.
Fares will rise by 10% next month.
What will Jane's fare be after the rise?

First find the increase.

Increase = 10% of 80 p
= 0.1 × 80 p = 8 p
New fare = 80 p + 8 p
= 88 p   *Old fare + increase*

14 Peter is paid £4.00 an hour.
   He is given a 10% pay rise.
   Find Peter's new hourly pay.

15 Jo bought apples for 20 p a kilogram.
   She sold the apples at a profit of 30%.
   How much did she charge for a kilogram?

16 A vintage car cost £5000.
   Its value has increased by 12%.
   What would the car cost now?

17 In the last two years, the number of rabbits on Hadley Common has grown from 600 by 12.5%. How many rabbits are there now?

18 A jar of coffee powder has been repackaged.
   The old jar contained 125 grams of instant coffee.
   The new jar contains 5% more coffee.

   a What is the weight of coffee powder in the new jar to the nearest gram?

   The old jar cost £2.64.
   The cost of the new jar is 6.5% more than the cost of the old jar.

   b How much does the new jar cost, to the nearest penny?

O USING PERCENTAGES
PERCENTAGE DECREASE

> A decrease is calculated on the quantity **before** any change.

Example
£80 is reduced by 30%.
Find the decrease.

Reduction = 30% of £80
         = 0.3 × £80
         = £24

Example
Find the new quantity when 500 grams is reduced by 15%.

First find the reduction.

Reduction = 15% of 500 g
         = 0.15 × 500 g
         = 75 g

Now take off the reduction.

New quantity = 500 g − 75 g
            = 425 g

Find the decrease when

1. £50 is reduced by 10%
2. £10 is reduced by 50%
3. 200 kg is reduced by 5%
4. £450 is reduced by 12%
5. 60 p is reduced by 20%.
6. The price of a shirt is £15.60. It is reduced by 10% in a sale. How much is taken off the price?
7. For a promotion a shop reduces the price of a 60 p loaf of bread by 25%. What is the reduction in price?
8. The number of seats in a cinema has been reduced by 15%. There used to be 460 seats. How many seats have gone?
9. A telegraph pole is 12 m tall. Its height is reduced by 10%. How much is taken off the height? 
10. A raw beef burger weighs 250 g. It loses 20% of this weight when it is cooked. How many grams is this?

Find the new quantity when

11. £80 is reduced by 20%
12. £160 is reduced by 10%
13. 80 grams is reduced by 5%
14. 30 m is reduced by 25%
15. £800 is reduced by 12%.

16. The price of a pair of shoes is reduced from £44 by 25%. What is the reduced price?

17. **30% OFF ALL MARKED PRICES**
    Find the cost of a tie marked £7.50.

18. Joe weighs 110 kg and is overweight. His doctor tells him to lose 10% of his weight. What weight does Joe need to get down to?

19. What is the bargain price of a desk marked £57?
    SPRING BARGAINS
    20% OFF MARKED PRICE
    if purchased by 31 March

20. In 1991, 4568 people were killed on the roads in Great Britain. By 1996, this number had been reduced by 20%. How many people were killed on the roads in 1996? Give your answer to the nearest person.

21. In 1994, the UK emitted 132 million tonnes of carbon dioxide. In 1995 this had reduced by 2.8%. How many tonnes were emitted in 1995? Give your answer to the nearest million tonnes.

O USING PERCENTAGES
ONE QUANTITY AS A PERCENTAGE OF ANOTHER

Example

Find 10 p as a percentage of 400 p.

$$\frac{10}{400} \times 100\% = \frac{10}{4}\% = 2\frac{1}{2}\%$$

$10 \text{ p} = 2\frac{1}{2}\%$ of 400 p.

Put 10 p over 400 p, then multiply by 100.

Example

My bus fare has increased from 40 p to 50 p.
Find the percentage increase.

The increase is 10 p. *First find the increase.*

Remember, a change is always found as a percentage of the original quantity, so find 10 p as a percentage of 40 p.

The percentage increase
= 10 p as a percentage of 40 p
= $\frac{10}{40} = \frac{1}{4} = 25\%$

1 Find 50 p as a percentage of 200 p.

2 Find 10 p as a percentage of 40 p.

3 Find £25 as a percentage of £250.

4 Find 15 cm as a percentage of 150 cm.

5 Find 36 g as a percentage of 180 g.

6 Find 10 g as a percentage of 1000 g.

7 Find 5 ml as a percentage of 250 ml.

8 Find 2 apples as a percentage of 25 apples.

9 Find £1.50 as a percentage of £2.50.

10 Find £1.50 as a percentage of £4.

11 Find £3 as a percentage of £2.

12 Find £10 as a percentage of £4.

13 Find 60 p as a percentage of £3.
(Did you remember to change £3 to 300 p?)

14 Find 200 g as a percentage of 1 kg.
(Did you remember to change 1 kg to 1000 g?)

15

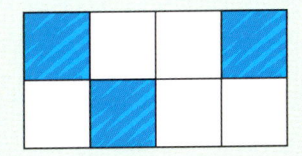

What percentage of this shape is blue?

16

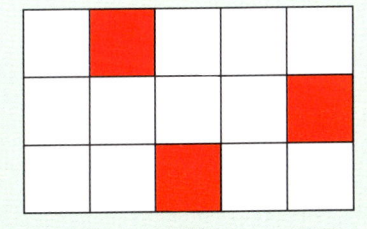

What percentage of this shape is red?

17 Raj is paid £5 an hour.
He gets a pay rise of £2.
Find his percentage rise.

18 The price of a battery goes up from £1.50 to £1.80.
Find the percentage increase.

19 The price of a computer has fallen from £800 to £600.
Find the percentage decrease.

20 The number of flights from London to Nice falls from 8 a day in high season to 3 a day in low season.
Find the percentage decrease.

21 Bottles are filled from a 10 kg sack of salt.
250 g of salt is wasted by spilling.
What percentage is wasted?

22 The number of people living in London is about 8 000 000.
This number is expected to grow by 160 000 in ten year's time.
What percentage growth is this?

23 The cost of a one-day travel card on London tubes and buses is £4.10.
It is expected to rise to £4.30 at the next fare increase.
What percentage increase is this?
Give your answer correct to 1 decimal place.

O USING PERCENTAGES
MIXED PERCENTAGE QUESTIONS

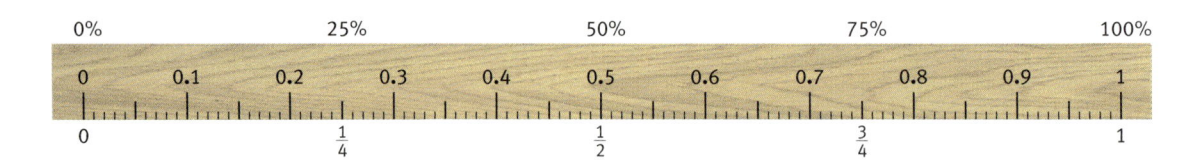

1 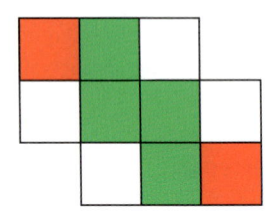 There are 10 squares in this shape.
   a How many squares are red?
   b What percentage of the shape is red?
   c What percentage of the shape is green?
   d 30% of this shape must be coloured blue. How many squares must be coloured blue?

2 Andy got 45 out of 75 in a test.
Find his percentage mark.

3 Look at these numbers.
   0.2,   15%, $\frac{3}{5}$,   150%, $1\frac{1}{2}$,   1.6
   a Which are the same size?
   b Which is the largest?
   c Which is the smallest?

4 SALE — 25% off marked prices
   a What sum is taken off a tie marked £12.00?
   b Find the sale price of a pair of shoes marked £48.40.

5 This question was given to 200 people.
   Should all nuclear power stations be closed?
   Yes ☐   No ☐   Don't know ☐
   47% of replies ticked 'Yes'.
   a What percentage did **not** tick yes?
   $\frac{1}{8}$ of the people ticked 'Don't know'
   b What percentage ticked 'don't know'?
   15% of the 200 people refused to answer.
   c How many refused to answer?

6 Amy buys a new car on credit.
She has to make a down payment of 5% of the price.
The car costs £9500.
What is the value of the down payment?

7 Jason is paid £180 a week.
He gets a pay rise of 2.5%.
What is Jason's pay after the rise?

8 When Una was born, she was given £100 in a savings account.
When Una was 18, the sum had grown to £287.
What was the percentage increase?

9 The *Local Times* sells in three areas. The chart shows the proportions of its sales in these areas. 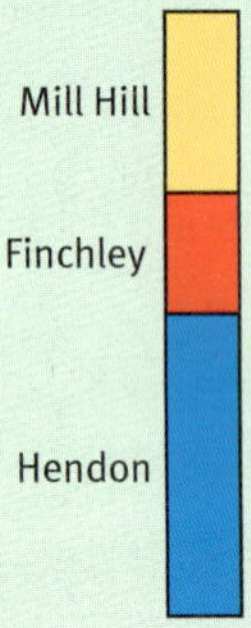
   a Use a ruler to find the fraction of sales in Hendon.
   b What percentage of the sales were in Finchley?

10 Peter invested £500 in a savings account.
The interest paid was 5% per annum.
   a How much interest did Peter get after 1 year?
   b Peter added this interest to the money in his account.
   How much interest did Peter get at the end of the second year?

11 In July, the annual rate of inflation was 2.4%.
Ann's hourly pay is increased in line with inflation each year in July.
Her pay was £6.50 an hour.
What is it after the increase?
Give your answer to the nearest penny.

12 A washing machine costs £450 plus VAT.
VAT is charged at 17.5%.
What is the price of the machine including VAT?

P ALGEBRA
FUNCTION MACHINES AND FORMULAS IN WORDS

1. This function machine can be used to find the cost of hiring a car.

   Number of days → Multiply by 25 → Add 30 → Cost in £

   Find the cost of hiring a car for 5 days.

2. Number of miles → Divide by 5 → Multiply by 8 → Number of kilometres

   Use this function machine to find the number of kilometres equal to
   a 50 miles   b 120 miles   c 64 miles.

3. These are the instructions for roasting a turkey.

   > Roast at 180° for 40 minutes per kilogram plus 20 minutes.

   How long does it take to roast a turkey weighing a 6 kg b 7.5 kg?
   c Copy and complete this function machine.
   Number of kilograms → ☐ → ☐ → Roasting time

4. You can use this rule to find, roughly, the temperature in degrees Celsius from the temperature in degrees Fahrenheit.

   > Subtract 30 from the Fahrenheit temperature and then halve the answer.

   a Use this rule to find, roughly, the temperature in degrees Celsius of i 52 °F ii 120 °F.
   b Make a function machine for these instructions. Start with the number of degrees Fahrenheit.

5. The cost of a holiday in £, can be worked out from this formula:

   Cost in £ = 150 + number of nights × 20

   a Use the formula to find the cost of a holiday lasting 14 nights.
   b Draw a function machine for this formula.

6. This rule converts kilometres to miles.

   Number of miles = (number of kilometres ÷ 8) × 5

   a Use this rule to convert 240 kilometres to miles.
   b Draw a function machine for this rule.
   c Now look at the function machine for question 2. What is the connection between these two machines?

7. This function machine changes kilograms to pounds.

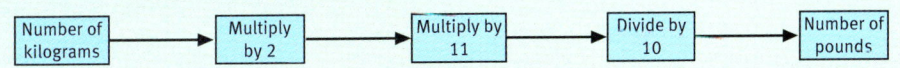

   Number of kilograms → Multiply by 2 → Multiply by 11 → Divide by 10 → Number of pounds

   a Use this function machine to change 2.5 kilograms to pounds.
   b Draw a function machine to show how to change pounds to kilograms.

8. This function machine gives a quick, but very rough, conversion from Euros(€) to £.

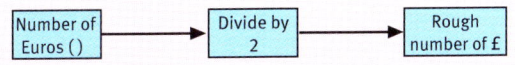

   Number of Euros (€) → Divide by 2 → Rough number of £

   a How many £, very roughly, is 34 €?
   b Use the function machine backwards to give, very roughly, the number of Euros equivalent to £5.

P ALGEBRA
ADDING AND SUBTRACTING LETTER TERMS

$x + x = 2x$

Simplify

1. $a + a$
2. $x + x + x$
3. $b + b + b$
4. $y + y + y$
5. $x + x + x + x + x$

Write out in full

6. $3x$
7. $2b$
8. $4y$
9. $6y$

$2 \times x = x \times 2 = 2x$

Simplify

10. $4 \times a$
11. $2 \times y$
12. $3 \times x$
13. $t \times 5$
14. $x \times 7$
15. $s \times 10$

$2x + 3x = 5x$

Simplify

16. $3y + 4y$
17. $2x + 5x$
18. $7x + 2x$
19. $2a + a$
20. $t + 4t$
21. $s + 6s$
22. $x + 3x + x$
23. $5a + a + 4a + a$

$4x - 2x = 2x$

Simplify

24. $5x - 2x$
25. $6a - 3a$
26. $5y - y$
27. $3l - 2l$
28. $4z - 3z$
29. $8p - p$
30. $3p + p$
31. $8y - 2y$
32. $6x - 5x$
33. $6x + 5x$
34. $7s - s$
35. $3a + 7a$

$3x + 5$ cannot be simplified.

Example

Simplify $2x + 3 - x + 1$

Put the x terms together and the number terms together.

$2x + 3 - x + 1 = 2x - x + 3 + 1$
$= x + 4$

Simplify

36. $4x + x - 2$
37. $y + 4 + 2y$
38. $2a - 3 + 4a$
39. $4 - 3b + 5b$
40. $6 - 2p + 8p$
41. $2a + 3 - a + 1$
42. $5p + 2 - 1 + 3p$
43. $8 + 9a - 7a + 7$
44. $7x - 5 + 10 - x$

Example

Simplify $2x + 3y - x + 2y$

Put the x terms together and the y terms together.

$2x + 3y - x + 2y$
$= 2x - x + 3y + 2y$
$= x + 5y$

Simplify

45. $3t + 6t - 4s$
46. $2p + 6q - p$
47. $2a + b + a$
48. $x + 2y + 4x - y$
49. $5a + 7d - 3d + 8a$

50.

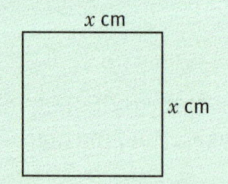

   (square with sides x cm)

   Write down an expression for the perimeter of this square. Remember to simplify your answer.

51.

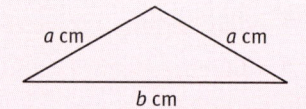

   (triangle with two sides a cm and base b cm)

   a. Write down an expression for the perimeter of this triangle. Remember to simplify your answer.

   b. What is the name of this type of triangle?

52. One pencil costs d p.
    One ruler costs f p.

    a. Write down an expression for the cost of 1 pencil and 1 ruler.

    b. Write down an expression for the cost of 4 pencils and 6 rulers.

P ALGEBRA
MULTIPLYING LETTER TERMS

$x \times x = x^2$

Simplify

1. $y \times y$
2. $a \times a$
3. $l \times l$
4. $p \times p$

$x \times x \times x = x^3$

Simplify

5. $a \times a \times a$
6. $k \times k \times k$
7. $t \times t \times t$
8. $b \times b \times b$

$x \times y = xy$

Simplify

9. $x \times z$
10. $a \times b$
11. $p \times q$
12. $s \times M$
13. $a \times f$
14. $A \times B$
15. $P \times r$

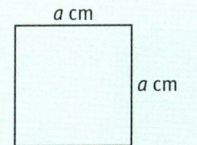

16. A square with sides a cm.

   a Write down an expression for the perimeter of this square. Simplify your answer.

   b Write down an expression for the area of this square. Simplify your answer.

Example

Simplify $4p \times p$

$4p \times p = 4 \times p \times p$
$= 4 \times p^2$
$= 4p^2$

Simplify

17. $3x \times x$
18. $2a \times a$
19. $y \times 4y$
20. $3s \times s$
21. $4x \times y$

Example

Simplify $2x \times x \times y$

$2x \times x \times y = 2 \times x \times x \times y$
$= 2 \times x^2 \times y$
$= 2x^2y$

Simplify

22. $3a \times a \times b$
23. $2a \times b$
24. $6 \times p \times q \times q$
25. $x \times 4y$
26. $10 \times a \times b \times a$

Example

Simplify $2x \times 3y$

$2x \times 3y = 2 \times x \times 3 \times y$
$= 2 \times 3 \times x \times y$
$= 6 \times x \times y$
$= 6xy$

Simplify

27. $3x \times 2$
28. $a \times 4a$
29. $3 \times 2x$
30. $5 \times 3y$
31. $2a \times 4a$
32. $3t \times 5t$
33. $4x \times 2x$
34. $5y \times 4y$

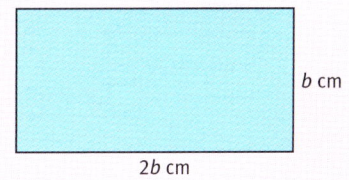

35. A rectangle with height b cm and width $2b$ cm.

   a Write down an expression for the perimeter of this rectangle.

   b Write down an expression for the area of this rectangle.

36. One packet of crisps costs x pence. One can of drink costs y pence.

   a Write down an expression for the cost of 5 packets of crisps. Simplify your answer.

   b Write down an expression for the cost of 5 packets of crisps and 4 cans of drink.

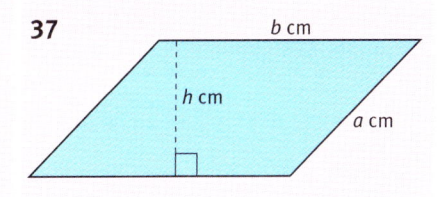

37. A parallelogram with base b cm, slant side a cm, and height h cm.

   a Write down the mathematical name of this shape.

   b Write down an expression for the perimeter of this shape.

   c Copy this sentence and fill in the missing letter.

   The height of the shape is ..... cm.

   d Write down an expression for the area of this shape.

38. A coach costs £P to hire for a day.
   A ticket for the theatre costs £t per person.
   Write down an expression for the total cost of taking 20 people to the theatre by coach.

P ALGEBRA
USING NEGATIVE NUMBERS

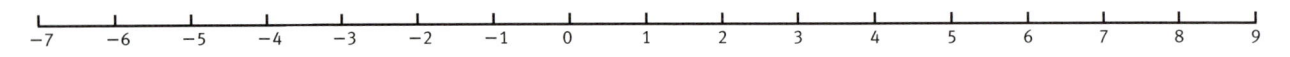

> **Example**
>
> Simplify $3 - 5$
>
> $3 - 5 = -2$ 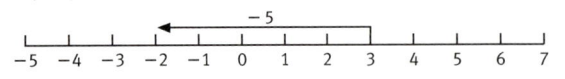

Simplify

1 a $5 - 6$ **b** $3 - 7$
2 a $-1 - 3$ **b** $-2 - 4$
3 a $-3 + 4$ **b** $-1 + 2$
4 a $-1 + 1$ **b** $2 - 2$
5 a $3x - 5x$ **b** $2y - 6y$
6 a $-2x - 4x$ **b** $-3a + 3a$
7 a $2 - 6 - 1$ **b** $5 - 10 + 2$
8 a $2x - 7x + x$ **b** $6b - 10b - 2b$

> **Example**
>
> Simplify $5x - 2y + 8y - 8x$
>
> Group like terms together.
>
> $5x - 2y + 8y - 8x = 5x - 8x - 2y + 8y$
> $= -3x + 6y$

Simplify

9 a $4 + x - 9$ **b** $2y - 8 + 4y$
10 a $2 + 3y - 9$ **b** $5 + 2x - 10$
11 a $3a + 7 - 4 - 6a$ **b** $3x + 7y - 4y - 6x$
12 a $2a + b + 7a - 8b$ **b** $5s - 7t - 2t - s$
13 b $5p - 3q + 7q - 6p$ **b** $12a + 6b - 20a - 8b$

> **Example**
>
> Expand $2(5 - 3x)$
>
> $2(5 - 3x) = 2 \times 5 - 2 \times 3x$
> $= 10 - 6x$

Expand

14 a $3(x + 2)$ **b** $4(2x + 1)$
15 a $5(7y - 4)$ **b** $3(5 - 6x)$
16 a $4(6a - 1)$ **b** $5(2 - x)$

17 a $x(x + 3)$ **b** $a(a - 4)$
(Did you remember that $x \times x = x^2$?)
18 a $a(a + 3)$ **b** $x(2x + 3)$
19 a $t(t - 7)$ **b** $2s(s + 6)$
20 a $2a(a - 3)$ **b** $4b(b + 8)$

> **Example**
>
> Simplify $2(x + 4) + 5(x - 2)$
>
> Expand the brackets.
>
> $2(x + 4) + 5(x - 2) = 2x + 8 + 5x - 10$
> $= 2x + 5x + 8 - 10$
> $= 7x - 2$

Simplify

21 a $2(x - 2) + 5$ **b** $5(2a + 3) - 8$
22 a $a + 2(a + 4)$ **b** $2x + 3(x - 2)$
23 a $2(a + 3) + 3(a + 2)$ **b** $4(x + 1) + 3(x - 1)$
24 a $4(s - 1) + 2(s + 4)$ **b** $6(x + 3) + 2(3 - x)$

25

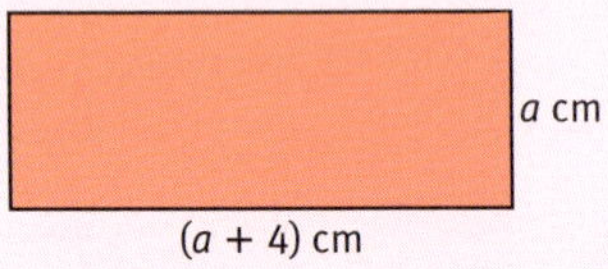

Rectangle with sides a cm and $(a + 4)$ cm.

a Find an expression for the perimeter of this shape.
b Find an expression for the area of the shape. Remember to simplify your answers.
c Write down the name of the shape.

26

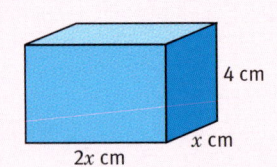

Box with dimensions $2x$ cm, x cm, and 4 cm.

a Find an expression for the area of the base of this box.
b Draw a net for this box.
Use your net to find an expression for the surface area of the box.

P ALGEBRA
MAKING AND USING A FORMULA

1. One nectarine costs 45 pence.
   Graham buys n nectarines.

   a. Write down an expression for the cost of n nectarines.

   The total cost is C pence.

   b. Write down a formula connecting C and n.

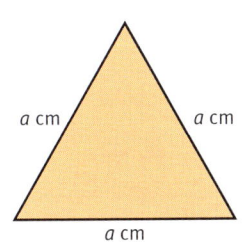

2.

   a. Write down an expression for the perimeter of this triangle. Simplify your answer.

   b. The perimeter of this triangle is P cm. Write down a formula for P in terms of a.

   c. Find P when $a = 1.5$.

   d. What is the special name of this triangle?

3. Input → Multiply by 2 → Add 3 → Output

   a. The input number is 3. What is the output number?

   b. The input number is x. Write down an expression for the output number.

   c. The output number is y. Write down a formula connecting y and x.

4.

   a. Write down the mathematical name of this shape.

   b. Find an expression for the perimeter of this shape.

   c. The perimeter of this shape is P cm. Write down a formula for P in terms of x and y.

   d. Find P when $x = 2.5$ and $y = 1.9$.

5. The area of a circle is given by the formula

   $$A = \pi r^2$$

   where A is the area and r is the radius of the circle.
   Use the formula to find the area of a circle whose radius is 14 cm. Use $\pi = \frac{22}{7}$.

6. Kylie uses this formula to work out the time, t minutes, it will take her to travel D miles in London.

   $$t = 6D$$

   How long will a journey of $4\frac{1}{2}$ miles take?

7. Look at this sequence:

   1, 5, 9, 13, ...

   a. Write down the 10th term of this sequence.

   b. Write down an expression for the nth term of this sequence in terms of n.

   c. The nth term of the sequence is N. Find a formula for N in terms of n.

   d. Find N when $n = 75$.

8. Jim uses this formula to work out his weekly pay.

   $$W = \frac{450n + 600m}{100}$$

   where W is his pay in £,
   n is the number of hours worked on weekdays,
   m is the number of hours worked over the weekend.

   Jim works 30 hours on weekdays and 10 hours over the weekend. What is Jim's weekly pay?

9. This formula converts a temperature in degrees Celsius, C, to degrees Fahrenheit, F.

   $$F = \frac{9}{5}C + 32.$$

   Find 35 °C in degrees Fahrenheit.

P ALGEBRA
SUBSTITUTING POSITIVE AND NEGATIVE NUMBERS

> Multiplying by a negative number changes the sign.
> e.g. $2 \times (-3) = -6$

Example

Find the value of $4x$ when $x = -3$.

> $4x$ means $4 \times x$. Substitute -3 for x.

$4x = 4 \times (-3)$
$ = -12$

1. Find $3y$ when   **a** $y = 3$ **b** $y = -4$.
2. Find $2p$ when   **a** $p = 6$ **b** $p = -2$.
3. Find $5a$ when   **a** $a = 3$ **b** $a = -3$.
4. Find $8b$ when   **a** $b = 1.5$ **b** $b = -\frac{1}{2}$.

Example

Find the value of $2x - y$ when $x = -5$ and $y = 3$.

$2 \times (-5) - 3 = -10 - 3$
$ = -13$

5. Find the value of $3x + y$ when $x = -3$ and $y = 1$.
6. Find the value of $2a - b$ when $a = 7$ and $b = 4$.
7. Find the value of $5m + n$ when $m = -2$ and $n = 1$.
8. Find the value of $7x - y$ when $x = -7$ and $y = 3$.
9. Find the value of $2p - q$ when $p = -4$ and $q = 4$.
10. Find the value of $4a - b$ when $a = -1$ and $b = 6$.

> Multiplying by a negative number changes the sign.
> e.g. $(-2) \times (-3) = +6 = 6$

Example

Find the value of $x^2 - 2x$ when $x = -2$.

$x^2 - 2x = (-2) \times (-2) - 2 \times (-2)$
$ = 4 + 4$
$ = 8$

11. Find the value of $-3a$ when $a = -3$.
12. Find the value of a^2 when $a = -2$.
13. Find the value of $-2b$ when $b = -4$.
14. Find the value of s^2 when $s = -5$.

15. Find the value of $x^2 + 3x$ when $x = -2$.
16. Find the value of $b^2 - 4b$ when $b = -5$.
17. Find the value of $n^2 + 6n$ when $n = -3$.
18. Find the value of $y^2 + 2y$ when $y = -2$.
19. Copy and complete this table.

x	-2	-1	0	1	2
$3x - 4$					

20. Copy and complete this table.

x	-3	-2	-1	0	0.5	1	2
x^2							

21. $y = 3 - 4x$

Copy and complete this table for values of y.

x	-2	-1	0	1	2	3	4
$y = 3 - 4x$							

22. Given $s = 5t - 10$
    a find s when $t = 4$
    b find s when $t = 3$.

Example

Simplify $2(3 - x) - 4(2 - 3x)$

> Expand the brackets.

$2(3 - x) - 4(2 - 3x)$
$= 2 \times 3 + 2 \times (-x) - 4 \times 2 - 4 \times (-3x)$
$= 6 - 2x - 8 + 12x$
$= -2 + 10x$

23. Simplify $2(x - 4) - 2(2x - 5)$.
24. Simplify $3(a + 5) - 4(2a - 3)$.
25. Simplify $5(2 - x) - 3(2 - 3x)$.
26. Simplify $8(2 - y) - 8(1 - 2y)$.
27. The formula for changing a temperature in degrees Celsius, C, to degrees Fahrenheit, F, is

$$F = \frac{9C + 160}{5}$$

Find $-10\,°C$ in degrees Fahrenheit.

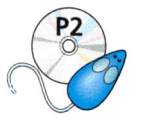

P ALGEBRA
SOLVING EQUATIONS

Example

Solve the equation $x + 2 = 5$

$x + 2 = 5$
$x + 2 - 2 = 5 - 2$ ← Take 2 from both sides.
$x = 3$

Solve the equations.

1 a $x + 3 = 7$ **b** $x + 1 = 9$

2 a $x + 3 = 5$ **b** $x + 7 = 10$

3 a $x + 2 = 6$ **b** $x + 4 = 9$

Example

Solve the equation $6 = x + 4$

$6 = x + 4$
$6 - 4 = x + 4 - 4$ ← Take 4 from both sides.
$2 = x$
$x = 2$

Solve the equations.

4 a $25 = x + 12$ **b** $7 = x + 6$

5 a $4 = x + 2$ **b** $12 = 8 + x$

6 a $17 = 14 + x$ **b** $25 = x + 10$

Example

Solve the equation $x - 5 = 4$

$x - 5 = 4$
$x - 5 + 5 = 4 + 5$ ← Add 5 to both sides.
$x = 9$

Solve the equations.

7 a $x - 3 = 6$ **b** $x - 2 = 7$

8 a $x - 1 = 4$ **b** $x - 6 = 2$

9 a $x - 4 = 1$ **b** $x - 8 = 5$

10 a $1 = x - 8$ **b** $17 = x - 24$

Example

Solve the equation $3 = 4 - x$

$3 = 4 - x$
$3 + x = 4 - x + x$ ← Add x to both sides.
$3 + x = 4$
$3 + x - 3 = 4 - 3$ ← Take 3 from both sides.
$x = 1$

Solve the equations.

11 a $5 = 9 - x$ **b** $2 = 11 - x$

12 a $12 - x = 10$ **b** $6 - x = 1$

Example

Solve the equation $2x = 4$

$2x = 4$
$2x \div 2 = 4 \div 2$ ← Divide both sides by 2.
$x = 2$

Solve the equations.

13 a $2x = 6$ **b** $3x = 9$

14 a $2x = 14$ **b** $4x = 12$

15 a $15 = 5x$ **b** $18 = 3x$

Example

Solve the equation $2x + 1 = 3$

$2x + 1 = 3$
$2x + 1 - 1 = 3 - 1$ ← Take 1 from both sides.
$2x = 2$
$2x \div 2 = 2 \div 2$ ← Divide both sides by 2.
$x = 1$

Solve the equations.

16 a $2x + 3 = 5$ **b** $3x + 2 = 8$

17 a $5x - 1 = 14$ **b** $6x - 5 = 19$

18 a $7x + 3 = 17$ **b** $5x + 3 = 18$

19 a $4x + 3 = 19$ **b** $2x - 9 = 37$

20 Given that $y = 4x - 7$
  a find y when $x = 4$
  b find x when $y = 9$.

21 Given that $x - y = 8$
  a find x when $y = 3$
  b find y when $x = 12$.

22 The cost, £C, of hiring a van for n days can be worked out from this formula.

$$C = 100 + 12n$$

It cost Anne £160 to hire this van.

How many days hire did Anne pay for?

P ALGEBRA
GRAPHS OF STRAIGHT LINES

1 a Copy and complete the table for $y = 2x - 1$.

x	-1	0	1	2
$y = 2x - 1$				

b Plot these points on a copy of the grid.

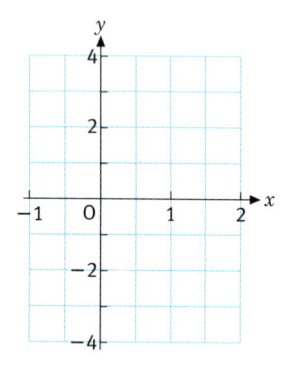

c Join these points to draw the graph of $y = 2x - 1$.
d Find the value of x when $y = 2$.
e Find the value of y when $x = 0.5$.

2 a Copy and complete the table for $y = 4 - x$.

x	0	1	2	3	4
y	4				

b Plot these points on a copy of the grid.

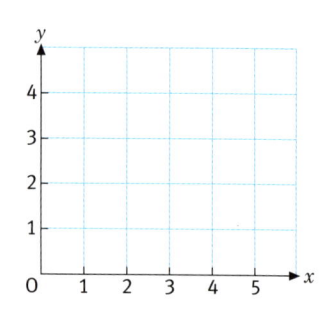

c Join these points to draw the graph of $y = 4 - x$.
d Copy and complete this table for $y = x$.

x	0	2	4
y		2	

e Plot these points on your grid and draw a line through them.
f Write down the coordinates of the point where the two lines cross.

3 a Plot the points (2, 0) and (6, 4) on a copy of the grid. Join these points with a straight line.

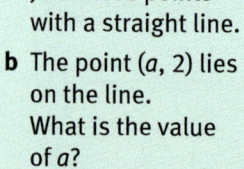

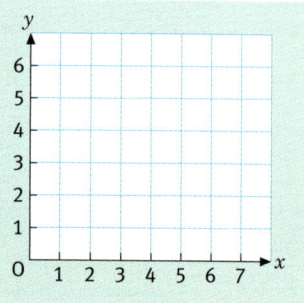

b The point $(a, 2)$ lies on the line. What is the value of a?

c The line is extended. Copy and complete the following mapping for points on the line.

$2 \rightarrow 0$
$6 \rightarrow 4$
$8 \rightarrow$
$x \rightarrow$

4 Use the graph you drew for question **3** for this question.

a On the same axes draw the graph of $y = 5 - x$.
b Write down the coordinates of the point where the two lines cross.
c Write down the solution of the equation $x - 2 = 5 - x$.

5 a Copy and complete the table for $y = 3x + 2$.

x	-2	-1	0	1	2	3
y	-4				8	

b Draw a graph of $y = 3x + 2$ on graph paper. Use a scale of 1 cm for 1 unit on both axes and scale the x-axis from -3 to 4 and the y-axis from -5 to 12.

c Use your graph to find x when $y = 9$.
d What is the value of y when $x = -0.5$?

6 You are given that $2x + y = 6$.

a Find y when $x = 1$.
b Copy and complete the table for values of y for other values of x.

x	-1	0	1	2	3
y					

c Draw the graph of $2x + y = 6$ on the same axes as you used for question **5**.
d Write down the coordinates of the point where the two lines cross.

Q AREAS OF TRIANGLES AND PARALLELOGRAMS

AREA OF A TRIANGLE

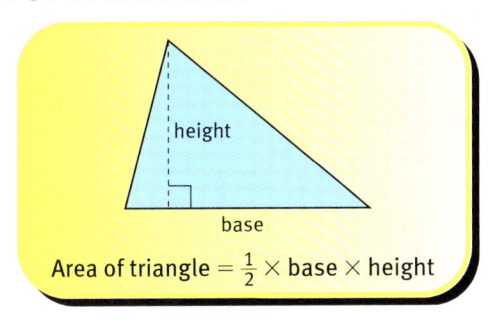

Area of triangle = $\frac{1}{2}$ × base × height

Sometimes the line showing the height is outside the triangle.

Example

Find the area of this triangle.

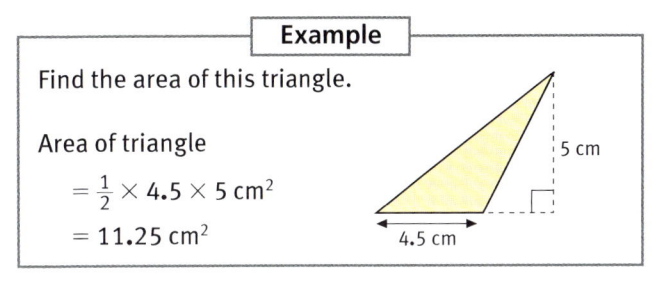

Area of triangle
$= \frac{1}{2} \times 4.5 \times 5$ cm^2
$= 11.25$ cm^2

1 Copy each triangle and draw a broken line to show its height.

a   b   c   d

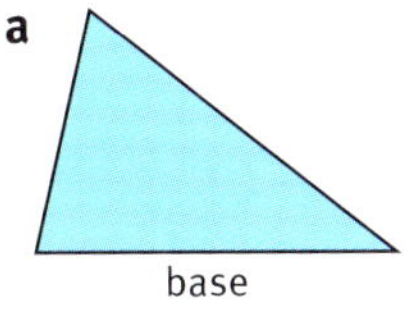

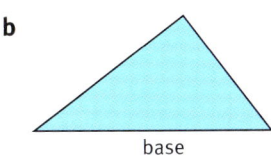

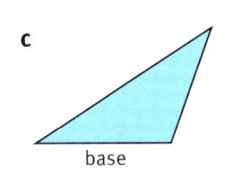

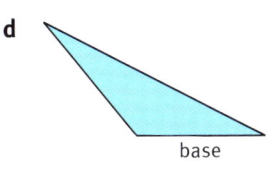

Find the area of each triangle.

2 7 cm, 8 cm

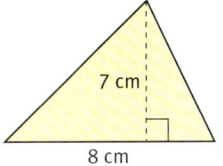

3 3 cm, 6 cm

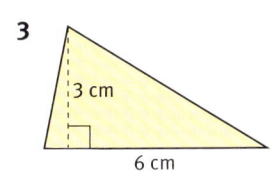

4 12 cm, 9 cm

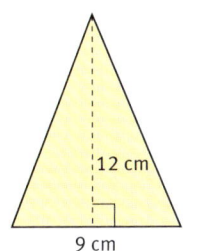

5 20 cm, 22 cm

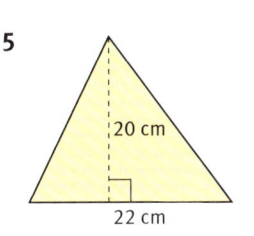

6 3 cm, 12 cm

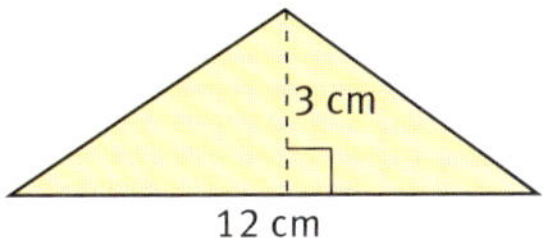

7 3.4 cm, 4 cm

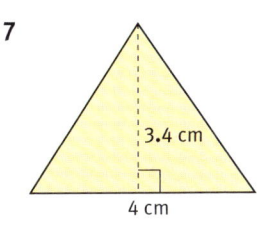

(Did you remember to divide by 2?)

Find the area of each triangle.

8 12 cm, 7 cm

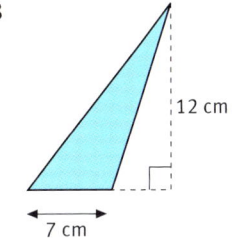

9 5 cm, 4.8 cm

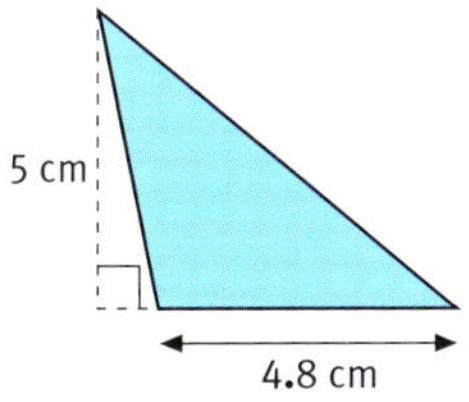

10 18 m, 14 m, 15 m

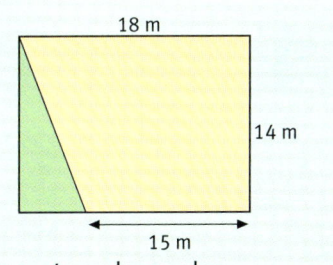

Sally has a rectangular garden.
The triangular piece is grass and the remainder is for vegetables.
  a Work out the height and base of the triangle.
  b Find the area of the grass.
  c What is the area of the whole garden?
  d What area is used for vegetables?
  e What fraction of the garden is grass?

11 14 cm, 8 cm, 10 cm, 4 cm (triangles A, B, C)

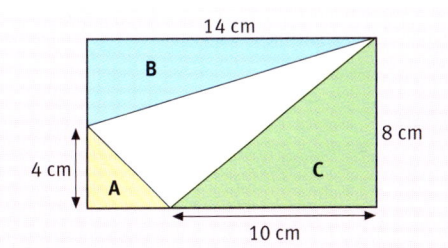

The triangles **A**, **B** and **C** are cut off this metal sheet.
Find a the area of triangle **A**
      b the area of triangle **B**
      c the area of triangle **C**
      d the area of the triangle that remains.

Q AREAS OF TRIANGLES AND PARALLELOGRAMS
AREAS OF COMPOUND SHAPES INVOLVING TRIANGLES

Example

Find the area of this metal plate which is a car part.

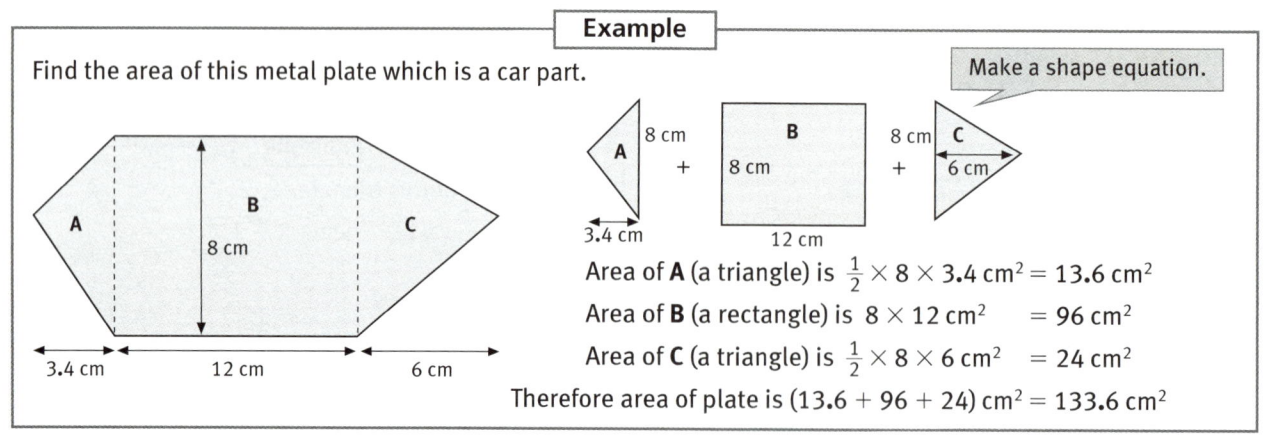

Make a shape equation.

Area of **A** (a triangle) is $\frac{1}{2} \times 8 \times 3.4$ cm² = 13.6 cm²
Area of **B** (a rectangle) is 8×12 cm² = 96 cm²
Area of **C** (a triangle) is $\frac{1}{2} \times 8 \times 6$ cm² = 24 cm²
Therefore area of plate is (13.6 + 96 + 24) cm² = 133.6 cm²

1 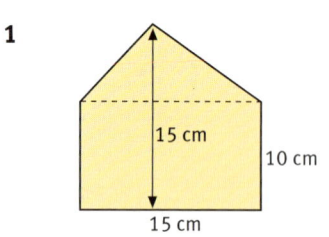
a Draw a shape equation to show how this shape divides into a triangle and a rectangle. Put all the measurements you need on each diagram.
b Find the area of
  i the triangle   ii the rectangle.
c Find the area of the whole shape.

2 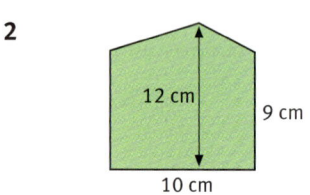
a Show, using a shape equation, how this shape can be divided into a rectangle and a triangle.
b Find the area of each shape.
c Find the area of the whole shape.

3 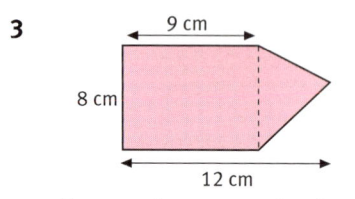
a Draw a shape equation for this shape.
b Find the area of this shape.

4 Work out the area of this piece of wood.

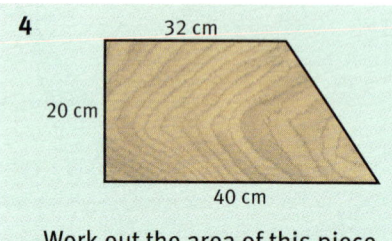

5 Work out the area of the end wall of this building.

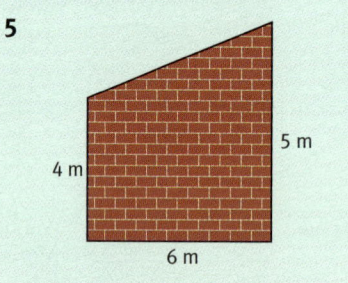

6 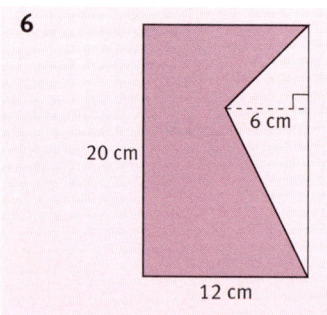
a Work out the area of the rectangle.
b Work out the area of the triangle.
c Find the area of the coloured shape.

Work out the area of each coloured shape.

7

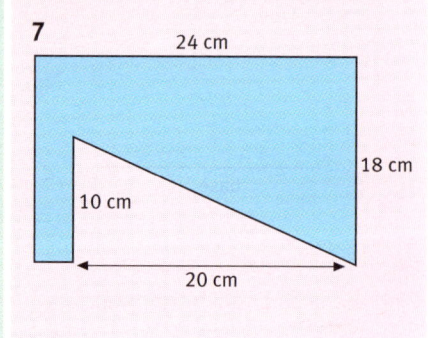

8

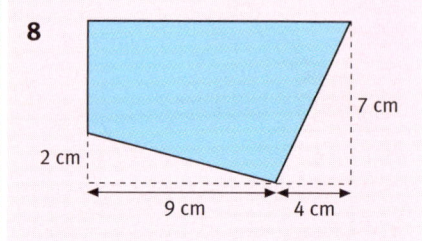

9

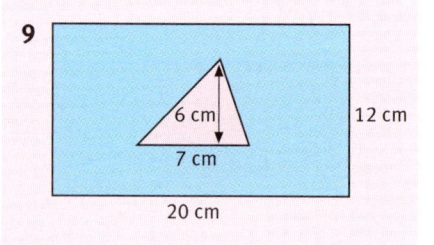

10

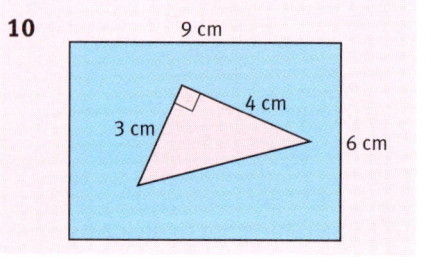

86

Q AREAS OF TRIANGLES AND PARALLELOGRAMS

AREA OF A PARALLELOGRAM

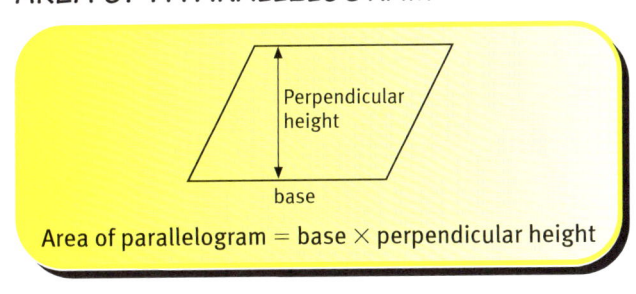

Area of parallelogram = base × perpendicular height

1 Copy each parallelogram and draw a broken line to show its height.

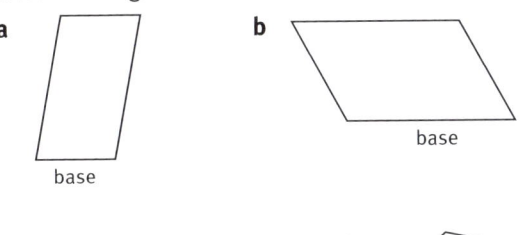

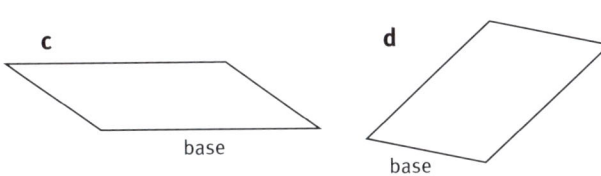

a b c d

Find the area of each parallelogram.

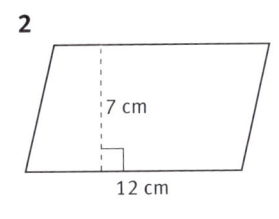

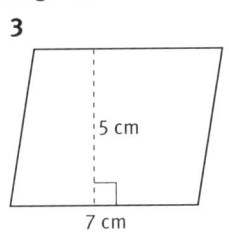

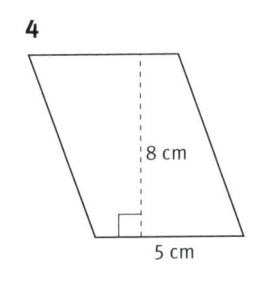

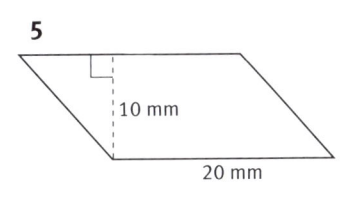

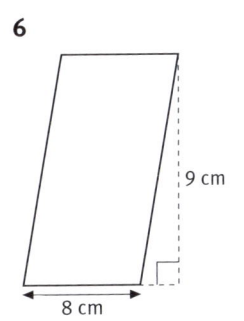

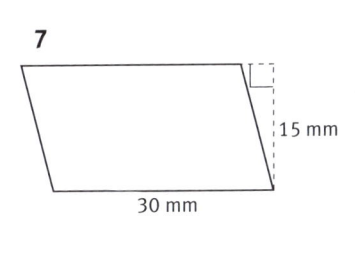

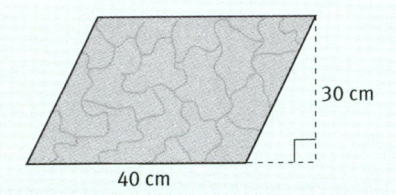

2 7 cm, 12 cm

3 5 cm, 7 cm

4 8 cm, 5 cm

5 10 mm, 20 mm

6 9 cm, 8 cm

7 15 mm, 30 mm

8 30 cm, 40 cm

The diagram shows a concrete paving slab, which is a parallelogram. Steve lays twenty similar slabs to form a patio. Find
a the area covered by one slab
b the area of the patio.
c Draw a diagram to show how these slabs tessellate to form a patio.

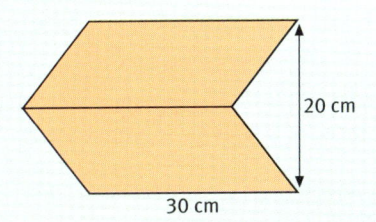

9 20 cm, 30 cm

Work out the area of this arrowhead which is made from two identical parallelograms.

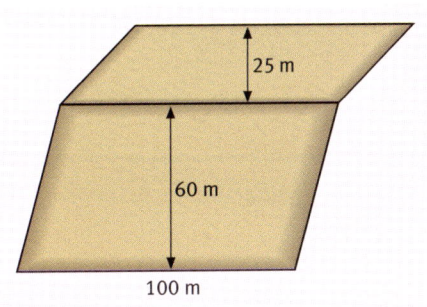

10 25 m, 60 m, 100 m

The diagram shows two plots of building land. Both plots are parallelograms.
Find the area of
a the larger plot b the smaller plot.

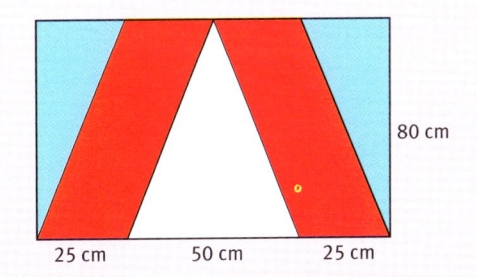

11 80 cm, 25 cm, 50 cm, 25 cm

A rectangular flag measures 100 cm by 80 cm. It is coloured red, white and blue.
The shapes coloured red are parallelograms.
Find the area of the flag that is
a red b white c blue.

R SUMMARISING DATA
MODE AND MEDIAN

> The mode is the value that occurs most often.
> The mode of the lengths
>   12 cm, 10 cm, 12 cm, 9 cm, 12 cm, 10 cm
> is 12 cm.

Find the mode for each set of values.

1. Molly's marks in five tests: 6, 7, 7, 8, 9.

2. The sizes of the last eight pairs of shoes sold in a shop: 5, 6, 6, 7, 7, 8, 8, 8, 9, 10.

3. The sums of money spent in a newsagents by the last ten customers:
   £2.75, 45 p, 40 p, £1.55, £3.85, 40 p, £1.91, 70 p, 40 p, £5.95.

4. The colours of nine cars in a car park: blue, red, black, black, red, white, red, black, red.

> The median is the middle value when the values have been arranged in order of size.
>   8, 14, 15, 23, 49
>   ↑
>   Median
>   6, 8, 10, 11, 16, 24
>   2 middle values
> The median is $\frac{10+11}{2} = \frac{21}{2} = 10.5$

5. Write down the median for each set of values.
   a. 3, 15, 19, 20, 21
   b. 1, 3, 9, 11, 19, 21.

6. Rearrange each set of values in order of size. Then write down the median value.
   a. 13, 5, 19, 7, 11
   b. 92, 104, 118, 34, 46, 88, 144
   c. 9, 16, 8, 10, 15, 19.

7. This bar chart gives the results of rolling a dice many times.

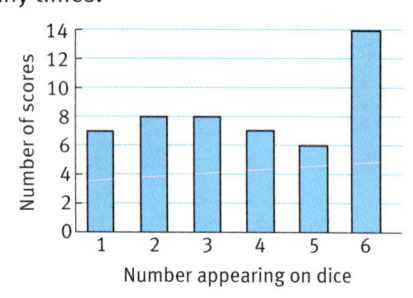

   a. What is the modal score?
   b. How many times was the dice rolled?

8. Thirty pupils took part in a competition. The points they scored were grouped and are given in the frequency table.

Points scored	Number of pupils
1–5	1
6–10	3
11–15	7
16–20	7
21–25	9
26–30	3

   a. Write down the modal group of points scored.
   b. How many pupils scored 10 or less?
   c. How many pupils scored at least 16?
   d. Penny scored 5.
      She said she had the lowest mark.
      Could this be true?
      Give a reason for your answer.

9. This list gives the time taken, in seconds, for a secretary to answer the telephone on 28 occasions.

   14.3 17.2 11.9 16.2 11.1 4.2 5.4
   12.3 21.5 12.0   9.3 11.3 19.4 23.8
   11.4   7.2 10.3 13.8   5.8 12.7 24.0
    6.4 18.3 13.7 14.2   3.8 12.6 14.4

   a. Copy and complete the frequency table below.

   > ≤ means 'less than or equal to'.

Time (t seconds)	Tally	Frequency
0 ≤ t < 5		
5 ≤ t < 10		
10 ≤ t < 15		
20 ≤ t < 25		

   b. Find the modal group for this data.

R SUMMARISING DATA
MEAN AND RANGE

> Mean = $\dfrac{\text{Sum of all values}}{\text{Number of values}}$
>
> The mean of 11, 5, 10, 16, 18 is $\dfrac{60}{5} = 12$

1 Find the mean of
  a 1, 7, 9, 3
  b 12, 15, 13, 10, 24, 16
  c 3, 6, 9, 12, 15.

2 Six people got the following marks in a test:
  7, 8, 4, 8, 4, 5
  What is the mean mark?

3 Five boys agreed to pool their money.
  The amounts each put into the pool were
  £6, £7, £8, £10, £14.
  a How much was in the pool?
  b If all five boys had put in equal amounts how much would each have given?
  c What was the mean amount put into the pool?

4 Don spent a week on holiday in Cyprus.
  The mid-day temperatures during the week were

Mon	Tues	Wed	Thurs	Fri	Sat	Sun
82°	79°	86°	82°	84°	88°	83°

  Work out the mean, giving your answer correct to
  a the nearest whole number
  b the nearest tenth of a degree.

> The range is the difference between the largest and smallest values.
> The range of 11, 5, 10, 16, 18 is $18 - 5 = 13$

5 Find the range of
  a 16, 9, 23, 6
  b 34, 2, 48, 16, 3
  c 12 cm, 79 cm, 72 cm, 44 cm, 11 cm, 39 cm
  d £2.45, £1.88, 98 p, £1.05, 66 p, £1.99.

6 Eight pupils were asked how much it had cost them to come to school on the bus.
  The amounts were
  60 p, 45 p, 80 p, 55 p, 30 p, 94 p, 55 p, 45 p.
  a What is the range of these fares?
  b Work out the mean fare.

7 The boot sizes of the players in a rugby team are
  8, 9, 7, 9, 10, 12, 9, 12, 8, 9, 7, 8, 10, 11, 9
  a How many players are there in the team?
  For these sizes find
  b the mode   **c** the mean
  d the range   **e** the median.

8 A page of a novel was chosen at random and the number of letters in each of the first fifty words on that page was counted. The numbers were

9	2	7	3	6	5	4	3	5	5
3	8	5	7	3	5	4	4	2	6
1	4	2	10	5	4	5	7	3	4
3	2	4	6	3	2	5	8	6	3
7	3	3	4	5	5	2	3	8	8

  a Copy and complete the following table.

Number of letters	Tally	Frequency
1		
2		
3		
4		
5		
6		
7		
8		
9		
10		

  b Find the mode of these numbers.
  c How many letters are there altogether in the fifty words?

9 A postman delivers letters to 50 houses.
  The mean number of letters per house is 3.
  How many letters does he have to start with?

10 The mean of the numbers 5, 5, 5, 9, 10, 10, 12 is 8.
  Find **a** the range **b** the median **c** the mode.
  Another number, 12, is added to the list.
  d Which of the values
  i median **ii** mean **iii** range **iv** mode
  will change? Give reasons.

11 In five tests, Peter's average mark was 8 out of 10.
  The range was 4 and his median mark 7.
  In a sixth test Peter scored 9.
  a Does his mean mark change?
  b Does the range change?
  Give reasons for your answers.

R SUMMARISING DATA
COMPARING DISTRIBUTIONS

1 Mr Parsons gave his class a geography test.
Here are the marks for the boys:

6 9 7 8 6 10 4 2 9 5 6 7 8

a Work out the mode.
b What is the median score?
c Find the range.

The median mark for the fifteen girls was 8 and the range was 5.

d By comparing the two sets of results explain whether the boys or the girls did better on the test.

2 Rena wants to take her family on holiday. The choice is between Panodorm or Messa de Mar. To decide which resort to go to, Rena looks up the number of hours of sunshine at each resort during the same 14 days last year.

The figures were:

Panodorm

6 7 6 10 8 9 5
8 6 5 7 6 7 8

Messa de Mar

10 6 8 7 10 7 8
9 7 6 9 10 9 6

Rena worked out the mean and range of the number of hours of sunshine for each place.

Panodorm
Mean number of hours of sunshine: 7
Range: 5 hours

Messa de Mar
Mean number of hours of sunshine: 8
Range: 4 hours

a Describe in words how Rena worked out the mean number of hours of sunshine in Panadorm.
b Describe how she calculated the range in Messa de Mar.
c Rena wants a holiday with as much sun as possible.
Which resort would you suggest that she takes her family?
Explain your choice, using both the mean and range in your answer.

3 A group of pupils took an English test.
The frequency diagram shows the distribution of their marks.

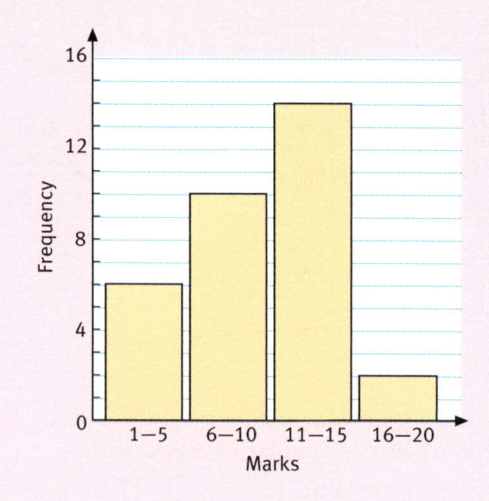

a How many pupils scored between 11 and 15 marks?
b How many pupils took the test?

The same group of pupils took a mathematics test. The frequency polygon shows the marks that some of the pupils got in this test.

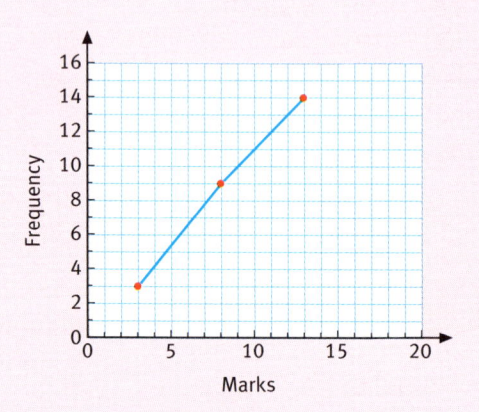

c In the mathematics test six pupils scored between 16 and 20 marks.
Use this information to complete the frequency polygon.
d Compare the marks scored by the pupils on the mathematics test with the marks they scored on the English test.

90

R SUMMARISING DATA

INVESTIGATION

'Most people find it easier to estimate a length than an area.' Investigate.

1. Start by writing your own hypothesis, that is write down, in your own words,
   what your investigation is going to test. For example:
   'My hypothesis is that people are better at estimating lengths than they are at estimating areas'.

2. Next you have to decide what you need to find out.
   When you have decided, write it down.
   For example, (use your own words): *'I need to find out what some people think
   the length of a line is and what they think the area of a shape is.'*

3. Now decide what line and what shape you are going to use.
   Will you draw a line and a rectangle (this is a simple shape) yourself?
   Or will you use some objects in the room, a table top, a picture frame or the floor for example?
   When you have decided, write down what you are going to use
   and include drawings of them or descriptions in your investigation.
   Remember to write a proper sentence, for example, *'I will ask people to estimate the .....'*

4. Now ask some people to estimate the length of your line and the area of your shape.
   Decide how many people to ask.
   Collect your information in a table like this one.

	Tim's estimate	Cora's estimate		
Line (length = ...)				
Shape (area = ...)				

5. Next find the difference between the true length and the estimated length: this is the error.
   Then find this error as a percentage of the real length: this is the percentage error.
   Do the same for the area.
   You can enter the percentage errors in a table like this one.

	Tim's % error	Cora's % error		
Line				
Shape				

6. Now you can summarise the percentage errors for the length; the range and the mean are useful.
   You can also draw a bar chart to illustrate the percentage errors in the length.
   To do this you must first make a frequency table like this:

% error	Tally	Frequency
0%–10%		
11%–20%		

7. Repeat question **6** for the area.

8. Now compare the errors made when estimating a length with the errors made when estimating an area.
   You must use your results to justify what you write.
   You can choose from:
   *'My investigation shows that people are
                       better at estimating lengths than they are at estimating areas because ......'
                       better at estimating areas than they are at estimating lengths because ......'
                       no better at estimating lengths than they are at estimating areas because ......'*

S SOLIDS
FACES, EDGES AND VERTICES

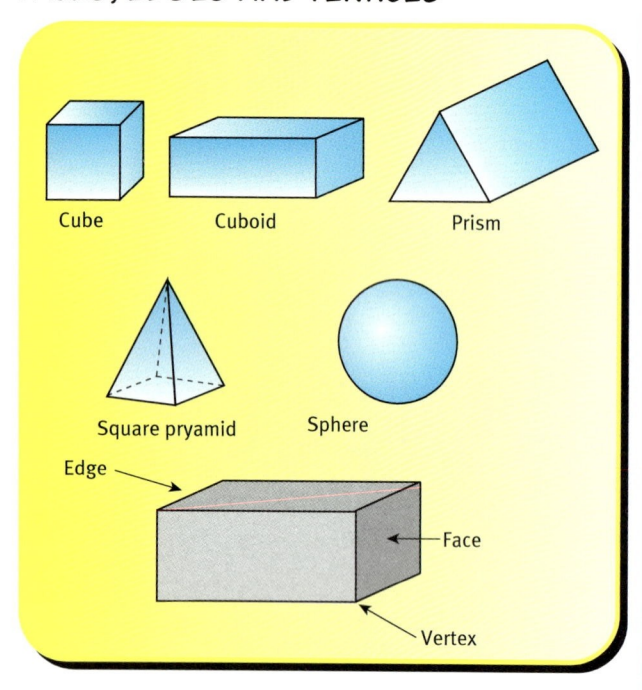

Cube   Cuboid   Prism

Square pyramid   Sphere

Edge — Face — Vertex

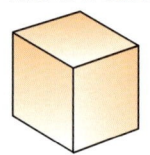

1 This is a cube.
  a How many faces does it have?
  b How many edges are there?
  c Stuart said that a cube has 6 vertices.
    Is he correct?
    Give a reason for your answer.

2 Write down the name of each solid and give the number of faces, edges and vertices.
  a   b   c

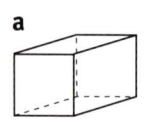

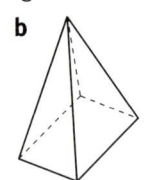

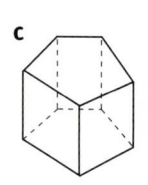

3 a Write down the name of this solid.
  b How many triangular faces does it have?
  c How many rectangular faces does it have?

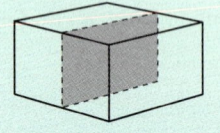

4 This cuboid has three planes of symmetry. One of them is shown. Draw **sketches** to show the other two.

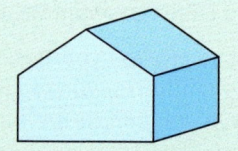

5 a How many planes of symmetry does this prism have?
    Illustrate your answer with suitable sketches.
  b Draw the constant cross-section for this solid.

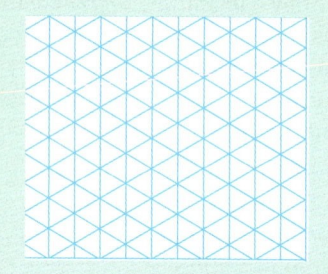

6 Use isometric graph paper like this to draw
  a a cube
  b a cuboid which is 5 units long, 4 units wide and 3 units high.

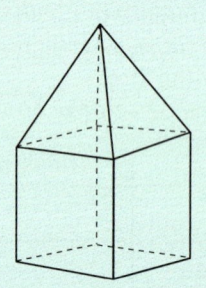

7 Copy each statement and fill in the blanks.
  a This solid is made from a ...... with a ...... on the top.
  b This solid has ...... triangular faces and ...... square faces.
  c This solid has ...... edges.
  d This solid has ...... vertices.

8 The cross-section of this prism is a regular hexagon.
  a Work out
    i the number of faces
    ii the number of edges
    iii the number of vertices.
  b How many planes of symmetry does this solid have: 6, 7 or 8?

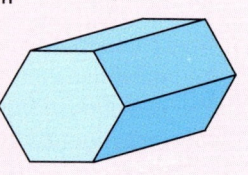

S SOLIDS

NETS

1 This is a net of a cube. The edges are 4 cm.

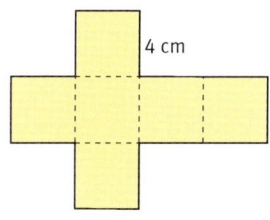

  a Draw the net on 1 centimetre squared paper and cut it out.

  b Fold it along the broken lines to show that it makes a cube.

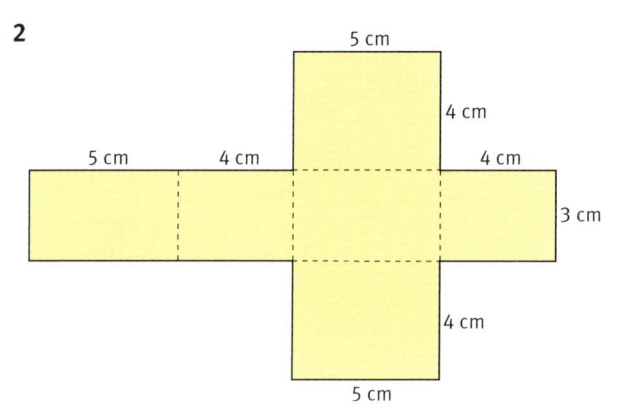

2

  a Draw this net on squared paper.

  b Cut it out and fold it along the dotted lines. Stick the edges together.

  c How many faces are rectangles measuring 5 cm by 4 cm?

  d How many faces are rectangles measuring 4 cm by 3 cm?

  e What are the measurements of the remaining faces?

  f What is the name of this solid?

  g Draw another arrangement of the rectangles that will fold to give the same solid.

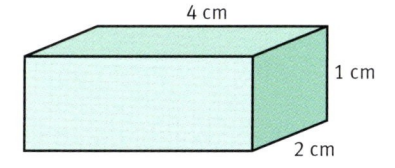

3

This cuboid is 4 cm long, 2 cm wide and 1 cm high.

  a How many faces does it have?

  b **Sketch** the faces and show their measurements.

  c On squared paper draw a net for this solid. Show the measurements of the rectangles forming the net.

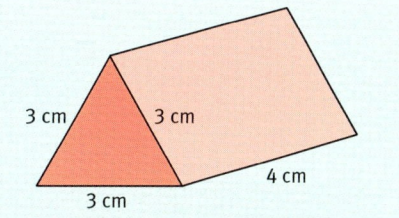

4

The cross-section of this solid is an equilateral triangle of side 3 cm.
The solid is 4 cm long.

  a What name is given to this shape?

  b How many faces does it have?

  c Describe the shapes of the faces.

  d **Sketch** a net for this solid, marking in any measurements.
     Do not draw an accurate full scale net.

5

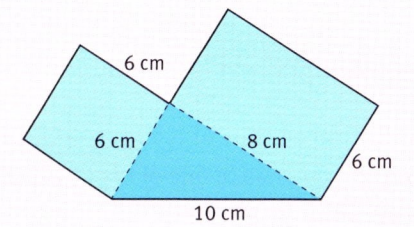

This diagram shows part of the net of a triangular prism.
It is drawn accurately but some of the faces are missing.

  a How many faces are missing?

  b Draw a **sketch** of the complete net. Mark in the measurements.

6

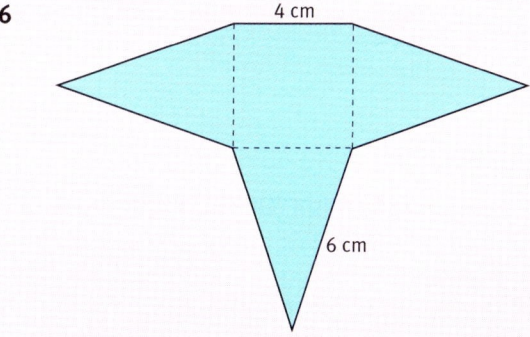

This is part of the net for a pyramid with a square base.

  a What shape is missing to complete this net? Show it on a sketch, marking any measurements.

  b Draw an accurate full size net for this pyramid.

  c Give sketches to show the other possible positions for the missing shape.

93

S SOLIDS
SURFACE AREA

1

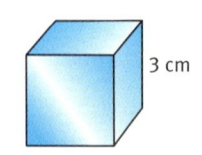

Ray has a cube with an edge of 3 cm.
a How many faces does it have?
b What is the area of one face?
c Work out the total surface area of the cube.

2

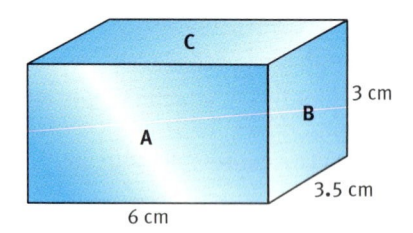

Ceri has a cuboid measuring 6 cm by 3.5 cm by 3 cm.
a Find the area of one of the smallest faces.
b Work out the area of one of the largest faces.
c Which letter: **A**, **B** or **C** refers to a face **not included** in either **a** or **b**?
d Work out the total surface area of the cuboid.

3

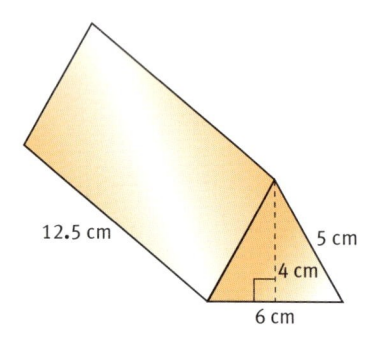

When a triangular prism rests on a table it covers a rectangle measuring 12.5 cm by 6 cm.
The prism is 4 cm high.
Each sloping edge is 5 cm long.
a Draw a cross-section for this solid. Mark its base and height.

Work out
b the area of the cross-section
c the area of a sloping face
d the area of the base
e the total surface area of the prism.

4

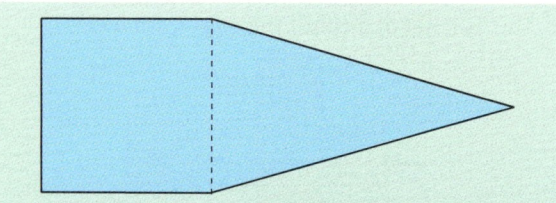

This is an incomplete net for a pyramid with a square base.
The length of the base of the triangle is 5 cm and the height of the triangle is 6 cm.

a How many more triangles exactly the same as the one shown above are needed to complete this net?
b Draw a **sketch** to show a complete net.
c What are the measurements of the base of the pyramid?
d Work out the area of one triangular face.
e Work out the area of the base.
f Find the total surface area of the pyramid.

5

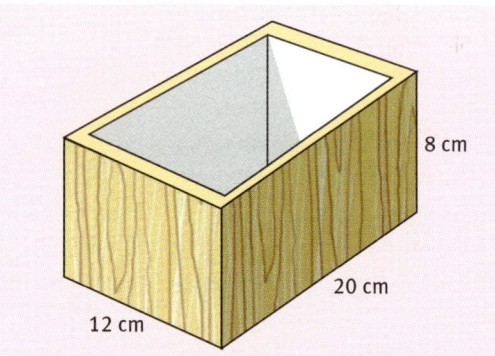

Sid makes an open wooden box measuring 20 cm by 12 cm by 8 cm.

a Find the total surface area of the four vertical sides.
b The sides and the base are everywhere 0.5 cm thick.
Work out the measurements of the inside of the box.
c The inside of the box is covered completely with material.
Draw a net for this material.
d Find the area of material needed to cover the inside of the box.

S SOLIDS

PLANS AND ELEVATIONS

> The **plan** of an object is what you see by looking down on it from above.
> An **elevation** is what you see by looking at an object from a side.

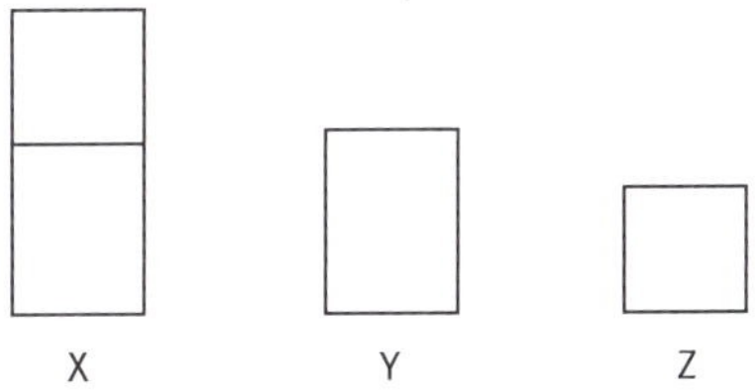

In the questions that follow all measurements on diagrams are in centimetres. Draw a rough sketch first and put all the known measurements on it.
Use 1 cm squared paper for your answers.

Example

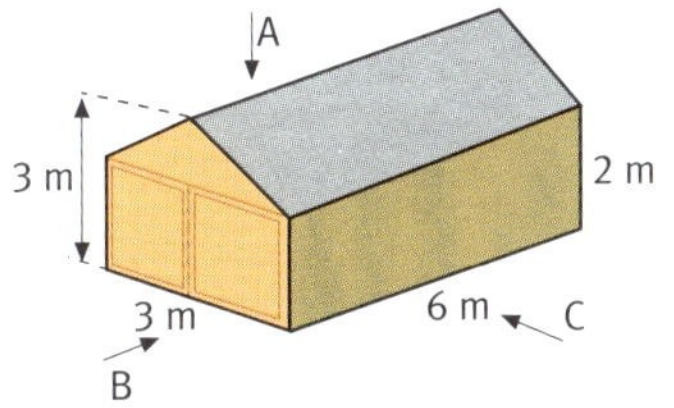

Here is the plan for this garage. It is what you see by looking at the garage from above (direction A).

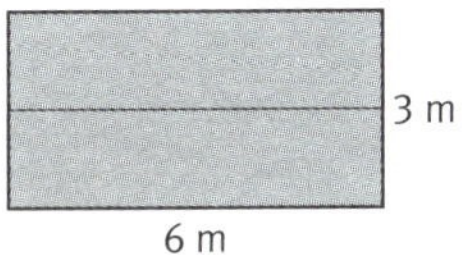

This is the elevation from direction B.

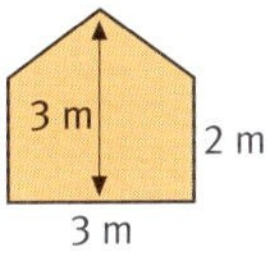

This is the elevation from direction C.

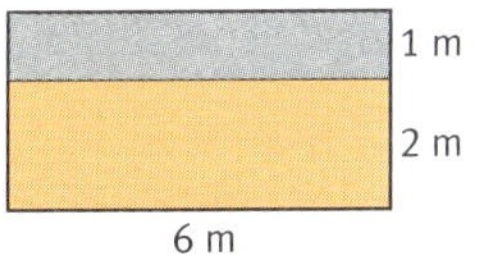

2 For this wooden block draw
  a the plan
  b the elevation in the direction of the arrow.

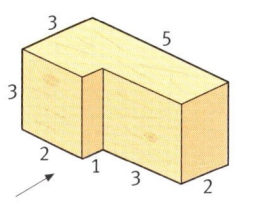

3 This cylinder has a radius of 3cm and a height of 5 cm.
  a Draw a plan for the cylinder.
  b Draw the elevation in the direction of the arrow.
  c Is the elevation the same from any direction?

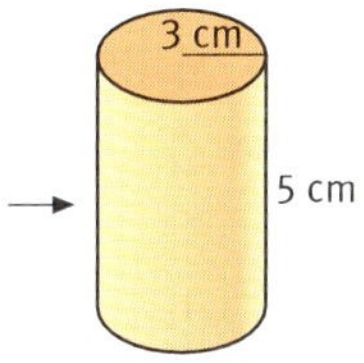

4 This block is used to cut off lengths of piping.
  a Draw its plan. 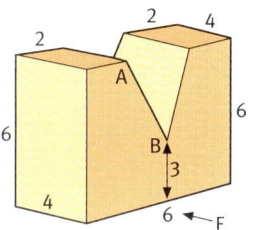
  b Draw the front elevation from direction F. Measure the length of AB.

1
  a Which of the following diagrams is a plan of this metal object?

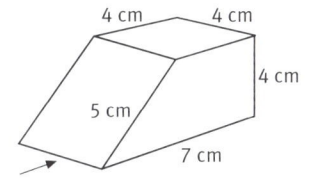

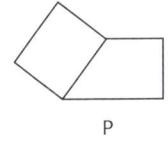

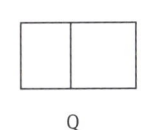

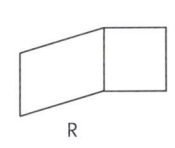

  P   Q   R

  b Which of the following diagrams is the elevation in the direction shown by the arrow?

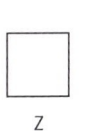

  X   Y   Z

5 The sketch shows a model for two steps.
Draw **a** the plan
  b the side elevation (S)
  c the front elevation (F).

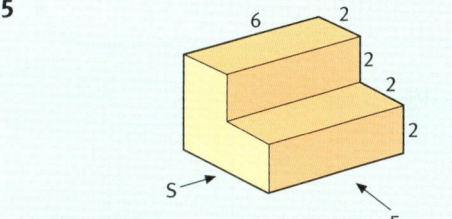

6 A cube of side 4 cm has a corner removed as shown in the sketch.
Draw **a** a plan
  b the side elevation (S)
  c the front elevation (F). Measure CD.

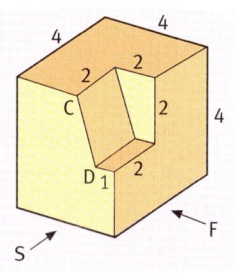

T CIRCLES
CIRCUMFERENCE OF A CIRCLE

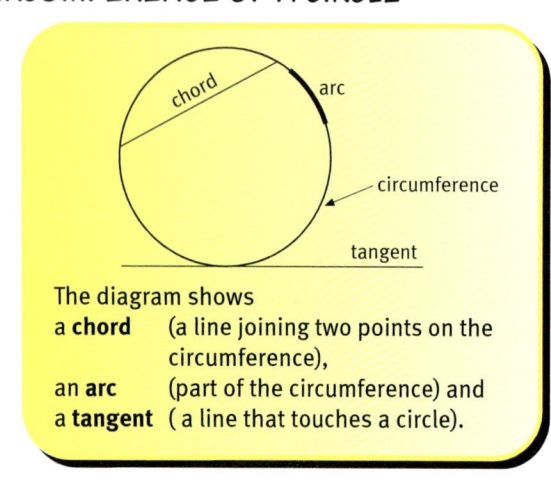

The diagram shows
- a **chord** (a line joining two points on the circumference),
- an **arc** (part of the circumference) and
- a **tangent** (a line that touches a circle).

1 Draw a circle and mark three points around its circumference. Letter these points A, B and C.
  a Draw the chord AB.
  b Draw the tangent at C.
  c Use a coloured pen or pencil to draw the arc BC.

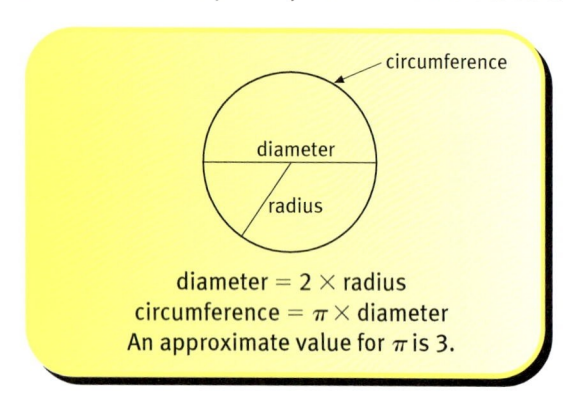

diameter = 2 × radius
circumference = π × diameter
An approximate value for π is 3.

2 Write down the radius of each circle.
  a 12 cm   b 5 cm   c 18 cm

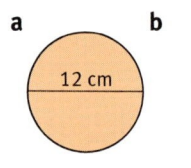

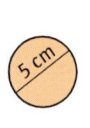

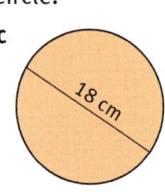

3 The diameter of a circle is 36 cm. Write down its radius.

4 The radius of a wheel is 17 cm. Write down its diameter.

5 The radius of a circular running track is 35 m. What is the diameter of the track?

6 The diameter of a circular tablecloth is 1.4 metres. Find the radius of the cloth.

Example
The diameter of a coin is 25 mm. Estimate its circumference.

circumference = π × diameter

Estimate is 3 × 25 mm = 75 mm

7 Use π = 3 to estimate the circumference of each circle.
  a 5 cm   b 9 cm   c 15 cm   d 4 cm

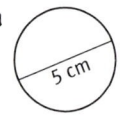

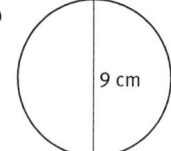

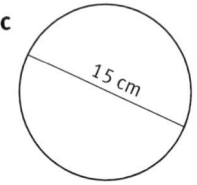

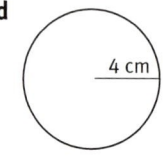

8 The diameter of this clock face is 24 cm. Estimate its circumference.

9 Use the value of π on your calculator to find the circumference of each circle.
  a 8 cm   b 12.6 cm

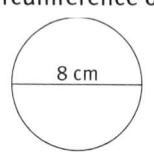

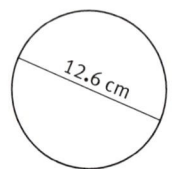

10 Use the value of π on your calculator to find the circumference of each circle.
  a 7.5 cm   b 4.4 cm

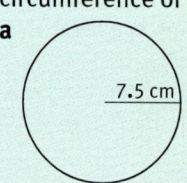

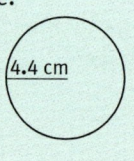

11 The radius of a cycle wheel is 33 cm.
  a What is the diameter of the wheel?
  b How far will the bike move forward for one turn of a wheel? Give your answer in
    i centimetres ii metres.
  c Mike cycles 100 metres. How many complete turns must the wheels make to cover this distance?

T CIRCLES
AREA OF A CIRCLE

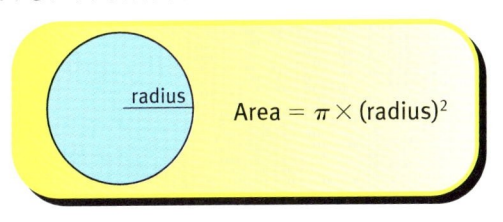

Area = π × (radius)²

Example

The diameter of a coin is 28 mm.
Find **a** its radius **b** its area.

a Radius = $\frac{1}{2}$ diameter

= $\frac{1}{2}$ × 28 mm = 14 mm

b Area is π × 14² mm²
= π × 196 mm²
= 615.7... mm²
= 616 mm² (correct to nearest whole number)

1 Use π = 3 to estimate the area of each circle.
   a 4 cm   **b** 7 cm   **c** 16 cm

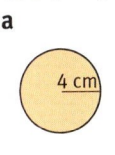

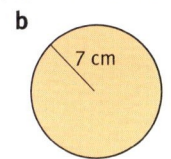

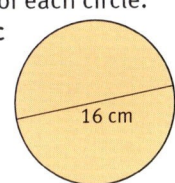

2 Use the value of π on your calculator to find the area of each circle.
Give your answers correct to the nearest whole number.
   a 2.5 cm   **b** 4.3 cm

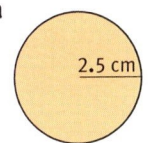

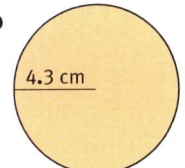

3 Use the value of π on your calculator to find the area of each circle.
Give your answers correct to the nearest whole number.
   a 7 cm   **b** 9.4 cm

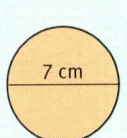

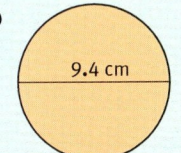

4 The radius of a circular tablecloth is 0.7 metres.
Work out the area of the tablecloth.

5 The diameter of a dining table is 1 metre.
   a What is the diameter in centimetres?
   b Find the area of the tabletop in square centimetres.

6 Sim has two plates.
The diameter of one plate is 16 cm.
The diameter of the other plate is 24 cm.
   a Work out the area of each plate.
   b Peg says that the area of the larger plate is more than twice that of the smaller plate.
   Sim disagrees.
   Who do you agree with?
   Give a reason for your answer.

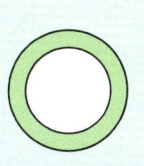

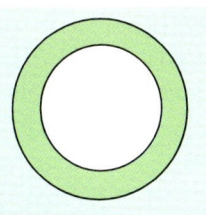

7 A circular lawn has a radius of 5 m.
The contents of a bottle of weedkiller will treat 50 m².
Is one bottle enough to treat the whole lawn?
(Give a reason for your answer.)

8 Nia cuts the largest possible circle from a sheet of paper measuring 12 cm by 12 cm.
   a What is the area of the circle?
   b What area of paper is wasted?

9 Steve is cutting discs of diameter 10 cm out of a sheet of foil measuring 60 cm by 40 cm.
   a What is the area of the foil?
   b Work out the area of one disc.
   c How many discs can Steve cut out along the length of the sheet?
   (The first 5 are shown in the top row of the diagram.)
   d How many discs can Steve cut out down the width of the sheet?
   (The first 3 are shown in the left-hand column.)
   e How many discs can he get from one sheet?

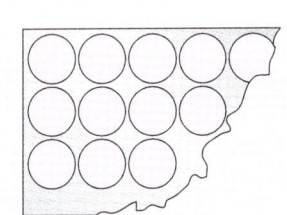

10 A ladies' cloak is a semicircle (half circle) of radius 110 cm.
Work out the area of material used.

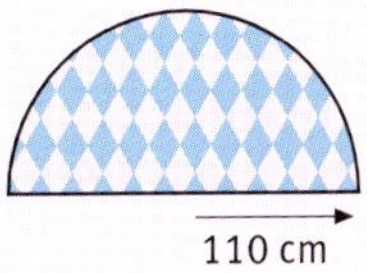

97

U VOLUMES
COUNTING CUBES

1. **a** How many 1 centimetre cubes like this do you need to cover the bottom (base) of this box?

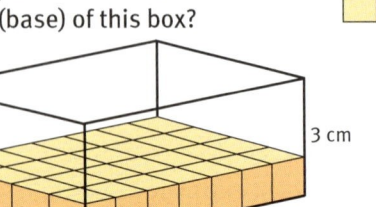

   b How many layers of cubes do you need to fill the box?

   c How many one centimetre cubes do you need to fill this box?

2. How many centimetre cubes do you need to make each stack?

   a   **b** 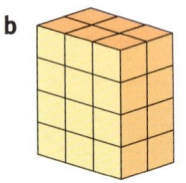   **c**

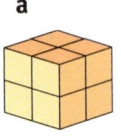

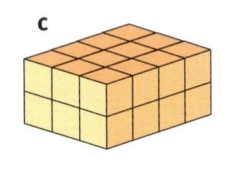

3. Rebecca has a box like this.

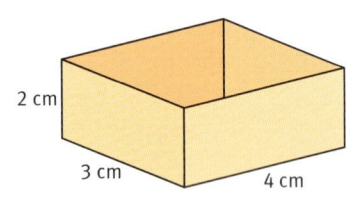

   She wants to know how many 1 cm cubes will fit into the box.
   a She covers the base with one layer of cubes. How many cubes will fit in?
   b She puts another layer in. Will this fill the box? Give a reason for your answer.
   c How many cubes are there in the box when it is full?
   d What is the volume of the box?

4. How many 1 cm cubes are needed to fill each box?
   a 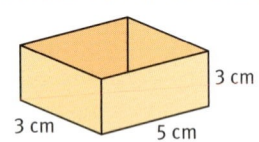
   b

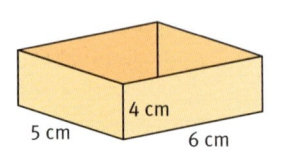

5. Find the volume of each stack of loose 1 cm cubes.

   a   **b** 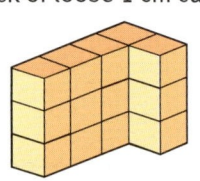   **c** 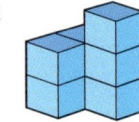   **d**

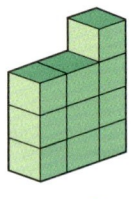

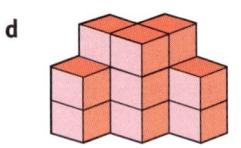

6. This box is full of 1 cm cubes.

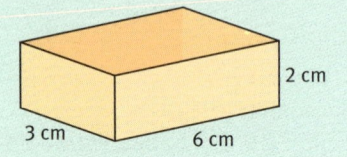

   a How many cubes are there in the box?

   Some of the cubes are used to cover the base of this box.

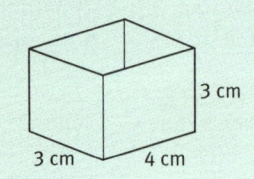

   b How many cubes will do this?
   c Are there enough cubes to fill this box? Give a reason for your answer.

7. **a** How many 1 cm cubes have been used to make this solid shape?

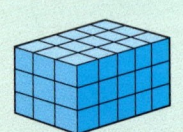

   b A line of cubes through the middle is taken out. How many centimetre cubes are left?

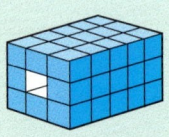

8. How many cubes of edge 2 cm can be stored in a cubical box with edge 6 cm?

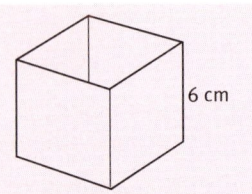

98

U VOLUMES
VOLUME OF A CUBOID

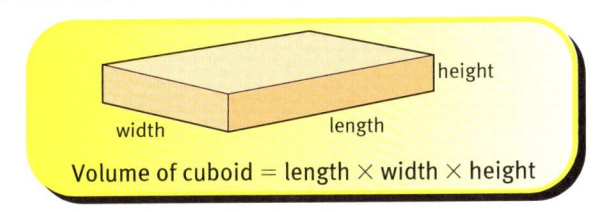

Volume of cuboid = length × width × height

Find the volume of each cuboid.

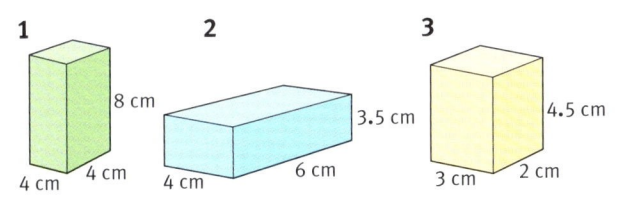

1 4 cm × 4 cm × 8 cm

2 4 cm × 6 cm × 3.5 cm

3 3 cm × 2 cm × 4.5 cm

4 A solid made from a cube (2 cm × 2 cm × 2 cm) on top of a cuboid (10 cm × 5 cm × 5 cm).

This solid is made from a cube and a cuboid. Use a 'shape equation' to find the volume of this solid.

5 The base of a wooden block measures 20 cm by 10 cm. The block is 12 cm high.

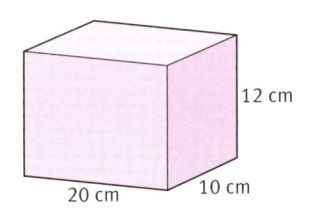

 a Work out the area of the base.
 b Work out the volume of the block.

1 litre = 1000 cm³

6 Helen's jug holds 2000 cm³. How many litres is this?

7 George buys a 2½ litre bottle of water. How many cubic centimetres is this?

8 Alison's kettle holds 1.5 litres. How many cubic centimetres is this?

9 The label on Charlotte's bottle of cola says that it contains 1800 cm³. How many litres is this?

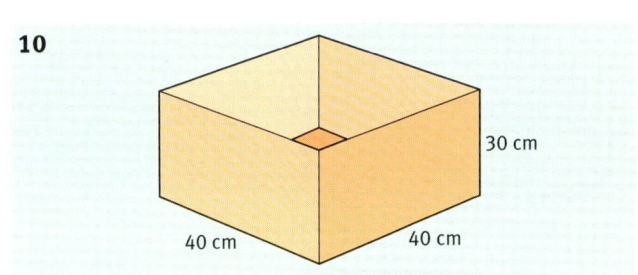

10 The base of a water tank measures 40 cm by 40 cm. The tank is 30 cm deep. Water is poured into the tank until the depth of water is 25 cm.
 a Work out the volume of water in the tank in cm³.
 b How many litres is this?

11 This block measures 4 cm by 3 cm by 3 cm and has a volume of 36 cm³.

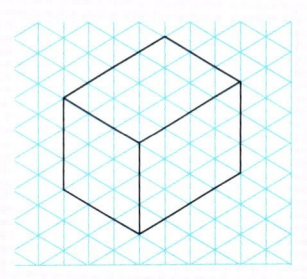

Sketch, on a similar grid, another block that has a volume of 36 cm³.
Write down
 a its length
 b its width
 c its height.

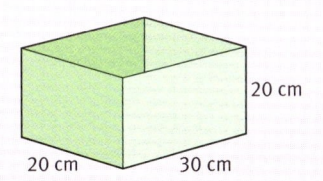

12 An **open** cardboard box has a rectangular base measuring 30 cm by 20 cm. The box is 20 cm deep.
 a Work out the volume of the box.
 b Sketch a net for this shape, writing in the measurements. (You do not need graph paper for this.)

U VOLUMES
USING VOLUMES

1

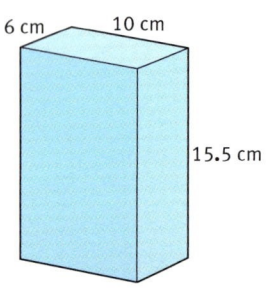

6 cm, 10 cm, 15.5 cm

This box contains grass seed.
a Work out the volume of seed in the box.

b

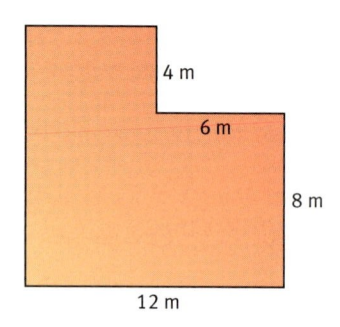

4 m, 6 m, 8 m, 12 m

Ken want to seed this plot.
Find its area.

c A full box contains enough seed to cover 12 m² of ground.
How many boxes of seed should Ken buy to seed this plot?

2

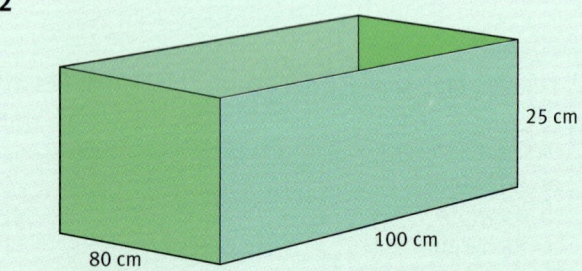

80 cm, 100 cm, 25 cm

This is an oil tank.

a What volume of liquid will the tank hold when it is full?
How many litres is this?
(1 litre = 1000 cm³)

b Oil is poured into the tank to a depth of 10 cm.
How many cubic centimetres of oil has been poured in?

c More oil is poured into the tank until the depth is 15 cm.
By what fraction has the volume of oil in the tank increased?

3

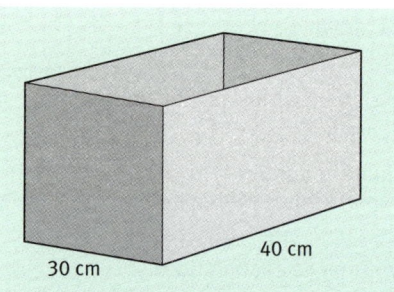

30 cm, 40 cm

The base of a tank measures 40 cm by 30 cm.
It is filled with water to a depth of 20 cm.

a What volume of water is in the tank?

b More water is poured into the tank until the depth of water is 22.4 cm.
Calculate the percentage increase in the volume of water in the tank.

4

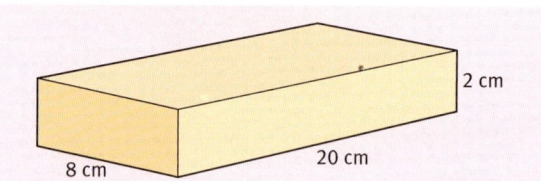

8 cm, 20 cm, 2 cm

Sally buys a block of ready-made pastry.
It is 20 cm long, 8 cm wide and 2 cm thick.

a Find the volume of the pastry.

b She rolls it out into a rectangle measuring 40 cm by 16 cm.
How thick is the pastry now?

5

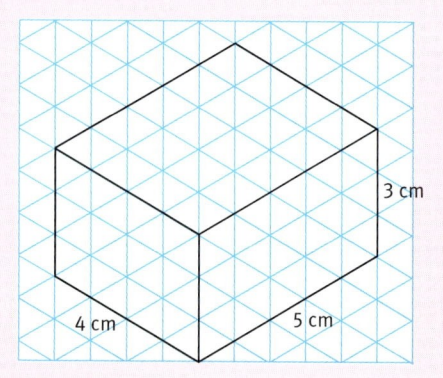

4 cm, 5 cm, 3 cm

A piece of cheese measures 5 cm by 4 cm by 3 cm.

a Work out its volume.

b On a grid like this one, draw another piece of cheese which has dimensions twice those of the given piece.

c How many pieces of cheese measuring 5 cm by 4 cm by 3 cm will fit into a box whose dimensions are twice those of one of the pieces?

V MORE ALGEBRA
MAKING EQUATIONS

1 a Write down an expression for the sum of the angles in this triangle.
  b Make an equation for this sum.
  c Find the size of **each** angle in this triangle.

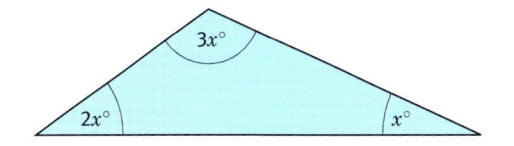

2 a Write down an expression for the perimeter of this shape.
  b The perimeter is 20 cm. Make an equation for a.
  c Solve your equation. How long is a side of this shape?
  d What is the mathematical name for this shape?

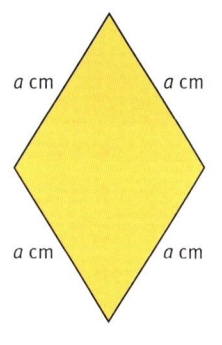

3 Sam is 4 years older than her brother Viv.
Viv is now x years old.
  a Write down an expression for Sam's age now.
  b Write down an expression for Sam's age in three year's time.
  c Write down an expression for Viv's age in three year's time.
  d In three year's time, Sam will be twice as old as Viv.
    i Write down an expression for twice Viv's age.
    ii Now make an equation.
  e Solve your equation to find Viv's age now.

4 Anwar thinks of a number, x. He then doubles it and subtracts 3.
  a Write down an expression for Anwar's answer.
  b Find the number that Anwar started with when his answer is 21.

5 The perimeter of this rectangle is 39 cm.
  a Make an equation for x.
  b Solve your equation.
  c Find the length of the longer side of the rectangle.

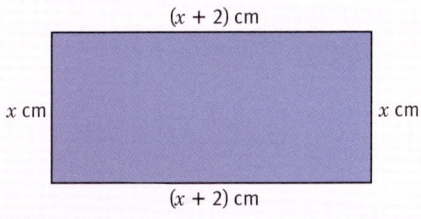

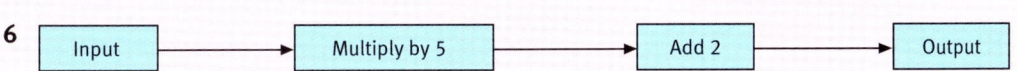

6 Input → Multiply by 5 → Add 2 → Output
  a The input number is x.
    Write down an expression for the output number in terms of x.
  b The output number is 17.
    Make an equation involving x.
  c Solve the equation to find the input number.

7 Given that $4x - 3 = 13$, find the value of $8 - 3x$.

V MORE ALGEBRA
MORE EQUATIONS

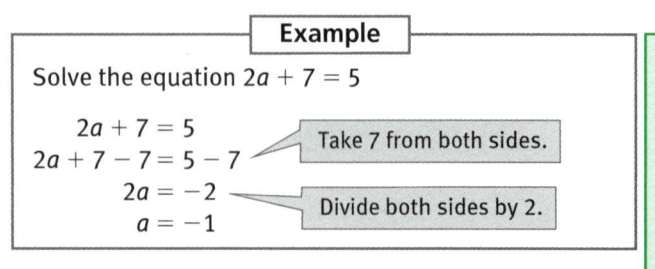

Example

Solve the equation $2a + 7 = 5$

$2a + 7 = 5$
$2a + 7 - 7 = 5 - 7$ — Take 7 from both sides.
$2a = -2$
$a = -1$ — Divide both sides by 2.

Solve the equations.

1. $x + 6 = 4$
2. $x + 3 = 1$
3. $3 + x = 2$
4. $4 + x = 1$
5. $1 = x + 4$
6. $2 = x + 5$
7. $2x + 5 = 3$
8. $3x + 7 = 1$
9. $1 = 6 + x$
10. $3 = 8 + x$
11. $7 = 3x + 10$
12. $12 = 5x + 22$

Example

Solve the equation $3 - 4x = 11$

$3 - 4x = 11$
$3 - 4x + 4x = 11 + 4x$ — Add 4x to both sides.
$3 = 11 + 4x$
$3 - 11 = 11 + 4x - 11$ — Take 11 from both sides.
$-8 = 4x$
$-2 = x$ — Divide both sides by 4.
$x = -2$

Solve the equations

13. $2 - x = -1$
14. $5 - 2x = 9$
15. $x + 2 = -4$
16. $2x + 1 = -5$
17. $x - 4 = -1$
18. $4x - 3 = -7$
19. $2 = 1 - x$
20. $9 = 3 - 2x$

Example

Solve the equation $2x + 3 = 8$

$2x + 3 = 8$
$2x + 3 - 3 = 8 - 3$ — Take 3 from both sides.
$2x = 5$
$x = 5 \div 2$ — Divide both sides by 2.
$x = \frac{5}{2} = 2\frac{1}{2}$

Solve the equations.

21. $2x + 1 = 4$
22. $5x + 2 = 3$
23. $5 - 2x = 4$
24. $4 - 2x = 1$
25. $5 = 3 + 3x$
26. $8 = 7 + 4x$
27. $2 = 7 - 2x$
28. $6 = 1 - 10x$
29. $9x + 1 = 4$
30. $4x - 3 = 3$

Example

Solve the equation $3x + 3 = 2x - 1$

$3x + 3 = 2x - 1$ — Take 2x from both sides.
$3x + 3 - 2x = 2x - 1 - 2x$
$x + 3 = -1$
$x + 3 - 3 = -1 - 3$ — Take 3 from both sides.
$x = -4$

Solve the equations.

31. $2x = 5 + x$
32. $1 + 3x = x$
33. $2x + 1 = 4 - x$
34. $4x - 2 = 3x + 5$
35. $4x + 1 = 2x - 3$
36. $x + 2 = 4 - x$
37. $3 - 2x = 5x - 4$
38. $3x - 1 = 9 - 2x$
39. $2 + x = 7x - 1$
40. $1 - 5x = 4x - 17$

41. The temperature, $T\,°C$, in my freezer t minutes after turning it on can be found from the formula
    $T = 25 - 2t$.
    a. Find the temperature in my freezer 15 minutes after it is turned on.
    b. The freezer turns off when the temperature gets to $-20°C$.
       How long does it take to get to $-20°C$?

42.

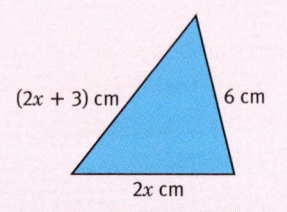

Triangle with sides $(2x + 3)$ cm, 6 cm, and $2x$ cm.

The perimeter of this triangle is 20 cm.
a. Form an equation for x and solve it.
b. Write down the lengths of each side of the triangle.

43. a. x → Take away 10 → Output
    Write an expression involving x for the output of this machine.
    b. x → Double → Add 1 → Output
    Write an expression involving x for the output of this machine.
    c. There is one value of x that gives the same output for both machines.
    Form an equation and solve it to find x.

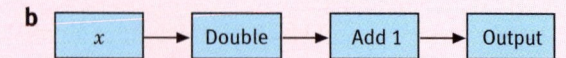

V MORE ALGEBRA
CURVED GRAPHS

1 a Copy and complete the table for $y = x^2 + 5$.

x	0	1	2	3	4	5	6
$y = x^2 + 5$			9			30	

b Draw a grid like this on graph paper. Plot the points from the table on your grid. Draw a smooth curve through your points to draw the graph of $y = x^2 + 5$.

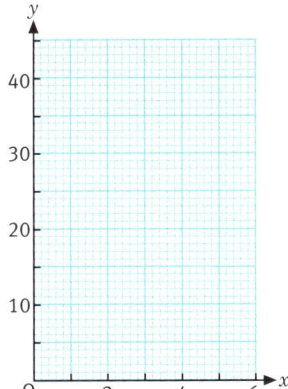

c Use your graph to find the value of x when $y = 25$.

2 a Copy and complete the table for $y = x^3 + 1$.

x	0	1	2	3	4
$y = x^3 + 1$					

b Draw a grid like this on graph paper.

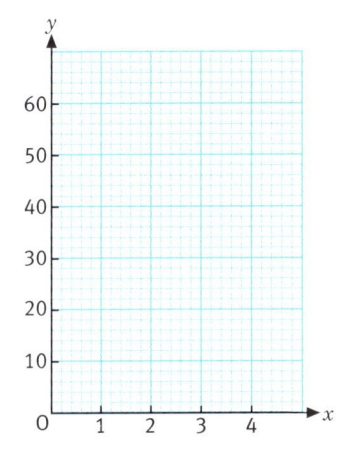

Plot the points from the table on your grid. Draw a smooth curve through your points to give the graph of $y = x^3 + 1$.

c Use your graph to find the value of x when $y = 30$.

d Use your graph to find the value of y when $x = 2.5$.

e Now use your calculator and $y = x^3 + 1$ to find the value of y when $x = 2.5$. Write a sentence to describe how accurate your graph is.

3 The graph of $y = x^2 + 1$ is drawn by plotting the points given in the table and drawing a smooth curve through them.

a Copy and complete the table.

x	−3	−2	−1	0	1	2	3
y	10				2		

b Plot these points on a grid like this and draw the graph of $y = x^2 + 1$.

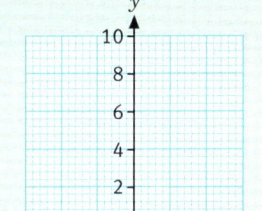

c Use your graph to find y when
  i $x = 2.5$ **ii** $x = -1.5$

d Use your graph to find the values of x when
  i $y = 3$ **ii** $y = 5$.

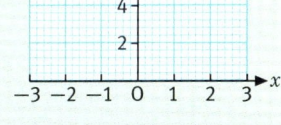

4 a Copy and complete the table of values for $y = x^2 + 2$.

x	−4	−3	−2	−1	0	1	2	3	4
$y = x^2 + 2$		11			3				

b Plot these points on a copy of a grid like this one. Hence draw the graph of $y = x^2 + 2$.

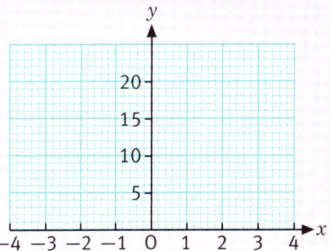

c Use your graph to find the value of y when $x = 1.5$.

5 a Copy and complete the table for $y = x^2 - 2$.

x	−3	−2	−1	0	1	2	3
$y = x^2 - 2$			−1			2	

b Plot these points on a grid like this. Hence draw the graph of $y = x^2 - 2$.

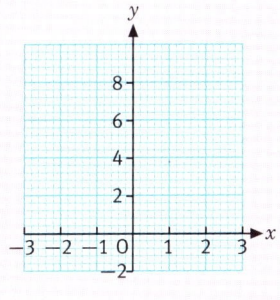

c Use your graph to find
  i the value of y when $x = -2.5$
  ii the positive value of x when $y = 3$.

V MORE ALGEBRA
USING BRACKETS

> Remember that multiplying by a negative number changes the sign.

Example

Simplify $3x - 5(4 - 2x)$

$3x - 5(4 - 2x)$
$= 3x - 20 + 10x$ — Expand the bracket.
$= 3x + 10x - 20$
$= 13x - 20$ — Put the x terms together and the number terms together.

Simplify

1. **a** $a + 3(2a + 6)$ **b** $p + 2(3 + 2p)$
2. **a** $2x - 3(4 - x)$ **b** $2s - 2(s - 3)$
3. **a** $2 - 2(2a + 3)$ **b** $2x - 3(x - 1)$
4. **a** $4(2x + 3) - 3(2x - 1)$ **b** $5(b + 1) - 2(b - 2)$
5. **a** $7(1 - x) - 2(2x - 3)$ **b** $4(1 - 2x) + 3(4 - x)$
6. **a** $5(2x + 1) - 3(2 - 3x)$ **b** $7(2a - 2) - 2(7a + 1)$

Example

Solve $3(5 - 2x) = 9$

$3(5 - 2x) = 9$
$15 - 6x = 9$
$15 - 6x + 6x = 9 + 6x$
$15 = 9 + 6x$
$15 - 9 = 9 - 9 + 6x$
$6 = 6x$
$x = 1$

Solve the equations.

7. **a** $2(x + 1) = 4$ **b** $2(2x - 1) = 6$
8. **a** $4(2x - 1) = 12$ **b** $3(x - 2) = 9$
9. **a** $5(1 - x) = 10$ **b** $4(1 - x) = 8$
10. **a** $4(2 - 5x) = 12$ **b** $7(1 + 2x) = 14$
11. This hexagon is regular.

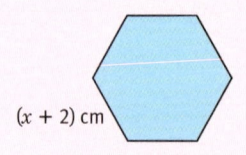

    $(x + 2)$ cm

    a Write down an expression for the perimeter.
    b The perimeter is 24 cm. Form an equation and solve it to find x.

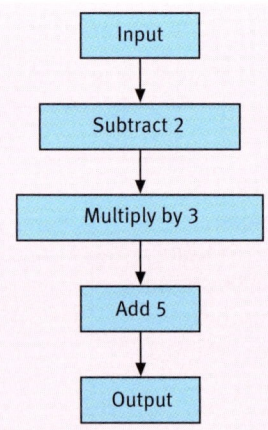

12. Input → Subtract 2 → Multiply by 3 → Add 5 → Output

    a The input number is x. Write an expression for the output number in terms of x.
    b Find the input number when the output number is 23.

13. Write down the common factor of
    a 12 and 9 **b** 8 and 10 **c** 3 and 15.

Example

What is the common factor of $4x$ and x^2?

Write both expressions out in full.

$4x = 2 \times 2 \times x$ and $x^2 = x \times x$ — x is a factor of both.

x is the common factor.

14. Write down the common factor of
    a $2x$ and 6 **b** 8 and $6x$ **c** 10 and $5x$.
15. Write down the common factor of
    a $2x$ and x^2 **b** x^2 and $3x$ **c** x^2 and $6x$.

Example

Factorise $2x^2 - x$.

x is a factor of both terms.

$2x^2 - x = x(2x - 1)$ — Put the common factor outside the bracket. Put the other factors inside.

Check: $x(2x - 1) = 2x^2 - x$

Factorise

16. **a** $6x + 3$ **b** $4x - 2$ **c** $3x - 6$
17. **a** $4 - 2x$ **b** $6 - 3x$ **c** $5 - 10x$
18. **a** $x^2 - 2x$ **b** $x^2 - 3x$ **c** $x^2 + 5x$
19. **a** $3x^2 + 9$ **b** $2x + x^2$ **c** $6x^2 - x$